# STRANGE HISTORY

BY THE BATHROOM READERS' INSTITUTE

PORTABLE PRESS
ASHLAND, OREGON

Strange History
Copyright © 2016 Portable Press
All rights reserved. No part of this publication may be reproduced,
distributed, or transmitted in any form or by any means, including
photocopying, recording, or other electronic or mechanical methods,
without the prior written permission of the publisher, except in the
case of brief quotations embodied in critical reviews and certain other
noncommercial uses permitted by copyright law.

Portable Press/The Bathroom Readers' Institute
An imprint of Printers Row Publishing Group
P.O. Box 1117, Ashland, OR 97520
www.bathroomreader.com
e-mail: mail@bathroomreader.com

Printers Row Publishing Group is a division of
Readerlink Distribution Services, LLC.

The Portable Press, Bathroom Readers' Institute, and Uncle John's
Bathroom Reader names and logos are trademarks of
Readerlink Distribution Services, LLC.

All correspondence concerning the content of this book should be
addressed to Portable Press/The Bathroom Readers' Institute,
Editorial Department, at the above address.

ISBN-13: 978-1-62686-583-9

Library of Congress Cataloging-in-Publication Data

Names: Bathroom Readers' Institute (Ashland, Or.)
Title: Strange history.
Description: Ashland, OR : Portable Press, 2016.
Identifiers: LCCN 2015031604 | ISBN 9781626865839 (pbk.)
Subjects: LCSH: American wit and humor. | History--Miscellanea. |
Curiosities and wonders.
Classification: LCC PN6165 .S88 2016 | DDC 081--dc23
LC record available at http://lccn.loc.gov/2015031604

First Printing
20 19 18 17 16   1 2 3 4 5

# STRANGE HISTORY

# Introduction

Welcome to the strangest book you'll ever read. The editors at Portable Press have collected thousands of bizarre facts and mind-blowing stories, from the recent past all the way back to prehistory, spanning all four corners of the globe (back in the days when the Earth had corners). So prepare yourself for a smorgasbord of oddities: kings, queens, commoners, criminals, gladiators, aliens, ghosts, gods, monsters, and much more.

But be forewarned: History wasn't always pretty. In fact, most of humanity's past was stinky, brutal, bloody, scary, and downright disturbing. But trust us, it's a lot more fun to read about it than it was to live it. So sit back and enjoy.

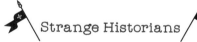

### Strange Historians

Publisher: Gordon Javna
Editor: Jay Newman
Interior design: Lidija Tomas
Cover design: Michael Sherman
Illustrator: Sophie Hogarth
Production Editor: Trina Janssen
Copyeditor: Dan Mansfield

# Things Don't Change

*We begin this strange journey with some quotations from ages past that sound like they could have been said last week.*

"What is happening to our young people? They disrespect elders and disobey their parents. They ignore the law. They riot in the streets inflamed with wild notions. What is to become of them?"

—Plato, 427–347 B.C.

"The young people of today think of nothing but themselves. They have no reverence for parents or old age. They are impatient of all restraint. They talk as if they know everything, and what passes for wisdom to us is foolishness to them. As for the girls, they're forward, immodest, and unladylike in speech, behavior, and dress."

—Peter the Hermit, A.D. 1050–1115

"No job worth doing was ever done on time or under budget."

—Khufu, Egyptian pharaoh, c. 2560 B.C., on building the Great Pyramid

"Nothing is more unpredictable than the mob, nothing more obscure than public opinion, nothing more deceptive than the whole political system."

—Cicero, 106–43 B.C.

"Great wisdom is generous; petty wisdom is contentious. Great speech is impassioned, small speech cantankerous."

—Zhuangzi, Chinese philosopher, 369–286 B.C.

"The Arrius Pollio Apartment Complex owned by Gnaeus Allius Nigidius Maius FOR RENT from July 1st. Streetfront shops with counter space, luxurious second-story apartments, and a townhouse. Prospective renters, please make arrangements with Primus, slave of Gnaeus Allius Nigidius Maius."

—Roman rental notice from Pompeii, 1st century A.D.

"It is better to hide ignorance, but it is hard to do this when we relax over wine."

—Heraclitus, Greek philosopher, 540–480 B.C.

"Quickly, bring me a beaker of wine, so that I may wet my mind and say something clever."

—Aristophanes, the "Father of Comedy," 456–386 B.C.

# Chee-Chee = Nasty! Nasty!

This strange Broadway musical, written in 1928 by the legendary duo of Richard Rodgers and Lorenz Hart, put an end to their long string of successful shows. Why? It may have been the squirm-inducing plot, based on a comic novel called *The Son of the Grand Eunuch*. (In case you don't know, eunuchs were men who had been castrated and then employed to guard the women's living areas.)

Rodgers and Hart set their story in ancient China. The emperor's grand eunuch, Li-Pi-Sao, tells his son, Li-Pi-Tchou, that he wants him to take over his job. But Li-Pi-Tchou is in love with a beautiful woman named Chee-Chee and doesn't want to become a eunuch. So the lovers flee and embark on a series of misadventures in which Chee-Chee has to award various thieves and bullies sexual favors in order to get herself and Li-Pi-Tchou out of one predicament or another.

The musical bombed. The review of *Chee-Chee* in the *London Observer* was entitled, simply: "Nasty! Nasty!"

# Three Strange Fads

**GOLDFISH SWALLOWING**: On March 3, 1939, Harvard University student Lothrop Withington Jr. swallowed a live goldfish to win a $10 bet. Days later, not to be outdone, a college student in Pennsylvania downed three goldfish seasoned with salt and pepper. When a fellow classmate upped the ante to six goldfish, the gauntlet had been thrown down, and the goldfish swallowing craze spread like wildfire on campuses across the United States. By the time the fad faded a few months later, thousands of goldfish had met gruesome ends.

**TOOTH–DYEING**: In 16th-century Europe, tooth dyeing was popular among upper-class women. In Italy, red and green were the most popular colors, while Russian women favored black.

**CROTCHLESS TUNICS**: In medieval England, wealthy gentlemen often wore clothing that left their "assets" exposed—by way of short-fitting tunics with no pants. (If the genitals didn't hang low enough, padded, flesh-coated prosthetics called briquettes would be used.)

# The Flea Killer

Queen Christina ruled Sweden from 1632 to 1654. What did she consider the biggest threat to her kingdom? Fleas. The queen hated hated HATED them and wanted each and every one she found in her palace killed...individually. To accomplish this feat (this was long before the invention of chemical insect repellents), she commissioned the construction of a tiny, one-inch-long cannon that was packed with tiny flea-sized cannonballs. Whenever she spotted one, she fired the tiny cannon at it and occasionally made a killshot.

> "Fools rush in where angels fear to tread."
> —**Alexander Pope**

# Thar Be Unicorns! (Or Not)

**MYTH:** Famed explorer Marco Polo saw unicorns in the 13th century. He described them as "ugly brutes."
**REALITY:** Historians believe that Marco Polo did see a horned animal—a rhinoceros.

**MYTH:** Unicorns are mentioned in the Bible nine times.
**REALITY:** The word seems to have first popped up in the 1611 version of the King James Bible. Scholars say it wasn't magic that put unicorns into the holy scripture, it was mistranslation and misunderstanding. The Hebrew word *re'em*—which was translated into English as "unicorn"— most likely referred to the *rimu*, a now-extinct species of ox.

**MYTH:** The horn of a captured unicorn, when ground into a powder, has medicinal qualities, such as the ability to destroy poison and purify water. In the 16th century, an intact unicorn horn was worth ten times more than gold. They were sold in pharmacies well into the 1700s.
**REALITY:** Shady merchants got their "unicorn horns" from the narwhal, a type of whale with a protruding tooth that looks like a horn.

# History...North Korea Style

In November 2012, the government-run North Korean Central News Agency announced that scientists there had found the burial site of a unicorn—the one that was said to have been ridden by King Dongmyeong, who had founded Korea (known as Goguryeo at the time) in 37 B.C. The site was located near a temple in the North Korean capital of Pyongyang. A rock engraved with "Unicorn Lair" marked the grave.

Sung-Yoon Lee, a professor of Korean studies at Tufts University, told *LiveScience* that the report was political propaganda. So why would the government claim that unicorns are real? To support Kim Jong-un, North Korea's leader. "It's symbolic," Lee said. North Koreans don't take reports like this literally the way Westerners would. Another professor said the report was mistranslated. What was found was not a unicorn's lair at all. It was the burial site of a *kirin*. What's that? A beast with a dragon's head, a deer's body, and the tail of a cow.

# A HOLE IN THE HEAD

Ever heard of *trepanning*? It involves boring a hole into the human skull for "medical" purposes. The practice goes way back—archaeologists have discovered Neanderthal skulls with nickel-size holes in them. During the Middle Ages, trepanning was used to release "demons" that people believed were the cause of mental illness. But then it fell out of favor as medical knowledge increased.

That is, until the groovy 1960s. A Dutch self-help guru named Bart Hughes tried to spearhead a modern-day trepanning comeback. His purpose: to expand his consciousness and increase his brainpower. So in 1965 Hughes, using a surgical drill, performed the procedure on himself (and then stitched up the skin over the borehole...himself). After bragging to reporters that he felt much better, Hughes was committed to a mental institution for observation.

Although his efforts didn't lead to a modern trepanning movement, he did gain a few followers who were just as weird as he was. Their story is on the next page...

# More Holes in More Heads

In the mid-1960s, an English painter—and Bart Hughes fan (see previous page)—named Joey Mellen wanted a hole drilled in his head, too, believing it would get him "permanently high." His girlfriend, Amanda Feilding, claimed that she had successfully trepanned herself. Afterward, she experienced euphoric highs.

The first time Feilding tried to drill into Mellen's melon, the hole wasn't deep enough. Then she botched the second attempt and Mellen lost a lot of blood—enough to require medical attention. After recovering in a hospital (under psychiatric watch), Mellen went home and drilled the hole himself. When he heard what he later called "an ominous sounding 'schlurp' and the sound of bubbling," he knew he'd successfully bored through his skull (but *unsuccessfully* drilled into his own brain).

Mellen survived, though, and the couple later had two children: Rock Basil Hugo Feilding Mellen (born 1979) and Cosmo Birdie Feilding Mellen (born 1985). So you can add "weird baby names" to the side effects of trepanning.

> "The doctors X-rayed my head and found nothing."
> **—Dizzy Dean, baseball player**

# Slang From the 1930s

**FROG-SKIN**: A dollar

**JUICY**: Enjoyable

**EGG**: A crude person

**ABERCROMBIE**: A know-it-all

**HOT SQUAT**: The electric chair

**ALL WET**: No good

**BIG IT**: A conceited person

**CITY JUICE**: A glass of water

**CRUMB**: A loser

**SWEET PATOOTIE**: An attractive woman

**WET SOCK**: A social misfit

**BOUNCING BETTY**: A car, especially a Ford

**BRODIE**: A mistake

**JUNGLE**: A hobo camp

**BLOW YOUR WIG**: Become very excited

**GROUNDER**: A cigarette picked up off the ground

**CHICAGO OVERCOAT**: A coffin

**DEAD HOOFER**: A bad dancer

**ABYSSINIA**: I'll be seeing you

**BOTCHED HISTORY**

"When the stock market crashed, Franklin D. Roosevelt got on the television and didn't just talk about the, you know, the princes of greed. He said, 'Look, here's what happened.'"

—VICE PRESIDENT JOE BIDEN, EXPLAINING THE EVENTS OF 1929 (10 YEARS BEFORE BROADCAST TV)

# Where Did the Time Go?

In 1996 German systems analyst Heribert Illig introduced a theory he called "phantom time hypothesis." Illig believes that the Early Middle Ages—the years 614 to 911—never actually happened and that all evidence of the 300-year period is faked. He said that in 1582, when Pope Gregory XIII replaced the Julian calendar with the Gregorian calendar (which we still use) in order to correct a ten-day error, he actually added 300 years. Among the historical evidence that Illig uses to support his claim are "fraudulent" records of Holy Roman Emperor Charlemagne, whom Illig says is actually a fictional character.

**LEONARDO DA VINCI'S PACKING LIST FOR A TRIP TO PAVIA IN 1510**
Spectacles with case, fork, firestick, bistoury, charcoal, boards, sheets of paper, chalk, white wax, forceps, pane of glass, fine-tooth bone saw, scalpel, inkhorn, penknife, nutmeg, boots, stockings, comb, towel, shirts, shoelaces, penknife, pens, a skin for the chest, gloves, wrapping paper, charcoal. (Get hold of a skull.)

# Borrrring

• In 1964 artist Andy Warhol released what is possibly the most boring movie ever made. Called *Empire*, the grainy, black-and-white silent film is just one continuous shot of New York City's Empire State Building on a night when nothing happened. Warhol filmed the building for six hours, but to make the movie even less interesting, he recorded it at a slower speed so it lasts eight hours.

• To many, the phrase "boring museum" is redundant, but some museums are more boring than others. Examples: the Cement Museum in Spain, the Wallpaper Museum in France, and the Occupational Health and Safety Museum in Germany.

• What's the world's most boring city? It could be Brussels, Belgium. According to a poll of 2,400 travelers conducted by the website TripAdvisor.com, aside from the famous waffles, there's not much of interest there.

• In 2010 British researcher William Tunstall-Pedoe designed a computer program that scanned all the news from every single day in the century to determine the most boring day of the 20th century. The "winner": April 11, 1954. On that day, no one famous was born, no one famous died, and there were no big news events. Even the weather was boring.

# Strange Toys of Yesteryear

### WITCH DOCTOR HEAD SHRINKER'S KIT

**The Product:** As it says—a (plastic) head-shrinking kit

**The Pitch:** "Into the deepest jungle went Pressman Toymakers, looking for something new. The secret they brought back for you is incredible! The Pressman Witch Doctor Head Shrinker's Kit! Plastic flesh, mixing cauldron, and petrifying potion. Just pour it into the mold and in minutes you can add monster hair! Paint it with the coloring kit included, or make up your own decorations. In 24 hours, the heads shrink, shrink down. Shrunken heads for all occasions! Collect 'em, swap 'em. Give them to your witch doctor friends. You can always cook up more, with Pressman's Witch Doctor's Head Shrinker's Kit."

### ROY ROGERS QUICK SHOOTER HAT

**The Product:** A cowboy hat with a hidden derringer cap gun

**The Pitch:** "Hi fellas! Say, that's a pretty tricky hat, isn't it? Partners, how would you like to surprise your pals like that? Well you can with my new Roy Rogers Quick Shooter Hat. It's by Ideal. Just press this secret button right here, and a replica of an authentic western pistol pops out and fires! It's your secret weapon, even when they think you're unarmed. So get Ideal's new Roy Rogers Quick Shooter Hat at your favorite store today. And you'll always be ready for anything!"

# An Irony of Orwellian Magnitude

In his 1949 novel *1984*, George Orwell warned that in the future, England would be ruled by "Big Brother," a government that constantly spies on its citizens to keep them in line.

It just so happens that in England today, there are a reported 5.9 million closed-circuit cameras watching the people. But one neighborhood in London is leading all of the others: On a single block in Canonbury Square in Islington, North London, there are 32 cameras trained on the streets, alleys, and even on peoples' properties. One of Canonbury Square's biggest claims to fame: George Orwell lived there while he was writing *1984*.

> "War is peace. Freedom is slavery. Ignorance is strength."
> —**George Orwell,** *1984*

# Loco Motive

On September 15, 1896, more than 40,000 people showed up in Crush, Texas, to watch two trains crash into each other. The stunt was organized by a railroad executive named Mark Crush to drum up business. The tiny town was erected just for the event. A special track had been built 50 feet from the crowd.

It should have been farther away.

At 5:00 p.m., two 35-ton trains traveling 45 mph slammed into each other in spectacular fashion. The force of the impact erupted the boilers on both locomotives, triggering massive explosions and hurtling debris into the crowd. Three spectators were instantly killed; dozens more were injured.

Crush (the town) was dismantled within a day; victims' families were compensated with free tickets on the M-K-T Railroad. Crush (the man) was fired...but then rehired when he convinced his bosses that he could spin the event into a public-relations piece about proper railroad safety. (Tip #1: Don't ram two trains into each other at full speed.)

# La Raverte's Big Secret

A 20-year-old bullfighter known only as "La Raverte" debuted in the Madrid bullring in 1900. What's odd about that? La Raverte was a female bullfighter. She remained a crowd favorite for seven years until 1908, when the Spanish government decided it was immoral for women to fight bulls, and La Raverte was banned from the ring.

But La Raverte wasn't worried. Why? Because she was really a he. At the conclusion of one of La Raverte's final bullfights, "she" took off her wig and fake breasts, revealing she was actually a man named Agustin Rodriguez.

So did La Raverte continue fighting bulls as a man? Nope. Bullfighting fans instantly turned on him, angered by the fraud. Within the year, Rodriguez fled Madrid and retired quietly in Majorca.

# Travel Back in Time to...
## That '70s Bathroom

**RUBBER DUCKIES.** After Bert and Ernie first sang the song "Rubber Duckie" on *Sesame Street* in 1970, the little yellow ducks became a bathroom fixture.

**AQUA VELVA AFTERSHAVE.** "There's something about an Aqua Velva man," said the beautiful blonde woman in the commercial, and millions of men believed her.

**JOHNSON'S "NO MORE TEARS" SHAMPOO.** The shampoo hit the market in 1953, but it wasn't until the 1970s that No More Tears became the best-selling American shampoo.

**AN EARTH-TONE BATHROOM SUITE.** "Earth tones" were in. Green wasn't green—it was *avocado*. Yellow wasn't yellow—it was *harvest gold*. Brown wasn't brown—it was *chocolate*. By today's standards, they're hard to look at (especially in combinations), but they were all the rage in the 1970s.

**FLOWER-SHAPED NONSTICK BATH DECALS.** The last remnants of the 1960s flower-power fad ended up keeping people safe when getting in and out of the tub.

**THE SHOWER MASSAGE.** The German company Hansgrohe introduced the first handheld, adjustable showerhead, the Selecta, in 1968. Soon they were everywhere. In 1974 Teledyne came out with the famous Original Shower Massage.

**A FUZZY TOILET SEAT COVER.** Basically a shag carpet on top of the toilet seat, it had one major drawback: When guys used the toilet, the thick cover would make the seat fall down...mid-stream, so to speak.

**TY-D-BOL.** In the 1970s, blue toilet water was clean toilet water. And then there was the Ty-D-Bol Man, that little guy in the captain's suit in the boat inside the toilet tank.

# Cinema Odd

In the 1960s, Paolo Cavara, Gualtiero Jacopetti, and Franco Prosperi were three budding documentary filmmakers with a problem: Documentaries bored them. They didn't want to paint sedate *National Geographic*–style pictures of foreign cultures. They wanted to show the lurid, shocking, and weird parts of human life that were rarely committed to film. The result: *Mondo Cane* (Italian for "A Dog's Life"). Released in 1962, the film was a 108-minute travelogue that visits 30 bizarre, violent, and odd places. It's sensational, exploitative, trashy...and really entertaining. Among the scenes recorded by *Mondo Cane* cameras:

- Asian cannibals eating a corpse
- The slaughtering of a bull and a pig
- A Taiwanese tribe eating a dog
- Ritualistic fattening of African women (to increase fertility)
- Sexualized tribal dancing
- A trip to a pet cemetery
- A South Pacific "cargo cult" that worships man-made objects

Critics called the film "vulgar" and "pornographic," but it was a hit. Surprisingly, the movie's theme song "More" was nominated for Best Song at the 1963 Academy Awards.

# FIVE FREAKY FACTS ABOUT...
## FOOD

- The first archaeological evidence of soup dates back to 6000 B.C. Main ingredient: hippopotamus.

- Sugar was first added to chewing gum in 1869...by a dentist.

- Besides human sacrifices, Aztecs offered the gods tamales.

- Abraham Lincoln's mother died from "milk sickness"—poisoning by milk from cows that had eaten the white snakeroot plant.

- Romans flavored food with garum, a paste made by leaving fish to rot for several weeks.

# The Skull Is in the Mail

When Germany conquered Tanganyika (a region of eastern Africa) in 1898, Chief Mkwawa, the leader of the Wahehe tribe, was killed. Mkwawa's head was sent to Germany, where it was displayed in a museum in Bremen. During World War I, the British kicked the Germans out of Africa, aided by the Wahehe. H. A. Byatt, the British administrator in charge, lobbied his government to return Mkwawa's skull in appreciation for the Wahehes' war effort. The return of the skull was even stipulated in the Treaty of Versailles, the 1919 agreement outlining the terms of Germany's surrender.

But the Germans denied taking Mkwawa's head, and the Brits didn't push the issue. Then, in 1953 Sir Edward Twining, the British governor of Tanganyika, vowed to track down the skull...and found it in the Bremen Museum among a collection of dozens of skulls taken in the 1890s. Mkwawa's skull was finally returned to the Wahehe in 1954.

# All-American Ghosts

**ALCATRAZ.** If you were to stay overnight on this island prison off San Francisco—which hasn't housed a living prisoner since 1963—you might be in for a long night. Park employees, guides, and even visitors have reported hearing the screams of long-dead inmates, footsteps of jackbooted guards, and the slamming of jail doors...that don't move.

**THE OLD HIGH SCHOOL IN BRUNSWICK, MAINE,** is full of tales about a drama student who died there many years ago. She was rehearsing a play on a balcony when she slipped and fell to her death. The building is now used for school board meetings...which are sometimes interrupted by slamming doors and books that fly off the shelves.

**BIG BAY POINT LIGHTHOUSE IN MICHIGAN** is said to be haunted by the ghost of its first keeper, Will Prior. (In fact, pretty much every lighthouse in America is said to be haunted.) If you visit Big Bay and see a red-haired ghost, that's Will Prior. Locals say he's harmless.

**HUNTRESS HALL AT KEENE STATE COLLEGE IN NEW HAMPSHIRE** is a freshman class dorm. Who else lives there? The college's benefactress (and the building's namesake), Harriet Huntress. Her wheelchair is stored in the attic. Students say it can be heard rolling around in the middle of the night.

**BELCOURT CASTLE IN NEWPORT, RHODE ISLAND,** is
famous for its ghosts, the spookiest of which is a spectral
monk who appears in front of a lion statue, walks away
from it, then disappears. Then he comes back and repeats
the whole process all over again.

**KEMPER ARENA IN KANSAS CITY, MISSOURI,** is the haunt
of former WWF wrestler Owen Hart. During a 1999 match,
Hart was being lowered from the ceiling to the ring when
the cable holding his harness snapped. He fell to the floor
and died instantly. Hart's ghost has been seen floating near
the ceiling...still wearing his mask and harness.

The ancient Romans had a god
named Verminus. His job: to
protect cows from worms.

# And the Cow Ran Away from the Spoon

On May 9, 1962, a Guernsey cow in Iowa named Fawn was picked up by a tornado and flew through the air for a few minutes before landing softly and safely at a nearby farm a half mile away. The flight is believed to be the longest (but not the first) unassisted solo cow flight in recorded history. Fawn landed in the pen of a Holstein bull at a neighboring farm before she successfully wandered home. (The brief encounter resulted in a calf.)

Amazingly, Fawn had a chance to beat her own record. In 1967 she was out grazing on a country road and was caught up in another tornado. She flew over a busload of gawking tourists and landed safely on the other side of the road. From then on, Fawn's owner locked her up whenever there was a storm warning.

## BOTCHED HISTORY

"John Wayne was from Waterloo.
That's the kind of spirit that
I have, too!"

—U.S. Rep. Michele Bachmann, speaking to a
crowd in Waterloo, Iowa. One problem: It was
John Wayne Gacy who was from Waterloo—a
serial killer (known as the "Killer Clown")
who murdered 33 people in the 1970s.
John Wayne the movie star was from another
town on the other side of Iowa.

# The Cabbage Patch Conspiracy

This kooky Cold War conspiracy theory goes like this: In the early 1980s, President Ronald Reagan feared that nuclear war with the Soviet Union was inevitable, and survivors would be horribly deformed. Their offspring would be even more gruesome. So Reagan ordered government scientists to expose human test subjects to radiation, then take samples of their DNA, and breed babies. Result: infants with mashed-in faces, beady eyes, and chubby limbs.

The government then hired Coleco Toys to make dolls based on the infants. Coleco explained their odd appearance with a fairy tale about the children growing in the ground, and released them to toy stores. The toys were a huge success. Mission accomplished.

A fun theory, but completely false. Cabbage Patch Kids first appeared in the 1901 novel *Mrs. Wiggs of the Cabbage Patch*. Coleco bought the rights to mass-produce the dolls in 1983—after Reagan took office.

The theory was started by college student Richard Joltes, who worked at a Sears in West Virginia. Why? Because he hated the dolls, so he started telling customers that "these things were designed to get people used to what mutants might look like after a nuclear war." Soon, other cashiers started doing it, too. Then the legend spread...and mutated.

# The Rise and Demise of the Polish Joke

Though rarely told today (thankfully), Polish jokes were a huge craze for much of the 20th century. (One example: Q: Why does the new Polish navy have glass-bottomed boats? A: So they can see the old Polish navy.)

Anyway.

You can blame Adolf Hitler for these jokes. In his quest to conquer Poland in the 1930s, Hitler pushed the racist "dumb Polack" stereotype so the rest of Europe wouldn't sympathize with the country's fate. The Nazi propaganda machine claimed, among other things, that Polish soldiers on horseback had once attacked German tanks with swords. That stereotype spread to the United States after the war, and by the 1960s, Poles had become a punch line. The TV show *Laugh-in* (1967–73) featured a regular segment dedicated to Polish jokes. Books of Polish jokes followed over the next decade.

The perception began to change in 1978 when Cardinal Karol Wojtyla became the first Polish pope (John Paul II). The fad tapered off after the fall of the Soviet Union in 1991.

# The Life of a Concubine

• Concubines were once a common part of life in numerous cultures. Who were they? To put it in modern terms, a concubine could be defined as "a man's live-in girlfriend and baby mama, only she doesn't get as much respect as his wife does."

• If a Mesopotamian wife couldn't have children, she had to find her husband a concubine who could.

• A Roman man could have one concubine, but only if he was unmarried. The relationship had legal standing, but his children had no birthrights.

• During the Chinese Qing dynasty (1644–1912), each emperor had up to 20,000 imperial consorts.

• In the 1640s, Sultan Ibrahim I of the Ottoman Empire sentenced 280 of his concubines to be drowned in the sea.

• Before imperial concubinage ended in Japan in the 1920s, half of Japan's emperors had been born to concubines.

• A valued gift given to concubines in China's Forbidden City: a back scratcher.

• In Mesopotamia, priestesses held high social rank—and some served as concubines. Men visited them out of "religious duty."

• Imperial consorts could raise their status by giving birth to a male heir. One named Wu had four sons by Emperor Gaozong and became empress of China.

• Roman husbands could have a young male concubine, but the husband had to retain the masculine authority of the household.

• Roman concubines were forbidden from worshipping Juno, the goddess of marriage.

• A Chinese emperor's eunuchs (castrated servants) were the only other men allowed near his consorts. They carried them to his bed by piggyback, since the women's bound feet prevented them from walking.

• In China, when Ming dynasty emperors died, their consorts were buried with them...sometimes alive.

• In India, Mughal rulers sometimes promoted a concubine to become their wife—and demoted their wife to concubine.

# Inside the Great Wall

The Chinese people refer to it as *Wan-Li Qang-Qeng*, or "10,000-Li-Long Wall" (a li is about a third of a mile). Today it's a popular tourist attraction, but 500 years ago, the Great Wall of China was one of the most dangerous places on Earth. Looming over the steep terrain—sometimes at a pitch of 75 degrees—the ornate structure was manned by more than a million soldiers. Watchtowers were placed at strategic intervals, some less than half a mile apart, others much farther, depending on the line of sight. The corridors within were narrow and confusing to any attackers who made it inside. The defenders would trap the invaders in labyrinthine passages that often led to dead ends.

Sentries were stationed on top of the towers to communicate impending dangers. Burning straw and dung, they sent signals to the soldiers by fire at night and smoke by day: A single fire or smoke plume meant 100 enemy soldiers were coming; two signals denoted 500; three warned of over 1,000 (which was not uncommon). Even more elaborate signals—flags, clappers, drums, bells, and later, gunpowder—could communicate exactly where along the Great Wall the danger was coming from. In only a matter of hours, every single general along the 4,000 miles of the wall could be alerted to an invasion and know whether—and where—they would need to send reinforcements.

# A Pox Upon Thee!

*May you never need a magical curse. But just in case...here are a few from yesteryear. Use them wisely.*

- May the desert wind blow angry scorpions up your robe.

- May malevolent hedgehogs soil your cornflakes.

- May you be swallowed by a whale with bad breath.

- May the dog really eat your homework.

- May you be trapped in an elevator with the world farting champion.

- May a family of ferrets nest in your knickers.

- May the fleas of a thousand camels infest your armpits.

- May your gastric juices keep you from sleeping at night.

- May you grow like an onion...with your head in the ground.

- May no one tell you about the spinach between your teeth.

- May you be smitten with an itch where you cannot scratch.

- May you find a half-eaten worm in your apple...after you swallow.

- May the lumps in your oatmeal hide cockroaches.

# Paper Clothing

This odd fashion fad was created in 1966 by the Scott Paper Company to promote its "Color Explosion" paper towels, napkins, and toilet paper. Scott probably never intended for people to take the paper dresses very seriously...but when the company received more than 500,000 orders in six months, dressmaking companies got into the act. A full line of paper clothing, including $8 maternity dresses, $12 men's suits, and even $15 wedding gowns, were available. For a time, disposable paper vacation wear appeared to be the wave of the future; travelers wouldn't have to pack—they'd just pick up paper clothes at their destination and throw them away at the end of the trip.

The fad really caught on: The Duchess of Windsor, Joan Kennedy, and even the Beatles were spotted wearing paper clothing. "Paper clothing is here to stay," *Time* magazine proclaimed in 1967. But it was wrong. Paper clothes ballooned out in unpredictable places, tore easily, and cost too much to replace constantly. The fad was dead by 1970.

"To be really medieval one should have no body. To be really modern one should have no soul. To be really Greek one should have no clothes."

—Oscar Wilde

# The Aquaman of Kent

Matthew Robinson, the second Baron Rokeby (1713–1800), was born into a noble Scottish family that lived in Kent, England. He inherited the title of baron in his 40s and served in the House of Lords.

But then something strange happened to Robinson: After he returned from a vacation in the German resort town of Aachen, he was obsessed with water. He started skipping work and spent most of his days swimming in the ocean. Each day, Robinson would walk to and from the beach wearing tattered peasant clothes; he'd swim for so long that he'd faint, requiring his servants to drag him out of the sea. The baron had drinking fountains installed along the path to the beach. If commoners were caught using them, Robinson didn't punish them—he gave them a gold coin to reward "their good taste."

His embarrassed family eventually talked him into installing a swimming pool at his home. He still spent most of the day swimming. He tried to prevent fainting by eating a roast leg of veal...underwater.

Later in his life, the Aquaman of Kent grew a really long beard (which was not the style at the time for aristocrats) that he kept tucked under his arm. He also switched to raw meat and never gave up swimming.

Robinson died peacefully in his sleep at the age of 87.

# The Final Days of King Charles II

**MONDAY:** On the morning of February 2, 1685, King Charles II of England was preparing to shave when he suddenly cried out in pain, fell to the floor, and started having fits. Six royal physicians rushed in and administered emergency "aid."

• They let (drained) 16 ounces of blood.

• Then they applied heated cups to his skin, which formed large round blisters, in order to "stimulate the system."

• They let 8 more ounces of blood.

• They induced vomiting to purify his stomach, and gave him an enema to purify his bowels.

• Then they force-fed him syrup of blackthorn and rock salt.

• They shaved his hair and put blistering plasters on his scalp. He regained consciousness. The treatment was working! So they gave him another enema.

• Then they applied hellebore root to the nostrils, more blistering plasters to the skin, and powdered cowslip flowers to the stomach.

• Special plasters made from pigeon droppings were attached to his feet. After 12 hours of care, they put the ailing king to bed.

**TUESDAY:** Charles woke and seemed much improved. The attending physicians congratulated themselves and continued the treatment.

• They let 10 more ounces of blood.

• They gave him a potion of black cherry, peony, lavender, crushed pearls, and sugar.

**WEDNESDAY:** He woke, had a fit, and was bled again.

• They gave him senna pods in spring water, and white wine with nutmeg.

• They force-fed him a drink made from "40 drops of extract of human skull" of a man who'd died violently.

• They made him eat a gallstone from an East Indian goat.

• They said that King Charles was on the road to recovery.

**THURSDAY:** The king was near death. He was blistered again, re-bled, repurged, and given another enema.

• He was given Jesuits' powder laced with opium and wine.

**FRIDAY:** Showing no improvement, the king was bled almost bloodless.

• Doctors scoured the palace grounds and created a last-ditch antidote containing "extracts of all the herbs and animals of the kingdom."

**SATURDAY:** The king was dead.

**POSTMORTEM:** It was rumored that Charles had been poisoned. Modern doctors think he may have been poisoned...by himself. He often played with mercury in an unventilated palace laboratory. Would the king have survived without treatment? Probably not. But at least his death wouldn't have been so excruciating.

# Where's Your Nose, Brahe?

Known as the father of astronomy, Tycho Brahe (1546–1601) compiled the world's first accurate set of astronomical tables. While a student at the university in Rostock, Germany, he and a fellow student, Manderup Parsbjergh, began quarreling over an obscure mathematical point. The argument went on for weeks until they decided to settle it with a duel...in the dark...with swords!

Parsbjergh sliced off a chunk of Brahe's nose. Brahe's vanity wouldn't let the disfigurement stop him from achieving greatness—in public, he wore an artificial nose made of gold and silver.

Irony Behind Bars

In 1853 a contractor named John Coffee built a new jail in the town of Dundalk, Ireland. During the project, Coffee went bankrupt. He became his jail's very first inmate.

# Jonah and a Whale of a Tale

In the early 1920s, the *Toronto Mail and Empire* ran an unbelievable story about two scientists named Dr. Schmierkase and Dr. Butterbrod who had discovered "the fossil of the whale that had swallowed Jonah." The next day, evangelists all over Toronto read the story from the pulpit, citing it as confirmation that the biblical story of Jonah and the whale was true. And the day after that, a rival newspaper ran a story reporting on the evangelists' speeches.

Then the story started spreading like wildfire...until the next day when the *Toronto Mail and Empire* ran a second story exposing the first one as a hoax, the work of a journalist named Charles Langdon Clarke. Clarke liked to spend his free time cooking up news items based on biblical stories, and then attributing them to fictional newspapers like the *Babylon Gazette* or the *Jerusalem Times* for added credibility. Anyone who spoke German would have had an inkling that the story was a joke—Dr. Schmierkase and Dr. Butterbrod translates as "Dr. Cheese" and "Dr. Butter Bread."

# Where Did the Neanderthals Go?

Neanderthals were a race of hominids that developed alongside early humans. They first appeared in Africa about 700,000 years ago and slowly migrated into Europe and the Middle East. They shared almost all the same genetic classifications with *Homo sapiens* (us), but differed in the final category, species (*Homo neanderthalensis*). After about 40,000 years of sharing territory with humans in Europe, the Neanderthals died out while *Homo sapiens* kept evolving. So why didn't the Neanderthals survive?

• **THEORY #1**: They weren't smart enough. It was long conventional wisdom that Neanderthals were not very intelligent, but recent findings suggest Neanderthals had bigger heads and brains than humans.

• **THEORY #2**: They weren't skilled hunters. Not true. It turns out that Neanderthal tools were actually more efficient than those crafted by early humans. Neanderthals are also believed to have had control over fire before *Homo sapiens* did, and to have cooked, rather than gathered, much of their food. (They actually ate healthier than most people do today.)

• **THEORY #3**: They couldn't communicate well. Recent studies have led some scientists to conclude that

Neanderthal voices were not incoherent grunts, as once believed, but high-pitched and melodic, and that their means of communicating may have been a combination of language, pitch, and song.

Far from being the brutish creatures of cliché, Neanderthals were probably the first hominids to bury their dead (they even left flowers on the grave sites). It is true that Neanderthals and humans looked different: Neanderthals were shorter and broader, with a heavier brow. But about the same percentage of Neanderthal and human DNA includes the genetic mutation that inhibits brown pigmentation, so Neanderthals were about as likely as humans to be pale-skinned, blond, or redheaded.

Native Africans, whose ancestors never lived alongside Neanderthals in Europe, have no Neanderthal DNA in their genomes—but pretty much all other people do. So when the last of them disappeared about 25,000 years ago, it's possible they had already assimilated into the larger human population.

Where did the Neanderthals go? Look in the mirror.

# The Undead of Crystal Palace

Built in 1865, Crystal Palace station in South London once handled 8,000 passengers per day. By the late 1920s, it had fallen into disrepair. During World War II, it was used as an air-raid shelter. German bombing during the Blitz shattered what was left of the glass roof, and by the time the war ended, rats far outnumbered commuters. Crystal Palace was demolished in 1961. The area is now covered by apartments and houses. All that remains of the station is a high retaining wall, a lone building, a stretch of tunnel beneath the road...and some ghostly inhabitants.

Legend has it that buried somewhere beneath the rubble of Crystal Palace station is a bricked-up train wreck from the early days of the line. The dead were purportedly entombed where they perished, along with the shattered remains of the locomotive. They are not resting in peace, however. Locals claim ghostly hands occasionally reach up from below to grab unwary pedestrians passing by aboveground.

## FIVE FREAKY FACTS ABOUT...
# WORDS

- Older than you might think: The word "earthling" appeared in print as early as 1593.

- First person to refer to a coward as a "chicken": William Shakespeare.

- The word "mouse" is from the ancient Sanskrit word *mus*, meaning "thief."

- Gelett Burgess, author of the children's poem "Purple Cow," invented the word "blurb."

- James Joyce coined the word "Klik-kaklakkaklaskaklopatzklatschabatta-creppycrottygraddaghsemmihsammi-hnouithappluddyappladdypkonpkot" in *Finnegan's Wake*. It means "an act of God."

# The Cloud People of Peru

Five centuries ago, deep in the mountainous jungles of what is now Peru, the Spanish conqueror Pedro Cieza de León encountered a tribe of people who were different from the ruling Incas. "They are the whitest and most handsome of all the people that I have seen," he wrote, "and their wives were so beautiful that because of their gentleness, many of them deserved to be the Incas' wives and to also be taken to the Sun Temple." In addition to being lighter-skinned than the Incas, these people were said to be much taller—and they had blond hair and blue eyes.

What they called themselves has been lost to history; the Incas called them the Chachapoyas, which anthropologists think meant "People of the Clouds." They lived in the dense forests that rise above the Marañón and Huallaga Rivers, a remote region of the Andes Mountains on the northern edge of the Amazon Rain Forest—so high above sea level that they're literally in the clouds.

Did they really have white skin? There are two fascinating theories as to how this may have occurred.

• **ADAPTIVE INDIANS.** Before retreating to the highlands, the Chachapoyas had dark complexions. But over the

centuries, the isolated population evolved lighter skin and taller stature due to the darker conditions and cooler climate.

• **JUNGLE VIKINGS**. Unlike just about every other dark-skinned native culture in the Americas—who crossed the Bering Strait from Asia thousands of years before—these people may have come from Europe. This gives credence to an Inca legend that says the Cloud People arrived on ships from the east. To the east is the Atlantic Ocean. So perhaps, during Europe's Dark Ages, Nordic tribes traversed the Atlantic and landed somewhere near the mouth of the Amazon River. Then, finding the temperature too hot and muggy, they migrated hundreds of miles into the mountains before settling in the cooler cloud forests.

So far, there's no conclusive DNA evidence to support either theory. If you want to see a remnant of the Cloud People, take a look at the beginning of *Raiders of the Lost Ark*: The idol that Indiana Jones attempts to "collect" is Chachapoyan.

# Smooth as Silk

Believe it or not, but one of the most profitable commodities in the ancient world came from the salivary glands of a caterpillar. According to Chinese records, the empress Si Ling-chi was watching silkworms (caterpillars of the *Bombyx mori* moth) in her garden in about 2700 B.C. when she discovered that their white cocoons contained shimmering threads inside. Noting that the threads would make a beautiful gown, she began to cultivate the caterpillars, discovered how to reel the silk fibers, and wove them into robes and other clothing. Thus she founded *sericulture*, the science of silk production. She even lent her name to it— the Chinese pronunciation of "Si Ling-chi" sounds similar to "silk."

The sheer, lightweight material became a profitable commodity worth its weight in gold. Silk even got its own trade route; from 139 B.C. through the 1400s, it was sold via the Silk Road across India, Arabia, Africa, and the Mediterranean. Silk was so valued that for 3,000 years, the secrets of where it came from and how it was made were extremely guarded—revealing them was punishable by death. Si Ling-chi was later deified for her discovery and given the name Seine-Than, or "goddess of silkworms."

# The Code of Hammurabi

Circa 1780 B.C., King Hammurabi of Babylon ordered his scribes to carve a set of 281 laws into an eight-foot-high stone column. At the top is a depiction of the king sitting on his throne. Below that, the text begins with a rambling message from Hammurabi, in which he calls himself "the exalted prince" and vows to "destroy the wicked and the evil-doers." Below that are the laws. Some you may be familiar with, such as "an eye for an eye." That's law #196: "If a man put out the eye of another man, his eye shall be put out." "A tooth for a tooth" is covered under law #200. There's no mention of prison. The only alternatives were fines, or, as in the case of the eye and tooth mentioned above, the occasional "pound of flesh." Here are some of the "crimes" that would have gotten you executed.

- Accusing someone of a crime without proof.
- Falsely accusing someone of a crime.
- Stealing the property of a temple or a court.
- Receiving the stolen property of a temple or a court.
- Stealing a slave.
- Helping a slave escape.
- Hiding a slave.
- Breaking and entering.
- Committing a robbery.

• Allowing conspirators to meet in your tavern.

• Violating a virgin who is promised in marriage to another.

Even an innocent bystander could be included in the death sentence. Take law #229, for example, which states that a house builder will be put to death if the house he built falls in and kills the owner. The next law, #230, adds a nuance: "If it kills the son of the owner, the son of that builder shall be put to death."

It gets worse.

• If a wife and her lover have their mates (her husband and the other man's wife) murdered, "both of them shall be impaled."

• If a robbery is committed during a fire, the criminal will be thrown into that "self-same fire."

• If a surgeon kills someone during surgery, his hands are cut off.

• If a slave says to his master, "You are not my master," his ears are cut off.

• If a husband accused his wife of adultery but can't prove it, the wife would be thrown into the water. If she floats, she's innocent. If not, she drowns.

If you want to see the Code of Hammurabi, it's on display at the Louvre Museum in Paris. (You may notice there's no law #13. That's because the ancient Babylonians were just as superstitious as we are.)

# Why Do We Say "In a Nutshell"?

The ancient Greek historian Pliny the Elder (A.D. 23–79) was known to stretch the truth a bit, especially when it came to the poems of Homer, which themselves were historical epics that embellished the truth.

In *Natural History*, Pliny claims that a copy of Homer's *Iliad*, written entirely on a piece of parchment, had once been found inside a nutshell. (There's no way this can be true—the *Iliad* is 15,690 lines long.) This amusing boast later became a Latin proverb, *in nuce Ilias*, or "the *Iliad* in a nutshell," which expresses the same meaning it holds today. The 16th-century English writer Stephen Gosson was the first to use the phrase without mentioning the *Iliad*, but it was popularized by frequent usage in the works of 19th-century writers Charles Dickens and Robert Browning. Today, the phrase "in a nutshell" means "a complicated concept or experience expressed succinctly."

# Outdated Concepts: Phrenology

Developed by the 18th-century Austrian anatomist
Franz Joseph Gall, phrenology was a pseudoscience
that held that 1) different personality traits were
located in different areas in the brain, and 2) the
shape of an individual's skull was influenced by the
size and shape of these areas of the brain. By carefully
measuring different parts of the skull, especially the
bumps, phrenologists believed it was possible to
gain insight into an individual's personality traits,
even to the point of evaluating their fitness for a
particular occupation, suitability as a potential mate,
and potential for criminal behavior. Though it was
never taken seriously by the scientific community,
phrenology
remained popular
throughout the
19th century and
still has a handful
of adherents today.

> "What progress we are making. In
> the Middle Ages they would have
> burned me. Now they are content
> with burning my books."
>
> **—Sigmund Freud**

# Kitty Cat Gods

**GRIMALKIN.** Its name comes from its color, gray, plus *malkin*, an archaic word for "cat." Scottish legend tells of this wraith, a human by day, a fierce panther roaming the Highlands by night. The huge cat has magical powers: It can appear in the form of a hare and then disappear at will. During the Middle Ages, the name grimalkin—and cats in general—became associated with the devil and witchcraft. Women tried as witches during the 16th, 17th, and 18th centuries were often accused of having a "familiar," a devilish companion animal. What kind of animal? Usually a grimalkin.

**JAGUAR SUN.** The Mayans of Central America worshipped the Jaguar Sun that rose each day in the east and journeyed west. After the sun set, the cat god would have to fight the lords of the underworld all night. But the cat god would win the battle and rise again in the morning. Warriors wore jaguar skins to help them in battle; shamans were said to be able to shape-shift into the big cats.

# More Strange Toys of Yesteryear

### LIONEL BALLISTIC MISSILE RAILCAR LAUNCHER

**THE PRODUCT:** How do you sell dull railroad trains during the Cold War era? By adding nuclear missile cars!

**THE PITCH:** "With a Lionel Train, you not only get locomotives and cars, but all sorts of missile and rocket equipment, too! You can learn to operate these Lionel missile launchers. And fire this ballistic missile launcher by pressing a button. Wow! And look! You can put this boxcar target together and blow it up again and again!" (Also available: the Lionel Turbo Missile Firing Car and the Lionel Aerial Target Car.)

### THE DING-A-LINGS

**THE PRODUCT:** Tiny battery-powered robots in the 1960s

**THE PITCH:** "You are witnessing the creation of an entire new world. A world of unbelievable excitement and fun. The world of the Ding-a-lings! Holy smokes, what's going on? It's Ding-a-ling Fireman coming to the rescue! He's got his own built-in pumper to save the day. Ding-a-ling Shoeshine gives you the brightest shine you've ever seen! Ding-a-ling Answer Man's got all the answers in his head. Push the lever, and he'll tell your future. Ding-a-ling Chef salts your food, and Ding-a-ling Gofer serves it to you! Stand back, world—there's a whole new one on the way. The wild, wonderful, wacky world of the Ding-a-lings!"

# Beasts of Burden

These days, we take zoos for granted, but they are actually a recent invention. If you wanted to see a wild animal from another country, you would have to travel to that country... or you would have to be very, very rich and powerful.

European royalty once had a strange fascination with exotic animals. They exchanged them like trading cards. In the 1200s, Holy Roman Emperor Frederick II owned a menagerie of hyenas, elephants, camels, lions, monkeys, cheetahs, and a giraffe. When he grew tired of the giraffe, he traded it to the sultan of Egypt for a polar bear.

In 1235 King Henry III of England had a collection of camels, lions, leopards, and lynx that he kept in the Tower of London. King Louis IX of France contributed an elephant—the first one ever seen in Great Britain. The animals were put on display for the royal family and its guests, but were also occasionally pitted against one another—tigers vs. lions, bears vs. dogs—to entertain royal visitors.

It would be several centuries before regular people got to see exotic animals at the zoo. Hoof it on over to the next page for that story.

# THE ZOO:
## AN OKAY THING TO DO!

When the royal family moved out of the Tower of London in the early 1700s, they left their menagerie of exotic animals behind. With no one to look after the creatures, someone came up with the idea of opening the collection to the public. Price: three halfpence, or, if you preferred, a dog or cat to feed to the lions.

In 1826 an explorer named Sir Stamford Raffles founded the London Zoological Society, named for the ancient Greek word *zoion*, which means "living being." Two years later, the society moved the animals from the Tower of London to Regent's Park. But the Zoological Park was closed to the public—the animals were "objects of scientific research," Raffles explained, "not of vulgar admiration."

It wouldn't be until 1846 that the Zoological Society finally opened its doors. Reason: Membership attendance was dwindling. Now, anyone with a penny could go to the "zoo," as it was being called—thanks to the popularity of the song "Walking in the Zoo Is an Okay Thing to Do." Sample lyrics:

*So when there comes to town my pretty cousin Loo*
*I took her off to spend a Sunday in the Zoo*
*I showed her the aquarium, the tiger, the Zebu*
*The elephant, the Eland, that cuss the Kangaroo*

# The *Titan* and the *Titanic*

*Eerie coincidence...or clairvoyant prediction?*

In 1898 Morgan Robertson wrote a novel called *Futility, or the Wreck of the Titan*, about the maiden voyage of an "unsinkable" luxury liner. Robertson's *Titan* was 800 feet long, weighed 75,000 tons, had three propellers and 24 lifeboats, and carried rich passengers. Cruising at 25 knots, the *Titan*'s hull was ripped apart when it hit an iceberg in April. Most of the passengers were lost because there weren't enough lifeboats.

Fourteen years later, the real-life "unsinkable" *Titanic* took off on its maiden voyage. It was 882.5 feet long, weighed 66,000 tons, had three propellers and 22 lifeboats, and carried rich passengers. Late at night on April 14, 1912, sailing at 23 knots, the *Titanic* ran into an iceberg that tore a hole in its hull and upended the ship. At least 1,517 people drowned because there weren't enough lifeboats.

After the disaster, reporters asked Robertson, an experienced seaman, if he was clairvoyant. "No," he replied. "I know what I'm writing about, that's all."

BOTCHED

HISTORY

"Titanic 100 years ago. wOw.
Global warming couldve saved
Titanic. Sad to say."

—FORMER BASEBALL PLAYER JOSE CANSECO,
TWEETING ON THE 100TH ANNIVERSARY
OF THE *TITANIC* DISASTER. (STRANGELY,
HE WAS KIND OF CORRECT.)

# TICKLED TO DEATH

Roman emperor Claudius I died in A.D. 54. Most historians claim that his wife, Julia Agrippina, tried to murder her husband by feeding him poison mushrooms. According to historians, that's not what did him in: Afterward, Claudius's doctor attempted to induce vomiting by tickling his throat with a feather. The feather got stuck in the emperor's throat, and he choked to death.

> "We must laugh at man to avoid crying for him."
> —Napoleon Bonaparte

# Smart People Talk History

"History is a relentless master. It has no present, only the past rushing into the future. To try to hold fast is to be swept aside."

—John F. Kennedy

"History is a vast early warning system."

—Norman Cousins

"History doesn't repeat itself, but it rhymes."

—Will Rogers

"God cannot alter the past, though historians can."

—Samuel Butler

"We live in a world where amnesia is the most wished-for state. When did 'history' become a bad word?"

—John Guare

"History is the sum total of things that could have been avoided."

—Konrad Adenauer

"History is merely gossip."

—Oscar Wilde

"History is politics projected into the past."

—M. N. POKROVSKY

"A morsel of genuine history is a thing so rare as to be always valuable."

—THOMAS JEFFERSON

"Time after time, history demonstrates that when people don't want to believe something, they have enormous skills of ignoring it altogether."

—JIM BUTCHER

"Radical historians now tell the story of Thanksgiving from the point of view of the turkey."

—MASON COOLEY

"The obscurest epoch is today."

—ROBERT LOUIS STEVENSON

# I Fart in Your General Direction!

In 568 B.C., King Apries of Egypt sent a trusted general named Amasis to put down a mutiny among his troops. But when Amasis got there, the troops offered to make him their leader instead...and he accepted.

King Apries couldn't believe it. He sent a respected advisor named Patarbemis to bring Amasis back. Amasis responded to the king's entreaties by raising himself from his saddle and farting. Then he told Patarbemis to "carry that back to Apries." The king was so enraged by the message that he had Patarbemis's nose and ears hacked off. Committing such a barbarous act against such a respectable man was the last straw for many Egyptians—they turned pro-Amasis. With their support, Amasis's troops attacked and defeated Apries's army.

Amasis became King Ahmose and reigned for 44 years, from 569 to 525 B.C., which modern historians call one of Egypt's most prosperous periods.

# Lost to History: Ancient Greek Dramas

• Historians consider Aeschylus (525–456 B.C.) the "father of tragedy" because he invented that basic theatrical form and, thereby, all of Western theater. Much of what we know about ancient Greek gods, history, and life comes from Aeschylus's plays. But we could have known even more. Records suggest that Aeschylus wrote between 70 and 90 plays. While we know the titles, only the scripts for seven of those plays survive. Three of those (*Agamemnon*, *The Libation Bearers*, and *The Eumenides*) form *The Oresteia*, the only Greek tragic trilogy still in existence.

• Aeschylus wasn't the only Greek playwright whose work was lost. His successor as the leading playwright and documentarian of Athens, Sophocles (496–406 B.C.), wrote 123 plays, but only seven still exist today, including *Antigone*, *Oedipus Rex*, and *Electra*. His successor was Euripides (480–406 B.C.). Historical records indicate that he wrote as many as 80 tragedies, but the scripts of only 18 survive, including *Medea*, *The Trojan Women*, and *The Bacchae*.

# Crisis Averted (Bearly)

Late at night on October 25, 1962, a guard at a U.S. Air Force base in Minnesota spotted a dark figure climbing the fence. The guard shot and killed the mysterious invader. The fence was wired to detect intruders, and as the culprit fell, it set off an alarm. But the fence was incorrectly wired, and the alarm set off a second alarm hundreds of miles away at a base in Wisconsin. F-106 fighter jets armed with nuclear missiles immediately prepared to take off toward the Soviet Union in response to the intrusion. But the nuclear strike was quickly called off after an investigation determined the identity of the fence-climbing spy: a bear.

## FIVE FREAKY FACTS ABOUT...
# THE SILVER SCREEN

- Elizabeth Taylor had 65 costume changes in the 1963 film *Cleopatra*.

- Clint Eastwood was drafted into the U.S. Army during the Korean War. An expert swimmer, he once swam three miles back to shore after his plane crashed in the Pacific Ocean.

- Only "Oscar" to win an Oscar: writer/producer Oscar Hammerstein II.

- Actual footage of the *Hindenburg* crash was shown in the 1937 comedy *Charlie Chan at the Olympics*.

- It cost $3 million to build the *Titanic*... and $100 million to make the movie.

# VLAD TO MEET YOU

In 1897 Bram Stoker wrote the book *Dracula*. It turns out that the fictional vampire wasn't anywhere near as bad as the man who inspired it: Vlad the Impaler, who really did impale a lot of people.

But where did the name "Dracula" come from? Vlad's father was Prince Vlad II of Wallachia (now Romania). In 1431 Holy Roman Emperor Sigismund invited the prince to join the Order of the Dragon, a religious order of knights sworn to defend Christendom from the Muslim Turks. The prince traveled to Nuremberg to accept the honor, and returned carrying a large flag with the image of a dragon on it. Prince Vlad (who was a bloodthirsty tyrant like his son) soon became known as Vlad Dracul—"Vlad the Dragon" or, since dragons and devils were synonymous in 15th-century Romania, "Vlad the Devil." Prince Vlad's son, who was also named Vlad, was nicknamed Dracula, "Son of the Devil." So heinous were his atrocities that his name became a warning to misbehaving children: "Be good, or Dracula will get you!"

# Two Actors, Two Legs

• British actor Herbert Marshall lost a leg fighting in World War I, but he didn't let that stop him from his true passion: acting. Marshall spent 50 years as a romantic lead on the stage and on the screen, starring opposite such stars as Marlene Dietrich in *Blonde Venus* and Greta Garbo in *The Painted Veil*. Audiences never even knew that he wore an artificial leg—directors kept his onscreen movements to a minimum to hide it.

• Probably the most famous actress at the turn of the 20th century, Sarah Bernhardt suffered from a festering knee injury and had to have her leg amputated while touring in a production of *Jeanne Dore* in 1915. Fitted with a wooden leg, "the Divine Sarah" continued to tour in plays, acted in movies, and even performed at the front during World War I.

> "According to Greek mythology, humans were originally created with four arms, four legs, and a head with two faces. Fearing their power, Zeus split them into two separate parts, condemning them to spend their lives in search of their other halves."
>
> —Plato, *The Symposium* (385 B.C.)

# Tales from the Cryptids

## THE OGOPOGO MONSTER

Ogopogo is sometimes referred to as "Canada's Loch Ness Monster," and sightings go back to the 1800s. Lurking in the cold waters of British Columbia's Okanagan Lake, he was called Naitaka or "Lake Demon" by First Nations peoples. They say he was once a man who got possessed by a demon and then murdered another man, so the gods condemned him to live forever as a serpent. (He got the name "Ogopogo" from a 1924 English music hall song called "The Ogo-Pogo: The Funny Fox-Trot.")

There have been numerous eyewitness accounts over the years; one of the most famous took place in 1947 when several boaters saw the monster at the same time. According to a man named Mr. Kay, Ogopogo had...

> ...a long sinuous body, 30 feet in length, consisting of about five undulations, apparently separated from each other by about a two-foot space, in which that part of the undulations would have been underwater. There appeared to be a forked tail, of which only one-half came above the water. From time to time the whole thing submerged and came up again.

# Prehistoric Myth-conceptions

**MYTH:** Pterodactyls were dinosaurs.

**FACT:** Technically speaking, dinosaurs were land-dwelling reptiles with their legs positioned directly underneath their bodies. Pterodactyls were pterosaurs—flying reptiles which, when on land, crawled on all fours with their feet sprawled out to the sides, like lizards and crocodiles (which are also not dinosaurs).

**MYTH:** Fossils are the preserved remains of animals or plants.

**FACT:** Very few fossils are the actual remains of the organism itself (such as an insect trapped in amber). Most are actually *trace fossils*: When the dead plant or animal was covered by sediment, the organic matter decayed and was slowly replaced by minerals in the groundwater. Over time, very little (if any) of the original living thing was left, except for its cast, or shape. Now it's basically a rock.

# Storming the Castle

One of history's greatest last stands took place in the 16th century when Turkish sultan Suleiman the Magnificent sought to expand his Ottoman Empire eastward into Europe. In 1552, after more than 30 years of war and advances, a Turkish force of approximately 80,000 soldiers attacked a castle fortress in the town of Eger, one of the Kingdom of Hungary's last strongholds. Roughly 2,000 people, including 1,500 soldiers, vowed to defend their home against the 80,000 invaders.

The Turks had more than 150 pieces of artillery, including 15 huge cannons. They fired at the castle from every direction for days, and then for weeks...but they couldn't get inside. They made several attempts to storm the castle; they shot flaming arrows over the sides; they even dug under the walls and planted bombs...and they still couldn't get inside.

Finally, after 39 days of relentless attacks, during which roughly a third of the Hungarians inside were killed, the Turks finally gave up and left. The Hungarians, outnumbered almost 50 to 1, had won.

"Three cheers for war in general."
**—Benito Mussolini**

# Almost Assassinated

• **PRESIDENT ABRAHAM LINCOLN:** In August 1864, a would-be assassin took aim at Lincoln's head, but the bullet went straight through his tall top hat and missed his head completely.

• **GENERAL ULYSSES S. GRANT:** Less than a year later, on April 14, 1865, Lincoln was killed. (He had his famous hat with him, but it was sitting on the floor.) But it could have been even worse. Lincoln had invited General Grant and his wife, Julia, to accompany him and Mrs. Lincoln to Ford's Theatre. The Grants declined. "Had his assassination plot gone according to plan," Carl Sifakis writes in *The Encyclopedia of Assassinations*, John Wilkes Booth "would have killed not only the president, but a future president as well, General Ulysses S. Grant."

Why didn't the Grants go? Because Julia Grant detested Mary Lincoln. A few weeks earlier, while touring Grant's headquarters together, Mary snubbed Julia so many times in front of so many important people that Julia refused to spend another night in Mary's company. Grant, biographer William S. McFeely writes, "was left to make to the president the most classic—and limp—of excuses: He couldn't go because of the children."

# Windows 1

In 1900 sponge divers found the wreck of an ancient ship 140 feet underwater, near the Greek island of Antikythera. Many of the items retrieved from it were taken to the National Archaeological Museum in Athens, among them lumps of corroded bronze that looked like parts of a statue. But an archaeologist noticed some words inscribed on the metal and then found gears—and realized it wasn't a statue, it was a machine. Originally held together by a wooden box that fell apart when taken out of the water, the mechanism had dials on the outside and a complicated arrangement of wheels and differential gears inside. The inscription dated it between 100 B.C. and A.D. 30, and indicated that the contraption had something to do with astronomy.

A 1959 *Scientific American* article compared the object to "a well-made 18th-century clock." The "Antikythera mechanism," it said, was a model of the solar system which, like a modern computer, "used mechanical parts to save tedious calculation." Turned by hand, or perhaps by water power, the machine would calculate and display the position of the sun, moon, planets, and stars. The find meant that historians had to rethink their whole concept of the ancient Greek world...and their ideas about when computing machines were first invented.

# Did We Really Land on the Moon?

**NO WE DIDN'T**! "I received a call from a Margaret Hardin of Portland, Oregon. She said that she had met a hooker in Reno in 1970 who admitted to her that two NASA engineers told her the Moon trips were a hoax."

—BILL KAYSING, AUTHOR OF *WE NEVER WENT TO THE MOON: AMERICA'S THIRTY BILLION DOLLAR SWINDLE*

**YES WE DID!** "Bill Kaysing is wacky. His position makes me feel angry. We spent a lot of time getting ready to go to the Moon. We spent a lot of money, we took great risks, and it's something everybody in the country ought to be proud of."

—JIM LOVELL, *APOLLO 13* COMMANDER

**NO WE DIDN'T**! "An old carpenter asked me if I really believed it happened. I said, 'Sure, I saw it on television.' He disagreed; he said that he didn't believe it for a minute, that 'them television fellers' could make things look real that weren't. Back then, I thought he was a crank. During my eight years in Washington, I saw some things on TV that made me wonder if he wasn't ahead of his time."

—BILL CLINTON

**YES WE DID!** "The body of physical evidence that humans did walk on the Moon is simply overwhelming."

—Dr. Robert Park, physicist

**NO WE DIDN'T'!** "The event was so removed, however, so unreal, that no objective correlative existed to prove it had not been an event staged in a television studio—the greatest con of the century."

—Norman Mailer

**YES WE DID!** "Who are these Looneytoons that do not believe in science, history, personal endeavor, heroic feats, and rock-solid facts? Forgive me, but I find these folks an utter waste of time, the 'didn't happen crowd.' I wish they'd just all go back to their beer, and shuffleboard, and wondering if the Earth is really not, after all, going around the Sun."

—Bobby Charles, NASA Oversight Committee, 1999

# Real-Life Frankensteins: Jonathan Dippel

Jonathan Dippel was a theologian, alchemist, and trouble-maker. Born in 1673 in the real Castle Frankenstein in Germany, he may have served as the inspiration for Mary Shelley's 1818 novel *Frankenstein*.

Working in his lab, Dippel whipped up a concoction of human bones, blood, and bodily fluids that he called the "Elixir of Life." The drinker, he claimed, would live forever. (He also discovered that his elixir, when combined with potassium carbonate, made a useful dye known today as Prussian blue.) There's no evidence that Dippel tried to stitch body parts together, but he was fond of putting legs, arms, heads, and torsos—both animal and human—into huge vats and boiling them down in the hope of, as he called it, "engendering life in the dead." The resulting stench angered the townspeople; they demanded that he end the grotesque experiments or risk being expelled from the country. Dippel wouldn't give in, so he was exiled. He was rumored to have been later poisoned in Sweden.

"History is a long succession of useless cruelties."

—**Voltaire**

# Seven Up

- Ancient people considered 7 the number that governs the rhythm of life. Their lives revolved around the phases of the Moon, which has four cycles of seven days.

- Among the Sumerians, Babylonians, and Egyptians, there were seven sacred planets: the Sun, Moon, Mercury, Venus, Mars, Jupiter, and Saturn.

- The Sumerians named their gods after these seven planets and were the first to divide the week into seven days.

- The ancient Greeks called 7 the perfect number, as it was the sum of the triangle (3) and the square (4).

- In China, the seventh day of the first moon of the lunar year is called Human's Day. The Chinese mark this day as the birthday of all humans.

- According to the Bible, there are seven deadly sins. Here they are, along with the *Spongebob Squarepants* characters they inspired: 1. Sloth: Patrick, the lazy starfish; 2. Wrath: Squidward, the angry squid; 3. Gluttony: Gary, the ever-hungry snail; 4. Pride: Sandy, the proud Texas squirrel; 5. Envy: Plankton, the jealous...plankton; 6. Greed: Mr. Krabs, the money-hungry crustacean; 7. Lust: SpongeBob, the sponge who loves everyone.

# The Flaming Underpants That Inspired a Nation

The 1956 Olympics were held in Melbourne, Australia. Nine students from the University of Sydney thought it was appalling that the Olympic torch relay—created by the Nazis for the 1936 Berlin Games—was elevating the torch to the level of a religious icon, with thousands of Australians lining the streets of Sydney wherever the relay passed through.

So they devised a plan to protest the torch with a phony relay. In the real relay, cross-country athlete Harry Dillon was supposed to run through downtown Sydney and hand the torch to Mayor Pat Hills, who would then make a speech and give the torch to another runner. Moments before Dillon was to arrive, however, one of the protesters began running in the streets with a different kind of torch—a silver-painted chair leg topped with a flaming pair of underpants.

The crowd laughed at the prank, but then the underwear fell off and the runner panicked and ran away. Another student took up the torch, relit the underpants, and continued to run the route...and police thought he was the real deal. They escorted him all the way to the town hall, where he presented the flaming underpants to Mayor Hills.

# Forgotten Firsts in Robot History

**350 B.C.**: The first known robot is a mechanical wooden bird, powered by steam, built by the Greek mathematician Archytas of Tarentum.

**1927**: "Maria," a female robot, appears in Fritz Lang's science-fiction movie *Metropolis*. It's the first ever on-screen robot.

**1940**: Isaac Asimov publishes "Robbie" in *Super Science Stories*, the first piece of robot-themed fiction.

**1954**: George Devol receives the first patent for a robot. Five years later, his Unimate, a robotic arm, is installed at a General Motors plant in New Jersey. It moves pieces of hot metal from a die-casting machine.

**1966**: Shakey, developed by the Stanford Research Institute, becomes the first robot that can actually react to its surroundings. Using "reason," it can identify and move small objects.

**1968**: "Humanoid Boogie" by the British group Bonzo Dog Doo-Dah Band is released, making it the first pop song about robots.

**1969**: A remote-controlled robot washes the windows of the Tower of the Americas in San Antonio, Texas.

**1983**: Ropet-HR, built by Personal Robotics Corp., lobbies the House of Representatives for increased spending in robot technology. It is the first robot to address Congress.

**1983**: "Robot Redford" becomes the first robot to deliver a commencement address when it speaks to the graduating class at Anne Arundel Community College in Maryland.

**1984**: A robot named "Rebecca" runs for president of the United States as an independent. Her supporters say she's eligible because she was "born" in Maryland.

**2006**: A team at Carnegie Mellon University creates "McBlare," the first robot bagpipe player. (Was that really necessary?)

# Made-up Languages

**SOLRESOL ("Language"):** A "musical language" created by François Sudre, a French author, in the mid-1800s

**Features:** Sudre based his entire language on the musical scale: do, re, mi, fa, sol, la, and ti. Each word in Solresol is composed of one or more of these syllables. It's probably the only language in the world that can be translated directly into music, and vice versa. And not just music: Any system you can think of that has seven different components—seven hand signals, seven whistles, seven colors, etc.—can serve as a medium for communicating in Solresol.

### SAMPLE WORDS:

| | |
|---|---|
| *dodomi*: season | *midofasol*: orphan |
| *ladoti*: book | *dofafado*: Easter |
| *fadore*: corrupt | *laremila*: blue |
| *reredo*: July | *fafadosol*: surgeon |
| *tiremido*: deaf | *remitisol*: stairs |
| *sollamifa*: sculpture | *tilamido*: police |

**Fatal Flaw:** Sudre drew huge crowds at demonstrations where language students translated his violin playing into speech. But as much as the public enjoyed the show, most thought of Solresol as nothing more than a novelty act. It never caught on.

# Privy Digging 101

*Before trash collection, people threw lots of stuff down the outhouse hole. Today, antique collectors can find all sorts of interesting treasures down there. Want to try it yourself?*

**1**. Know where to dig. The outhouses themselves are long gone. In areas with harsh winters, the outhouse is likely to have been closer to the house. On city lots, look to the back of the property line, usually in a corner.

**2**. Pick an outhouse that's on private property. Privies on public land may be protected by historical preservation laws, which usually don't apply to private lands.

**3**. Ask before you dig. Getting permission to dig in someone's backyard may be easier than you think—just offer to share the artifacts you find.

**4**. Keep digging. Most of the best artifacts are likely to have sunk all the way to the bottom.

**5**. Check the sides and corners. When an outhouse is in use, material "mounds up in the center," just below where people sat, says privy digger Peter Bleed. "Things tend to roll off to the sides."

**6**. But wait, there's more! When one privy vault filled up, a new one was dug—frequently right next to the old one. So if you find one privy vault, don't stop! Look for more nearby.

# Magnum P.U.

*Hey, privy diggers (see previous page), time for some "Outhouse Detectives" mysteries!*

**Discovery:** A child's doll, recovered completely intact
**Mystery:** Most items that were disposed of in an outhouse were garbage. It's unlikely that a 19th-century family would have thrown away even an unbroken doll. And yet it's not unusual to find perfectly intact dolls at the bottom of an outhouse. What are they doing down there?
**Theory:** They ended up there by accident. "Lots of times, I think, little girls went to the bathroom and accidentally dropped their doll down there," said Michigan privy digger John Ozoga. "Dad wouldn't go get it."

**Discovery:** Three bottles of Wilkerson's Teething Syrup, recovered from an outhouse in St. Charles, Missouri. (It was used to help relieve a baby's teething pain.)
**Mystery:** What's remarkable about these bottles, privy diggers say, is that they are never found alone. Why?
**Theory:** The syrup's active ingredient is opium, which is highly addictive. Babies got hooked on the stuff, which meant that "parents had to keep on buying it to keep them from crying."

# We ♥ Lucy!

It was November 30, 1974, at a dig site in Hadar, Ethiopia. Don Johanson, an American paleoanthropologist, was about to quit searching for fossils because of the 110-degree heat. Before returning to camp, he and a colleague took a cursory look at one last slope because Johanson was "feeling lucky." There he saw a piece of fossilized bone on the ground, then another, and another.

The scientists knew they were onto something big. The fossils formed the partial skeleton of a very primitive, female apelike creature. That night, while celebrating their discovery, the researchers knocked back some beers while the Beatles' song "Lucy in the Sky with Diamonds" played in the background. Sometime during a night of partying, the Hadar expedition named their new find "Lucy."

Lucy was the size of a modern child; she stood about 3'6" and weighed around 60 pounds, but she was no kid. Scientists estimate that she was 21 years old when she died more than three million years ago. But was she the "missing link" between apes and humans?

Scientists expected the missing link to have a big brain and an apelike body. Lucy, however, had a small, chimp-sized brain with a lower body like a human's. For years people had believed it was the human brain that separated man from beast—now it seemed to be our pelvis and

locking knee joints. In 1979 Johanson and his colleague
Tim White officially categorized Lucy as *Australopithecus
afarensis* ("southern ape from East Africa"). She was related
to chimps but also related to *Homo habilis* and *Homo
erectus*—as well as us. But scientists don't think she is the
true missing link, or even if there is one. So maybe "Cousin
Lucy" is a better description. Either way, she changed the
way we think about our ancestors.

---

### BONUS LUCY FACT

In 1938 legendary film producer David O. Selznick
held auditions for a lead role in his upcoming film,
*Gone With the Wind*. He wanted a redhead. A young
starlet named Lucille Ball came in to audition, but it
was raining outside and she was soaked. She was led
to the producer's office and left alone to wait. Selznick
walked in as she was trying to dry her hair. He had
her quickly read the lines and dismissed her. She
didn't get the part.

Lucy never forgot. In 1957 she and her husband,
Desi Arnaz, by then two of America's biggest stars,
bought Selznick's old studio, renamed it Desilu, and
set up their headquarters...in the office that Lucy
remembered so well.

# The Last Stand at Thermopylae

In 480 B.C., Persia's King Xerxes I sought to add Greece to his empire and invaded with 80,000 soldiers. Several Greek city-states banded together to stop them. Led by King Leonidas of Sparta, 5,000 soldiers awaited the Persians at a narrow mountain pass near Thermopylae. Xerxes sent a message: "Surrender your weapons and you will live."

Leonidas's reply: "Come and get us."

Xerxes sent thousands of soldiers into the pass, but the Greeks repelled them. So Xerxes sent thousands more. They were stopped again. This went on for two days...until a Greek local told Xerxes about another pass—one that would allow the Persians to surround their outnumbered foes.

When Leonidas learned of the betrayal, he gathered 300 of his most skilled Spartan fighters (one of the few things the comic book and film 300 got right). Along with about 2,000 other fighters, they held off the Persians long enough to give the army time to escape. Attacked by the main force from the pass—and now by 10,000 more from the rear—the Greeks fought with spears, swords, hands, and teeth until every last one of them was dead, including Leonidas. The Greeks captured Xerxes and removed his head. Despite the victory, the Persians lost nearly 20,000 soldiers. A year later, they were crushed by the Greeks in the Battle of Plataea, and the Greco-Persian Wars were over.

# Kids on History

*These are actual answers to questions on students' tests
submitted to education websites by frazzled teachers.*

**Q:** What was Sir Walter Raleigh famous for?
**A:** He invented cigarettes and started a craze for bicycles.

**Q:** What is a fossil?
**A:** A fossil is an extinct animal. The older it is, the more extinct it is.

**Q:** Name the wife of Orpheus, whom he attempted to save from the underworld.
**A:** Mrs. Orpheus.

**Q:** What ended in 1896?
**A:** 1895.

**Q:** Name one popular queen.
**A:** Freddy Mercury.

**Q:** Name one of the Romans' greatest achievements.
**A:** Learning to speak Latin.

**Q:** Where was the Declaration of Independence signed?
**A:** At the bottom.

# Strange Cat History

• Some famous Italian paintings of the Last Supper show a cat at the feet of Judas. The fickle cat symbolizes Judas's role as traitor.

• In 1760 a "racy" book called *The Life and Adventures of a Cat* was published in England. The main character was a ram cat (as males were known back then) named Tom the Cat. The book was so popular that ever since then, males have been known as tomcats.

• Charles I ruled England from 1625 to 1649. According to legend, he had a lucky black cat. As civil war ripped the country, Charles became so convinced that his cat kept him safe, he assigned guards to watch it. Strangely enough, only one day after the black cat died, Charles was arrested, and was eventually sentenced to death by beheading.

• In a strange case of mass hysteria in 1844, a French nun began meowing like a cat for no apparent reason. Soon, all of the other nuns at the convent began meowing, too. It got so bad (and loud) that the villagers complained. French soldiers were dispatched to the convent and threatened to whip the nuns if they didn't shut up. After several hours, the nuns finally stopped meowing. They could provide no logical explanation for why they started to meow in the first place.

# Not So Mellow Yellow

Ever heard of alchemy? It was a medieval "science" and philosophy, and one of its goals was to find a way to turn base metals into gold through a process called *transmutation*. Scientists now know that this is impossible, but in the 1600s, it was a viable—and potentially lucrative—form of research.

An alchemist from Hamburg, Germany, named Hennig Brand believed the way to create gold was by chemically altering a very common substance: urine. At the time, it made sense. A prevailing theory of the day was that because urine and gold were both yellow, some advanced form of alchemy might be able to turn one into the other. With this in mind, Brand spent months collecting urine. When he'd accumulated 50 buckets of the stuff—mostly donated by local soldiers—he put them in his basement to "age," or allow the water to evaporate out and concentrate the urine.

One day in 1669, Brand was experimenting with his bucketloads of concentrated soldier pee and ended up with a vibrant blue-green substance that appeared to glow, both in the light and in the dark. But Brand couldn't get it to do anything else.

In 1675 another German alchemist named Daniel Kraft purchased Brand's blue goo and made a fortune showing it off to royalty and other wealthy Europeans. Kraft's act was basically magic tricks: He'd light candles with the stuff, throw it into gunpowder to make explosions, and write glowing blue-green words with it. It wouldn't be until 100 years later that the blue-green substance that Brand had discovered (and Kraft tried to take credit for) would be named: phosphorus. Today, phosphorus is abundant in manufacturing, commonly used in products such as soda, fertilizer, matches, flares, and fireworks. (And they don't have to get it from urine.)

**"Apollinaris, doctor to the emperor Titus, had a good crap here."**
**—ancient Roman graffiti scribbled on a wall in Pompeii**

# Two Random Origins

### THE POLICE CAR

The first occasion in which a car was used in police work occurred in 1899 when Sergeant McLeod of the Northamptonshire (England) County Police borrowed a Benz vehicle to pursue a man who was selling forged tickets for the Barnum and Bailey Circus. Top speed: 12 mph.

The first car regularly employed in police work was a Stanley Steamer acquired by the Boston Police Department in 1903. It replaced four horses.

### PET HAMSTERS

The natural habitat of golden (or Syrian) hamsters, as the pet variety is known, is limited to one area: the desert outside the city of Aleppo, Syria. (Their name in the local Arabic dialect translates to "saddlebags," thanks to the pouches in their mouths that they use to store food.) In 1930 a zoologist named Israel Aharoni found a nest containing a female and a litter of 11 babies in the desert and brought them back to his lab at the Hebrew University of Jerusalem. The mother died on the trip home; so did seven of her babies. Virtually all of the millions of domesticated golden hamsters in the world are descended from the four that survived.

# Pyramid Schemes

Some New Agers believe that the Egyptian pyramids were originally time machines, UFO bases, or gates to other dimensions. Thankfully, the Mayans of Mexico were somewhat more forthcoming—they left detailed documents that explain the astronomy behind the construction of their pyramids.

It turns out that the Mayans had a highly developed calendar system; they used astronomical events to set special dates for sacrifices and other rituals. Their pyramids were built on alignments that pointed toward the positions of the Sun, Moon, planets, and stars on these dates. It can't be proven that the Egyptian pyramids or the ziggurats of ancient Mesopotamia were built on the same kind of idea, but the astronomical alignments are similar, and so far no one has come up with a better explanation. So the next time you see an ancient pyramid, think "really big calendar."

## BOTCHED HISTORY

"My own personal theory is that Joseph built the pyramids [in Egypt] to store grain. Now, all the archaeologists think that they were made for the pharaohs' graves. But, you know, it would have to be something awfully big—when you stop and think about it, and I don't think it'd just disappear over the course of time— to store that much grain."

—BEN CARSON, NEUROSURGEON AND FORMER PRESIDENTIAL CANDIDATE

# Lost and Found...
# The Terra-cotta Warriors

While digging a well near Xian, China, in March 1974, a group of farmers struck what they thought was an oddly shaped rock. The rock turned out to be a life-size clay statue of a man's head with his hair in a topknot. The farmers had accidentally unearthed the first of an estimated 8,000 life-size warriors, chariots, charioteers, horses, and a cache of swords and spears buried and forgotten for more than 2,200 years.

The find was the terra-cotta army of China's first emperor, Qin Shi Huang, who died in 210 B.C. It's believed that the army was built to guard the mausoleum, one mile away. In the practice of the day, the emperor's childless concubines and all of the artisans who'd constructed the mausoleum were killed and buried with him. Although the tomb was mentioned in the works of a Chinese historian writing 100 years after the emperor's death, the army of figures was not.

> "I do not consider him to be as bad as depicted. He is showing an ability that is amazing, and he seems to be gaining his victories without much bloodshed."
> —**Gandhi, on Adolf Hitler**

# Bible Stories

• In 1631 a London bookmaker was printing an official edition of the Bible. But due to a goof, one important word was left out of all of the printings: "not." The section it was missing from: the Ten Commandments. Result: The book listed nine actual commandments...along with a sentence that read, "Thou shalt commit adultery." It became known as the "Wicked Bible."

• And speaking of wicked, in 1883 Noah Webster (of *Webster's Dictionary* fame) complained that the Bible was filled with smut: "Many words and phrases are so offensive, especially to females, as to create a reluctance in young persons to attend Bible classes and schools in which they are required to read passages which cannot be replaced without a blush." So Webster rewrote the entire Bible, removing the "filthiest" passages entirely and cleaning up the less offensive ones. Words such as "whore," "fornication," and "teat" gave way to milder expressions like "lewd woman," "lewdness," and "breast."

• Early 20th-century Ethiopian emperor Menelik II had an unusual habit: When he felt sick or uneasy, he'd eat a few pages out of a Bible. He was feeling especially sick after suffering a stroke in 1913, so he ate the entire book of Kings. A few days later, the emperor died of an intestinal blockage caused by the paper.

# Strange Savants

It's called Asperger's disorder, or "little professor syndrome." People who have Asperger's have many of the same traits as autistic people—social withdrawal, prodigious memory, interest in collecting and naming things, being prone to outbursts, and an obsession with order. They also display some symptoms that are unique to Asperger's: higher IQs, and unusual ability in science, complex calculations, and computer programming.

Dr. Hans Asperger, who gave the disorder its name in 1944, states it unequivocally: "For success in science and art—a dash of autism is essential." Here are a few noted geniuses who fit that model.

**ISAAC NEWTON (1642–1727):** Newton pioneered the laws of motion, the binomial theorem, and calculus. Reclusive, quirky, mindless of his personal cleanliness, he seldom spoke and was so obsessed with his work that he would forget to eat. At Cambridge, Newton was known for giving lectures...even if no one showed up to hear them. And rumor had it that Newton died a virgin. According to the French writer and philosopher Voltaire, "He was never sensible to any passion, was not subject to the common frailties of mankind, nor had any commerce with women."

**GLENN GOULD (1932–82):** This Canadian classical pianist was known by his friends and family as a control freak. Like

many savants, he had perfect pitch and a steel-trap memory. He also tended to sing along with his playing, which drove recording engineers crazy. But his gifted interpretations of Bach are considered some of the finest ever recorded.

**SAMUEL JOHNSON (1704–84):** The compiler of the first English dictionary had a tendency to startle people by shouting barnyard noises, or bits of the Lord's Prayer. Johnson would throw a tantrum if there were any changes in his daily habits.

**HENRY CAVENDISH (1731–1810):** The man who discovered hydrogen was one of the first people to accurately calculate the mass of the Earth, as well as the chemical composition of the atmosphere. He rarely left his house and went out of his way to avoid seeing anyone. Many discoveries credited to other scientists were found to have been made by Cavendish years earlier when his papers, which he never published, were examined after his death.

**THELONIUS MONK (1917–82):** Known as the high priest of bebop, this pianist and composer revolutionized jazz with his original compositions. He also had a unique performance style—personal tics that included unusual syncopations in his rhythms, as well as a tendency to dance around his piano. He spoke in a bizarre medley of grunts and random philosophical mutterings.

# FIVE FREAKY FACTS ABOUT...
# TRANSPORTATION

- From 1916 to 1920, Girl Scouts could earn an automobiling badge.

- A real train crossing a real bridge was blown up for the 1957 film *The Bridge on the River Kwai*.

- Hijacking an airplane wasn't officially outlawed until 1961.

- Before wipers, drivers smeared a mixture of onions and carrots on their windshields to repel water.

- Early names for the helicopter: instrument, screw, aerodynamic, pterophore, automoteur, aeroveliero, convertiplane, spiralifere, aerial carriage, aerial screw, stropheor.

# WHAT A DOLL

In 1918 Austrian artist Oscar Kokoschka was dumped by the musician, sculptor, and infamous Viennese socialite Alma Mahler. Devastated, Kokoschka commissioned Munich dollmaker Hermine Moos to craft him a life-size replica of his lost love. He sent Moos hundreds of intimate sketches of Mahler so Moos would get the dimensions of the wood exactly right. "Please pay special attention to the head and neck, to the rib-cage, the rump and the limbs," Kokoschka wrote. And: "Can the mouth be opened? And are there teeth and a tongue inside? I hope so."

Kokoschka finally received the doll in the spring of 1919. He could be seen driving through the streets of Vienna with "Alma" riding in the passenger seat. At parties it would be seated beside him; it would accompany him to his studio in Dresden. The couple even shared a box at the opera. The end came, so the story goes, at the close of a party in Dresden. At dawn, a drunken Kokoschka carried the doll out into his garden and beheaded it.

# Antiques Roadshow: The Top Finds

*Since 1997, millions have tuned in weekly to the PBS series* Antiques Roadshow *to see what treasures lie hidden in America's attics, pawn shops, and yard sales. Here are some of the most valuable items the show has ever discovered.*

**A NAVAJO BLANKET:** A man walked into a 2001 *Antiques Roadshow* taping in Tucson, Arizona, with his family's old blanket; it was handwoven with stripes of black, brown, blue, and white. He brought it in because family legend held that it had originally been a gift from the famed frontier scout Kit Carson. As it turns out, it's a national treasure—a Navajo blanket from the 1850s that was specially made for a chief. Fewer than 50 still exist. "When you walked in with this," appraiser Donald Ellis told the owner, "I just about died." The blanket now hangs in the Detroit Institute of Arts. Estimated worth: about $400,000.

**AN ANCIENT CHINESE STATUE:** The owner of this marble lion statue inherited it from her grandparents, who bought it in a curio shop on a vacation in China in the 1920s. It turned out to be, as Sotheby's appraiser Lark Mason said in a 2002 episode, "one of the finest examples of Tang dynasty art that's appeared in recent years." It was carved sometime between A.D. 618 and 907 and is worth about $250,000.

**A GOLD SWORD:** Before the Medal of Honor was first awarded in 1862, the highest honor an American officer could receive was a dress, or ceremonial, sword made of solid gold. In 1848 General William O. Butler was awarded such a sword for his service in the Mexican-American War. It was passed down through the generations to the man who took it to an *Antiques Roadshow* taping in Charlotte, North Carolina, in 2002...where it was appraised for $200,000.

**A SEYMOUR CARD TABLE:** The owner of this mahogany table bought it at a garage sale for $25. While cleaning it, she noticed its delicate inlay work and became curious, so she brought it to *Antiques Roadshow* in 1997. Appraisers Leigh and Leslie Keno were dumbfounded to find a label on the back identifying it as the work of father-and-son master cabinetmakers John and Thomas Seymour, English émigrés to Boston in the late 18th century. Estimated at $300,000, the circa-1797 table later sold at auction for $500,000.

# Love's Labour's Lost's Lost Sequel

*William Shakespeare wrote his plays quickly and in fragments, often handing scraps of paper to the actors to memorize. The plays weren't officially published until after his death, and they were based on those script fragments. Historians have found a total of 36 Shakespeare plays, but they think there may have been two more.*

• **LOVE'S LABOUR'S WON.** In 1598 English author Francis Meres listed nearly all of Shakespeare's known 36 plays... along with one called *Love's Labour's Won*, a sequel to *Love's Labour's Lost*. But Meres failed to include *The Taming of the Shrew*, leading scholars to believe for nearly 400 years that *Shrew* and *Won* were the same play. They were wrong. In 1953 an early 17th-century list of Shakespeare's plays was discovered that listed both *The Taming of the Shrew* and *Love's Labour's Won*.

• **CARDENIO.** There is a record of this play, an adaptation of Miguel de Cervantes's 1605 novel *Don Quixote*, being produced in 1613 by the King's Men, Shakespeare's theater troupe. The script has never been found.

# Movies You'll Never See

*From the birth of cinema in the 1890s until the late 1940s, the standard film stock was made of a nitrate base, which is highly combustible. Plus, it disintegrates quickly if it's not stored in a special low-oxygen, low-humidity, climate-controlled vault. Result: Hundreds of films are gone forever, including these:*

• **THE FAIRYLOGUE AND RADIO-PLAYS [1908].** The first-ever adaptation of L. Frank Baum's Oz books, it starred Baum interacting with drawings of his characters. The single print was in Baum's possession, but it disintegrated and was thrown out by his heirs.

• **THE WEREWOLF [1913].** The first werewolf film was lost in a 1924 fire.

• **CLEOPATRA [1917].** It starred silent-film icon Theda Bara in the title role and had a huge (at the time) budget of $500,000. All but 45 seconds were destroyed in a Fox Studios vault fire.

• **THE GULF BETWEEN [1917].** The first full-length color film made in the United States. Only a few frames are left.

# Hermitage, Sweet Hermitage

A by-product of the Industrial Revolution in the late 1700s: the Romantic era, in which writers, painters, and the well-to-do railed against modernization. Poets such as John Keats and William Wordsworth wrote about the virtues of solitude. The "humble hermit living off the land" became a symbol of the Romantic ideal...though few were willing to try it themselves. So wealthy Englishmen constructed "architectural follies" on their grounds—elaborate buildings that were primarily decorative, such as Roman temples and Egyptian pyramids, towers, grottoes—and hermit houses, or *hermitages*.

Most hermitages were pretty small. The one at Hagley Hall in Worcestershire was a closet-sized stone cave covered with roots, moss, and foliage. A Keats poem was hung

on the wall, just in case visitors didn't understand the connection. Many hermitages also included macabre decor, such as floors made of knucklebones. Marston House in Surrey was surrounded by a bone fence topped with real horse heads. And no hermitage was complete without a decorative human skull for contemplation.

# Hermits for Hire

Any wealthy nobleman had to have his own hermit—preferably a filthy, bearded old man—to live in his specially built hermitage. An English politician named Charles Hamilton advertised for a hermit to live in the forest at Painshill Park in Surrey...

> ...where he shall be provided with a Bible, optical glasses, a mat for his feet, a hassock for his pillow, an hourglass for his timepiece, water for his beverage, and food from the house. He must wear a camlet robe, and never, under any circumstances, must he cut his hair, beard, or nails, stray beyond the limits of Mr. Hamilton's grounds, or exchange one word with the servant.

Hamilton offered a payment of 700 guineas (more than $500,000 today), but there was a catch: The hermit wouldn't get a penny unless he followed every detail in the contract. Hamilton did find a man willing to shed his wares, but he lasted only three weeks—the "hermit" was fired for drinking at the local pub.

> "Whosoever is delighted in solitude is either a wild beast or a god."
> —**Aristotle**

# The Chariot Races

• Chariots date to around 3000 B.C. Carvings on Mesopotamian monuments show scenes of chariots being driven in battle parades.

• What animals pulled chariots for the first 1,000 years? Oxen.

• Chariot races were an Olympic event in ancient Greece, and it's thought that chariot drivers were the only athletes not to compete nude. (They wore white tunics.)

• In 2011 five chariots and several horse skeletons were found in the tomb of a Chinese nobleman. They were 2,500 years old.

• Archaeologists have said that King Tut died from injuries sustained during a chariot crash, but research conducted in 2015 disputes that. "It would not be possible for him [to drive a chariot], especially with his partially clubbed foot, as he was unable to stand unaided," said Professor Albert Zink, head of the Institute for Mummies and Icemen.

• The word "car" is derived from the Latin *carrum*, or "two-wheeled Celtic war chariot."

• Persian "scythed chariots" (circa 467 B.C.) had blades that protruded from the axles so that enemy soldiers could be cut down.

# How Can You Tell a Communist?

*FBI director J. Edgar Hoover was considered an expert on Communist infiltration. Here are excerpts from different interviews he gave from 1947 to 1950, telling Americans how to protect themselves against the Red Menace.*

**Q**: "How can you tell a Communist?"

**A**: "It is possible that a concealed Communist may hide in the most unsuspected and unlikely place. He is trained in deceit and uses cleverly camouflaged movements to conceal his real purposes. But he may frequently be detected by certain characteristics. He will always espouse the cause of Soviet Russia over that of the United States. His viewpoint and position will shift with each change in the Communist Party 'line.' He will utilize a language of 'double talk'— referring to the Soviet-dominated countries as 'democracies' and complain that the United States is 'imperialistic.' He will attempt to infiltrate and gain control of organizations and subvert them to the use of the party. My advice to the public is this: Be alert to the dangers of Communism. Report your information immediately and fully to the FBI."

**Q**: "Don't you draw a distinction between philosophical Communists and those who are tools of spy rings?"

**A**: "Any person who subscribes to these teachings, regardless of his reason, is working against American

democracy and for the benefit of Soviet Russia. Stalin is his omnipotent oracle from whom all wisdom flows. The Communist party is today a Trojan horse of disloyalty, coiled like a serpent in the very heart of America. It may mouth sweet words of 'peace,' 'democracy,' 'equality,' and flourish gay slogans of 'international solidarity' and 'brotherhood of men,' but its body and feet are from the Russian bear."

**Q**: "Are Communists trained to lie?"
**A**: "The concept of morality and fair play, as practiced in our democracy, is alien and repugnant to him. Moreover, the Communists employ a purposeful double-talk, roundabout style, known as 'Aesopian language,' designed to deceive and evade, to clothe their true thoughts. This technique, utilized by Lenin, is the very epitome of deceit."

**Q**: "What would you say to the charge that we are engaging in 'thought control' with our constant watching of Communists?"
**A**: "The FBI is concerned not with what Communists think, but with what they do—their actions, just as in any other field of its investigative activity. There is no scintilla of evidence to substantiate the charge that the FBI is engaged in 'thought control' activities."

# So Why *Did* the Chicken Cross the Road?

It sure wasn't to make people laugh. So why is the unfunny chicken joke so famous? Because people in the past didn't quite have the refined sense of humor we have today (honk honk!).

Historians have been unable to find a plausible answer to why this odd riddle is so popular, but they have found its origin. It first appeared in print in 1847 in a New York magazine called the *Knickerbocker*, on a page titled "Gossip with Readers and Correspondents." A reader wrote in: "There are 'quips and quillets' which seem actual conundrums, but yet are none. Of such is this: 'Why does a chicken cross the street?' Are you 'out of town?' Do you 'give it up?' Well, then: 'Because it wants to get on the other side!'" But whyyyy? We may never know.

# Stinkin' Thinkin'

Sure, it's one thing to know what history looked like, but to really get a feel for how life was in ancient times, it's important to know what history *smelled* like, too. That was the thinking behind a foul museum exhibit in England.

Held at the Deva Museum in Chester in 2013, the exhibit was called "The Roman Experience." Visitors could stroll through streets constructed to look as they did during Roman times. Hoping to provide an authentic experience, the staff wanted to add an authentic odor to the Roman latrines. They found one called "Flatulence" from Dale Air, a company that designs aromas for museums.

Unfortunately, Flatulence proved a bit too authentic, causing several schoolchildren to vomit. Museum supervisor Christine Turner apologized: "It really was disgusting." Dale Air director Frank Knight added, "We feel sorry for the kids, but it is nice to see that the smell is so realistic!"

# Crash Positions!

In 1947 an American Airlines pilot named Charles Sisto was flying a propeller-driven DC-4 aircraft carrying 49 passengers from Dallas to Los Angeles. Along with Sisto were his copilot, Melvin Logan, and John Beck, a DC-3 pilot who was learning how to operate the more sophisticated DC-4. While cruising along at 8,000 feet, Captain Sisto invited Beck to take the controls. Sisto thought he'd have a little fun at the rookie's expense—he fastened the gust lock, a device that locks up the rudder and the elevator and is supposed to be used only on the ground.

The plane started climbing. No matter what Beck tried, he couldn't level it out. Finally, Sisto decided that the joke had gone on long enough and unlocked the gust lock. Bad idea: Beck had left the controls set to an extreme position. The airplane went straight into a nose dive.

The sudden lurch threw Sisto and Beck out of their seats. They hit the ceiling—which happened to be where the propeller controls were located—and shut off three of the four engines. That actually slowed their descent and allowed Logan to level the plane just 350 feet from the ground. They made an emergency landing in El Paso.

At first, the pilots claimed that the autopilot had failed, but after a lengthy investigation, Sisto finally confessed to his ill-conceived practical joke. He was fired.

# Whores of Babylon

More than 4,000 years ago, ancient Babylonians (in modern-day Iraq) worshipped the goddess Ishtar, also known as the "Great Whore of Babylon." Ishtar was the goddess of war and sexual love, and the most powerful goddess in the Mesopotamian religion.

If you wanted to be part of her cult (and everyone did), you had to participate. Every female citizen was expected to go at least once in her life to the temple of Ishtar and offer herself to any male worshipper who paid the required contribution. There was no shame attached to being one of Ishtar's prostitutes—in fact, it was considered a sacred means of attaining divine union between man and goddess.

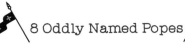
8 Oddly Named Popes

| | |
|---|---|
| **1.** Cletus | **5.** Linus |
| **2.** Fabian | **6.** Urban |
| **3.** Hyginus | **7.** Zosimus |
| **4.** Innocent | **8.** Lando |

# The "Killer Hawk" Newspaper Hoax

In January 1927, the *Chicago Journal* reported that a "killer hawk" had been seen preying on pigeons in the downtown area. The following day, other Chicago papers ran the story on their front pages, and continued doing so for five consecutive days—igniting considerable public hysteria in the process: A prominent banker offered a reward for capture of the hawk dead or alive; a local gun club sent shooters downtown to stalk the bird, with the help of local Boy Scout troops who joined in the hunt.

A week after the *Journal* ran the hawk story, its editors announced the start of a newspaper serial called "The Pigeon and the Hawk." The other papers, realizing they'd been tricked into publicizing a rival paper's promotion on their front pages for an entire week, never printed another word about the killer hawk.

> "News is what people don't want you to print. Everything else is ads."
> **—William Randolph Hearst**

# Close Encounters

• Did ancient Hindus see UFOs? The ancient Sanskrit poem *Mahabharata* tells of a technologically advanced, nonhuman race that created flying disks called *vimanas*, or "celestial chariots," that come in a variety of makes and models, from huge SUV-like vehicles for carrying troops, to single-person aircraft.

• In 1066 a "giant pearl" emerged from a Chinese lake. Witnesses claimed that it hovered briefly while a small door opened to reveal a brilliant light. Then it flew away.

• There were reports of glowing ships over the skies of Rome in 218 B.C. In addition, Roman historian Titus Livius (59 B.C.–A.D. 17) once reported seeing men wearing white clothing flying around in the sky.

• In the 1600s, a long, cylindrical craft was seen flying over Italy, Switzerland, and Scotland. Independently, crowds of people in each of these countries reported the sighting.

• In fourteen-hundred and ninety-two, Columbus sailed the ocean blue…and saw a UFO. He spotted it one night from the deck of the *Santa Maria*. He described it as a "light glimmering at a great distance."

• In 1896 a "winged cigar" with a giant headlight was spotted over California, spawning a rash of cigar-ship sightings across the United States.

# Boneheaded Baseballers

**NIGHT OF THE LIVING EDS:** In a baseball game in the early 1950s, Philadelphia Phillies right fielder Bill Nicholson hit a high pop-up that was destined to come down somewhere near the mound. Pittsburgh Pirates pitcher Bill Werle didn't want to catch it, so he called for one of his fielders to step in. "Eddie's got it! Eddie's got it!" he shouted. Then everyone in the Pirates' infield stood and watched as the ball landed on the grass...including catcher Eddie Fitzgerald, first baseman Eddie Stevens, and third baseman Eddie Bockman.

**FREE PASS:** In 1976 Phillies catcher Tim McCarver came up to bat with the bases loaded. Not known for his power, McCarver hit a deep fly ball. He watched it as he ran toward first base...and was elated when it sailed over the wall! McCarver put his head down and kept on running. One problem: Gary Maddox, the runner at first, held up to make sure the ball wasn't caught. McCarver ran right by him. By the time he realized his goof, it was too late—he was called out for passing a runner, thus negating his grand slam.

Asked how he did it, McCarver replied, "Sheer speed."

## BOTCHED
## HISTORY

"President Washington, President Lincoln, President Wilson, and President Roosevelt have all authorized electronic surveillance on a far broader scale."

—ATTORNEY GENERAL
ALBERTO GONZALEZ,
TESTIFYING BEFORE CONGRESS

# Greek Fire

Constantinople came under siege from the Arabs between 674 and 678, and might have fallen had it not been for the Byzantines' secret weapon: "Greek fire." Most likely invented by a Syrian engineer named Kallinikos (though it may have been the result of generations of experimentation), the manufacturing process was kept a strict secret, and the recipe has been lost to history. Historians think the weapon was probably a kind of burning oil that was ejected by siphons onto enemy ships, accompanied by smoke and a thunderous noise. The liquid burned in water, and, by some accounts, was ignited by water. The really weird part: Greek fire couldn't be extinguished with water, so any ship that was doused with it would continue burning until it was a floating pile of cinders. Greek fire could be put out only with sand, strong vinegar, or old urine.

Random Fact: The Harry Potter books have been translated into ancient Greek.

# Missing Parts

**ST. NICHOLAS'S BONES:** The real Saint Nick (who lived in ancient Greece and had a penchant for secretly giving gifts) was buried in the town of Myra, now a part of Turkey. In 1087, authorities in Bari, a rival town in Italy, hired pirates to steal the saint's bones. The pirates managed to make off with about half of them, which are still stored in Bari. The rest of the bones were stolen by Venetian sailors ten years later during the First Crusade and deposited in a church there. In 2009 Turkey demanded the bones back from Italy; it's still waiting.

**MUSSOLINI'S BRAIN:** Well, half of it, anyway. After the fascist leader was executed and Italy was occupied at the end of World War II, the American government took away part of Mussolini's brain, allegedly to study it, but mostly as a victory trophy. The Americans returned the brain to Mussolini's widow in 1966.

**NAPOLEON'S...LI'L SOLDIER:** It was allegedly removed during the French leader's autopsy in 1821 and given to a priest. The dried organ (said to resemble a "one-inch piece of beef jerky") ended up in the hands of a urologist in New Jersey, who paid $3,000 for it in 1977. The man stored it under his bed for 30 years, and his daughter inherited it after his death.

# World War III in 3-2-1...

At 1:00 a.m. on September 26, 1983, Soviet defense computers received a message that American-launched intercontinental ballistic missiles had been detected in the sky...and were on their way to Moscow. Colonel Stanislav Petrov was the officer in charge at the Serpukhov-15 bunker outside of Moscow; it was his job to monitor the early warning satellite network. In case of attack, he would notify his superiors, who would launch a nuclear counterattack.

But the computers registered only one missile launched from the United States. Petrov reasoned that the message was a false alarm—if the Americans were attacking, they'd launch several missiles, not just one. He was right. The "missile plumes" observed by radar turned out to be glare from the Sun.

Despite acting correctly, Petrov was demoted.

# Outdated Concepts: Blending Inheritance

This debunked way of thinking goes that hereditary characteristics of the father and mother are averaged, or "blended," in their offspring. For example, if a tall man has children with a short woman, the children will be of medium height. The problem with this theory is that if it were true, in relatively few generations the features that distinguish one person from another would fade away, and everyone would be the same. Yet over the thousands of years of humanity, it hasn't happened.

The theory of blending inheritance fell out of favor as botanist Gregor Mendel's theory of dominant and recessive genes gained acceptance at the turn of the 20th century.

"Any man can make mistakes, but only an idiot persists in his error."

—**Cicero**

# The Manhattan Hoax

In 1824 a retired carpenter named Lozier stood on a soapbox in New York City and announced that because of all the new buildings, the southern tip of Manhattan Island had become too heavy and was in danger of sinking. His fix: Saw the island off at the northern end, tow it out to sea, turn it 180 degrees around, and reattach it.

Claiming that Mayor Stephen Allen had put him in charge of the project, Lozier signed up hundreds of laborers, offering triple wages to anyone willing to saw underwater. He directed blacksmiths and carpenters to begin designing the 100-foot saws and 250-foot oars needed to saw the island and row it out to sea. He also arranged for the construction of barracks and a mess hall for his laborers, and the delivery of 500 cattle, 500 hogs, and 3,000 chickens.

After two months of planning, the date arrived for construction to begin. Scores of laborers, carpenters, blacksmiths, butchers, and animals—as well as a marching band and hundreds of onlookers—arrived at Spring Street and Bowery to see the historic project get underway. About the only person who didn't show up was Lozier, who'd suddenly left town "on account of his health." He was actually hiding in Brooklyn, and although there was talk of having him arrested, he wasn't. Why? The authorities didn't want to admit they'd been duped.

# Almost Assassinated

*Charles de Gaulle, president of France from 1959 to 1969, may have set a record as the modern world leader with the most attempts on his life—31. Some examples:*

• **SEPTEMBER 1961**: Assassins planted plastic explosives and napalm at the side of a road and set the bomb to go off when de Gaulle's car approached. But they detonated it too soon. De Gaulle's driver sped the undamaged car straight through the flames to safety.

• **AUGUST 1962**: A team of assassins, using submachine guns and hand grenades, planned to attack de Gaulle's motorcade. But the lookout failed to spot the cars until they were already speeding by. The perpetrators only managed to shoot out a window and a tire on de Gaulle's car. He escaped unharmed...except for a cut on his finger that he got while brushing broken glass off his clothes.

• **JULY 1966**: Would-be assassins parked a car full of dynamite on the road to Orly Airport. At the appointed time, de Gaulle's car drove past the car bomb...and nothing happened. Why not? The night before the attack was to take place, the assassins decided to commit a robbery to raise the money they would need to make their getaway. But they got caught—and were sitting in jail, unable to trigger the bomb.

# Behold the Werewolf!

• The first werewolf legends date back to ancient Greece. Plato wrote about a ceremony called the Lycaea that required human sacrifice in exchange for the powers of lycanthropy.

• "Werewolf" comes from the Old English *werwulf*. *Wer* was Old English for the Latin *vir*, or "man." So literally it means "manwolf."

• Want to become a werewolf? You might try drinking water that a wolf stepped in, eating wolf and human flesh mixed together, sleeping under a full moon on a Friday, or selling your soul to the devil for a magic wolf-skin belt.

• The French Inquisition recorded 30,000 cases of lycanthropy between 1520 and 1630.

• How can you tell if someone's a werewolf? Folklore says that if a person has a unibrow, a ring finger that's longer than the index finger, or hairy palms, he or she might be a werewolf.

• According to legend, Ireland's St. Patrick punished a wicked Welsh king named Vereticus by turning him into a wolf.

• Traditionally, there are two types of werewolves: *Voluntary* werewolves transform at will. *Involuntary* werewolves are cursed into taking wolf form, often because they've sinned (like Vereticus).

• In 1589 Peter Stubbe confessed to murdering 13 children and three adults in Bedburg, Germany. His excuse: He owned a magic wolf skin that transformed him into a werewolf. Stubbe was tortured for his crimes and beheaded, and then his body was burned.

• *Lycanthropy* refers to transformation into a wolf; *boanthropy*, a cow or ox; *ailuranthropy*, a cat; and *zoanthropy*, animals in general.

• The first use of silver bullets to kill werewolves dates to 1640. Legend has it that the German town of Greifswald was overrun by a pack of werewolves. When ordinary musket balls didn't kill them, a group of students melted the town's silver to make new ones. The silver musket balls did the trick, and silver's been the weapon of choice for killing werewolves ever since.

# Next of Skin

In 1881 a murderous train robber named "Big Nose" George Parrot was captured by angry townspeople in Rawlins, Wyoming, and hanged. After no next of kin claimed the body, two local doctors—Thomas Maghee and John Osborne—claimed it in the name of science. Dr. Maghee examined Big Nose George's brain (and gave the skullcap to his wife). Then he removed the skin from George's chest and thighs and mailed the flesh to a tannery in Colorado, where it was made into human "leather." Dr. Osborne then had the leather made into a coin purse, a doctor's bag, and a pair of shoes.

Osborne loved his Big Nose George shoes. He wore them while practicing as a country doctor, and when he was elected Democratic governor of Wyoming in 1892 (in what some claimed was a stolen election), he wore the shoes to his inauguration—which must surely make him the only elected official in U.S. history sworn into office while wearing another man's skin.

Let's hope so, anyway.

> **Q**: What are jinglebobs, heel chains, and rowels?
> **A**: Parts of a cowboy's spurs.

# The First Poet

The first writer ever known by name was a poet named
Enheduanna who lived 4,300 years ago. Born circa 2285
B.C., she was the daughter of a Sumerian ruler who
appointed her the high priestess of the moon god Nanna,
the patron saint for the city of Ur (in what is now southern
Iraq). As his high priestess, Enheduanna shared in Nanna's
glory and managed his property.

But Enheduanna's claim to fame came from the poems
and hymns she wrote for Inanna, the goddess of love,
fertility, and war. Enheduanna wrote that the gods made her
suffer by sending a rebel who took over Sumer. He demoted
her and even tried to bed her (the first recorded case of
sexual harassment). She then extols the power of Inanna,
who overthrew the rebel and made her priestess once again.
But in the poem "Lady of Largest Heart," Enheduanna
shows her disdain for the way Inanna treated her:

> I/ who spread over the land/
> the splendid brilliance/ of your divinity/
> you allow my flesh/ to know your scourging/
> my sorrow and bitter trial/
> strike my eye as treachery.

## FIVE FREAKY FACTS ABOUT...
# MUSIC

- The predecessor to the trombone was called the sackbut.

- The first rock star: In 1842 women fought over Hungarian composer Franz Liszt's handkerchiefs as souvenirs.

- In 2004 the first "robot conductor" led the Tokyo Philharmonic. The orchestra played Beethoven's Fifth.

- Sea shanties such as "Drunken Sailor" were the only songs allowed by the Royal Navy in the 1800s.

- During the Middle Ages, murdering a traveling musician was not thought a serious crime.

# THE WORST HOLE IN THE HISTORY OF GOLF

It happened during the 1913 Shawnee Invitational for Ladies. A golfer named M. H. Meehan hit a shot into a small tributary of the Delaware River. She could see it slowly floating down the lazy river. So, rather than take a penalty (which would have given her a do-over), Meehan decided that she was going to complete this hole, no matter what.

So she and her husband commandeered a rowboat. As he piloted the craft, she kneeled in the boat and frantically swatted at the drifting ball with her five-iron. (Meanwhile, the judges were counting her strokes.) Forty swats later, she finally hit the ball out of the water... and into the middle of a dense forest about 200 yards from the green. Once back on land, Meehan bush-whacked though the woods until the hole was in sight, then drove the ball toward it...where it wedged firmly between two rocks. She banged away for a dozen or so more strokes before freeing it from the rocks and getting it to the green.

Meehan finally sank the putt on stroke number 161.

# Men and Their Egos

### MINE'S BIGGER THAN YOURS

In 1931, just when the Manhattan Trust Company finished building the Empire State Building—which they thought was the world's tallest building—workers at the Chrysler Building hoisted a spire that had been hiding inside the structure up through the top of the roof to steal the coveted title.

### PULP SHAKESPEARE

"I've always thought that I might have been Shakespeare in another life," Quentin Tarantino once told *GQ* magazine. "I don't really believe that 100 percent, and I don't really care about Shakespeare, but people are constantly bringing up all of these qualities in my work that mirror Shakespearean tragedies. I remember in the case of *Reservoir Dogs*, writing this scene where the undercover cop is teaching Tim Roth how to be an undercover cop. When Harvey Keitel read it, he thought I had just taken Hamlet's speech to the players and broke it down into modern words."

Here's the spooky part: "I'd never read *Hamlet!*"

# How to Make a Shrunken Head

*A century ago, the Jivaro tribes living deep in the jungles of Ecuador and Peru collected the heads of their enemies and turned them into trophies. Want to try it yourself? Here's how:*

**STEP 1**: Find a head. Peel the skin away from the skull (hair and all). Sew the eye and mouth openings closed (to trap the soul inside so it won't haunt you). Turn the head inside out. Scrape away the fat using a sharp knife.

**STEP 2**: Cook the head. Add jungle herbs to a pot of water and bring to a boil. Add the head and simmer for one to two hours. Remove the head from the water.

**STEP 3**: Shrink the head. Fill the head with hot stones, rolling it constantly to prevent scorching. Repeat with smaller and smaller pebbles as the head shrinks. Mold the facial features between each step.

**STEP 4**: Give the head a facial. Hang the head over the fire to dry. Once dry, polish it with ashes. Moisturize with berries to prevent the head from cracking. Sew the neck hole closed and trim the hair. Now you're ready to impale it on a post and stick it in your front yard. (That'll keep those pesky neighborhood kids away.)

# The Curse of Macbeth

*In 1606 William Shakespeare wrote* The Tragedy of Macbeth. *In the Bard's quest for authenticity, he researched actual spells and curses used by English witches. True believers claim that witches were so angry that their secrets were being shared that they cursed the play. And the unfortunate actors and crewmembers have been paying the price ever since:*

• Shortly before the first performance, the male actor scheduled to play Lady Macbeth came down with a fever. Some accounts say he died.

• In the early 1900s, the Moscow Arts Company was doing a dress rehearsal when actor Constantin Stanislavski forgot his lines in the middle of the murder scene. He whispered for a prompt, but the prompter was silent. Then he yelled for a prompt, but the prompter remained silent. He found the prompter slumped over the script, dead. The show never opened.

• During a 1937 production at the famed Old Vic Theatre in England, the theater's founder, Lilian Baylis, suddenly died of a heart attack just before the play opened. Laurence Olivier, who was starring in the lead role, missed death by mere inches when a sandbag fell from the rafters.

• In 1948, during a production in Stratford, Connecticut, Diana Wynyard as Lady Macbeth announced that the curse was "ridiculous." She also decided it was silly to play her sleepwalking scene with her eyes open, so she closed them...and walked off the edge of the stage, falling 15 feet to the floor below.

• A 1942 run of *Macbeth* directed by John Gielgud was plagued by death. First, Beatrice Fielden-Kaye, playing one of the witches, died of a heart attack. Next, Marcus Barron, playing Duncan, died of angina. Another witch, Annie Esmond, died onstage while vigorously dancing around the cauldron. Finally, set designer John Minton committed suicide in his studio, surrounded by his designs for the *Macbeth* sets and costumes.

• A Russian film version of the play was canceled when nine members of the crew died of food poisoning.

• President Abraham Lincoln was quoting passages from *Macbeth* to his friends the evening before he was assassinated.

# What Goes Up...

Pilatre De Rozier, the first person ever to ascend in a balloon in 1783, tried to combine the two early methods of ballooning: hot air, which used ordinary air heated by an open flame, and hydrogen gas, which is lighter than air but is highly explosive when exposed to fire. (Helium, which is not explosive, was not discovered until 1868.) When he attempted to float across the English Channel on June 15, 1785, he used a "hybrid" balloon—one compartment filled with air heated by an open flame, the other filled with explosive hydrogen gas. About 15 minutes into the flight, the flame found the hydrogen, and de Rozier's ballooning career ended with a bang as he plunged more than 3,000 feet. De Rozier, the first person to ascend in a balloon, also became the first person to die in one.

Looney Law: In the 1950s, it was illegal for a flying saucer to land in a French vineyard.

# La Historio da Esperanto

Esperanto is a language created in 1887 by Lazarus Ludwig Zamenhof, an idealistic 28-year-old Polish ophthalmologist. He was troubled that his fellow Europeans deeply mistrusted each other. If only they spoke the same language, he figured, they could begin to see eye to eye. Zamenhof came up with a simplified hybrid version of all the Romance languages with only 16 rules of grammar and no irregular verbs (English has 728). He published his language under the pseudonym Dr. Esperanto, which translates as "one who hopes."

It may sound like a great idea, but after more than a century of lobbying, the "language of peace" has failed to take hold. The dream isn't dead, though: Even today, there are thousands of Esperanto speakers organized into clubs in more than 100 countries around the world.

In 1966 a low-budget horror movie called *Incubus* was filmed entirely in Esperanto. Directed by *The Outer Limits* creator Leslie Stevens, the movie was a weird cross between a Gothic melodrama and an art film. But Stevens didn't use Esperanto to promote the "language of peace"; he thought it would give the film an eerie atmosphere. It bombed.

**Final note:** *Incubus* starred 33-year-old William Shatner. (He didn't speak Esperanto, though—the cast learned their lines phonetically.) Shatner's next role: Captain James T. Kirk.

# Did We Really Land on the Moon?

**NO WE DIDN'T!** "While doing research at NASA, I uncovered one mislabeled reel from the *Apollo 11* mission. What is on the reel and what is on the label are completely different...It contains an hour of unedited footage that is dated by NASA's own atomic clock three days into the flight. Identified on camera are Neil Armstrong, Edwin 'Buzz' Aldrin, and Michael Collins. They are doing multiple takes of a single shot of the mission, from which only about ten seconds was ever broadcast. It means they did not walk on the Moon!"

—BART SIBREL

**YES WE DID!** "Let me say, as I sit here before you today, having walked on the Moon, that I am myself still awed by that miracle."

—BUZZ ALDRIN

**NO WE DIDN'T!** "You are a coward and a liar and a thief!"

—BART SIBREL, TO BUZZ ALDRIN IN 2002

**YES WE DID!** Aldrin responded to Sibrel's allegations by punching him in the face. The astronaut was not charged with assault after witnesses told police that Sibrel had repeatedly poked Aldrin with a Bible.

# The Evita Mummy

Former actress Eva "Evita" Perón became a crusader for the poor in 1940s Argentina. (Her husband Juan was the president of the country from 1948 to 1954.) When she died of cancer in 1952 at age 33, Juan Perón had her mummified and put on public display. The procedure took about a year and cost $100,000. The president fell from power while his wife was still lying in state, and he went into exile in Spain before he could arrange for her burial. Evita was put in storage in Buenos Aires. Then her body disappeared.

It turned out that anti-Perónists—making sure the body was never again used as a pro-Perón political symbol—had stolen the coffin, sealed it in a packing crate, and buried it in a Milan cemetery. In 1971—19 years later—a sympathetic Spanish officer told Perón where his wife was buried. Perón had her exhumed and brought to Spain. When Perón pried open the coffin, his wife was so well preserved that he cried out, "She is not dead, she is only sleeping!"

Rather than bury his beloved Evita again, Perón kept her around the house; he and his third wife, Isabel, propped her up in the dining room and ate with her every evening, even when they entertained guests. The arrangement lasted until 1973, when Perón returned to power in Argentina and left his beloved mummy in Spain. Later, Evita was brought across the Atlantic and buried in Argentina.

# PREHEATED CANADA GOOSE

On April 22, 1932, the townspeople of Elgin, Manitoba, were treated to delicious goose dinners that dropped right out of the sky. A flock of Canada geese were flying overhead during an electrical storm and ran afoul of some lightning. Fifty-two unlucky birds were electrocuted in midflight. After the charred birds plummeted into Elgin, the citizens gathered the geese, finished cooking them, and served them on dinner tables all over town.

## Name Game

Here are four titles that author F. Scott Fitzgerald considered and then rejected for his 1926 novel *The Great Gatsby*:

1. *Trimalchio's Banquet*

2. *The High-Bouncing Lover*

3. *Gold-Hatted Gatsby*

4. *Incident at West Egg*

# Edible Strange History

**GHOST SOUP:** In the Chinese province of Zhejiang in 2003, ancient skeletons were discovered in a cave during the construction of a resort. The discovery revived an ancient lost custom that locals had followed for thousands of years: "ghost soup." According to the tradition, the bones of long-dead female corpses were boiled down to a stock to make a soup, which was believed to cure a wide range of ailments.

**GERBER SINGLES:** This was Gerber Baby Food's attempt to sell food to adults. Launched in the 1970s, the line of gourmet entrées like sweet-and-sour pork and beef Burgundy had two major problems: The food came in baby food–style jars, and the name "Singles" was a turnoff to customers who were lonely to begin with. It flopped.

**THE BIG CHEESE:** The 1964 World's Fair in New York exhibited the world's largest piece of cheese—it was as big as a van and weighed 17.5 tons. It was made with 183 tons of milk, one day's production for 16,000 cows.

**PUNCH CRUNCH:** This 1975 spinoff of Cap'n Crunch had a pink box that featured Harry S., a hippo in a sailor suit, making goo-goo eyes at Cap'n Crunch. Many chain store owners perceived the hippo as gay and refused to carry the cereal. Marveled one Quaker salesman: "How that one ever got through, I'll never understand."

# The Untalented Mr. Ripley

Next time you make a choice to "go with the lowest bidder," keep this story in mind. Colonel James Ripley, chief of U.S. Army Ordnance in the Civil War, outfitted Union troops with 50-year-old short-range smoothbore rifles that dated to the War of 1812. He declined to buy the more modern, long-range Enfield rifles on the grounds that they were too expensive...and they were made in England, which Ripley still hated fiercely, even half a century after the War of 1812.

But the Enfield company eventually found a buyer: the Confederate army. At the first Battle of Bull Run in July 1861, the Confederates devastated the Union troops and suffered a third fewer casualties because their Enfield rifles could hit targets at 800 yards, compared to the Ripley's guns, which had a range of only 500 yards.

The Union did end up winning the Civil War, but according to some historians, Ripley's ill-fated gun order made it last two years longer than it should have.

Random Fact: In 1934 John Dillinger escaped from prison using a piece of wood shaped like a gun.

# Legends of the Big Dipper

**THE INDIANS:** Several Native American legends tell the same story of the night sky's most ubiquitous constellation: A party of hunters set out on a bear hunt. The first hunter carried a bow and arrow. The second hunter brought along a pot or kettle to cook the bear in. The faint star Alcor, just above the middle star of the Dipper's handle, was the pot. The third hunter carried a bundle of sticks to build a fire to cook the bear. In the fall, the first hunter shot the bear. Blood from the wounded animal stained the fall leaves in the forest. The bear died, was cooked, and was eaten. The skeleton lay on its back in the den through the winter months. When spring returned, the bear came out of the den and the hunters started to chase her again, and so it went from year to year.

**THE GREEKS:** Calisto was the daughter of the king of Arcadia, who caught the eye of Zeus. The god took her, and she later gave birth to a son named Areas. Hera, queen of the gods, changed Calisto into a bear in a jealous rage. Years later, Areas was hunting when he saw a bear. Not knowing it was his mother, Areas raised his spear. But Zeus rescued Calisto by placing her in the sky—where she remains today. The Greeks called Ursa Major *Arktos*, which means "Bear." This is where we get the word "Arctic."

## BOTCHED HISTORY

"I don't feel we did wrong in taking this great country away from them. There were great numbers of people who needed new land, and the Indians were selfishly trying to keep it for themselves."

—JOHN WAYNE

# PAPER WEIGHT

In 1965 an aspiring English publisher named Lionel Burleigh announced he was starting a newspaper called the *Commonwealth Sentinel*, which he promised would be "Britain's most fearless newspaper."

Burleigh did everything it took to make the paper a success—he promoted it on billboards, sold advertising space, wrote articles, and printed up 50,000 copies of the first issue so that there would be plenty to go around.

Burleigh remembered every detail, except for one very important thing: distribution. In fact, he had forgotten it completely until he received a phone call from the police informing him that all 50,000 copies had been deposited on the sidewalk in front of the hotel where he was staying. They were blocking the entrance. Could he please come and remove them? Britain's "most fearless paper" folded after just one day. "To my knowledge, we only sold one copy," Burleigh remembered years later. "I still have the shilling in my drawer."

# More All-American Ghosts

• **The Lizzie Borden House in Fall River, Massachusetts,** where Borden notoriously murdered her parents with an ax in 1892, is supposedly home to a ghost. Is it Borden herself, or one of her parents? No—it's the ghost of the family cat. Locals say that the invisible feline is friendly; it likes to rub up against tourists' legs and sit in their laps.

• **At the Vanderlip Mansion in Palos Verdes, California,** a legend goes that Mrs. Vanderlip killed her entire family (including the dogs) and then committed suicide. At night, witnesses have reported seeing the faces of the family staring out of the windows. The dogs run around and bark at squirrels in the woods behind the house.

• **The Hardee's in West Union, Iowa,** was built on top of a 19th-century cemetery. And now ghosts can be seen at the fast-food restaurant. Employees claim that they've seen objects move and can hear their names being called when nobody's there.

• **At the Radisson Suite Hotel in Ogden, Utah,** a ghost named Mrs. Eccles haunts the elevator. She died on the fifth floor, the story goes, so the elevator always stops there, whether anybody has pressed the button or not. You can't see Mrs. Eccles, but when she walks past, you can feel her brush against you and you can smell her perfume.

• **Late at night, the Duck Pond in Lithia Park in Ashland, Oregon,** emits an eerie blue light. It flickers for a few moments and then disappears. According to locals, the light is the ghost of a girl who was murdered at the pond in 1875.

• **In the desert outside Anthem, Arizona,** the ghosts of Native American warriors on horseback have been seen riding at night. And if they see you...they shoot (ghost) arrows at you.

# Lost and Found: The Lascaux Caves

There was a legend in the Dordogne region of France about a tunnel deep in the woods leading to a hidden treasure. In September 1940, four young boys and their dog, Robot, set out to find it. Robot found a deep hole hidden in the undergrowth. Thinking that this was the tunnel to the treasure, the boys lowered themselves down. The tunnel was an entrance to a cave complex, the upper walls and ceiling of which were covered with huge bulls painted in brilliant tones of red, black, and brown. Other rooms were painted with prehistoric horses, cats, and even rhinos.

The boys had discovered the most important prehistoric cave paintings ever found: images of animals that lived 15,000 years ago. The Lascaux caves came to be known as the Sistine Chapel of prehistoric art. Scientists believe the paintings were not for decoration but to pass along important information, as there is no evidence that humans ever lived in the caves.

> "Ben Franklin was a crafty and lecherous old hypocrite whose very statue seems to gloat on the wenches as they walk the States House yard."
> —**William Cobbett, English politician**

# Shipwrecks Aplenty

In 1829, four days out of Sydney, Australia, a heavy storm struck the vessel *Mermaid*, and drove it into a reef. All 22 on board jumped ship and swam to a large rock. After three days of waiting, another ship, the *Swiftsure*, found and rescued them. Five days later another storm struck. The *Swiftsure* was swept into a ridge and wrecked. Both crews escaped and waited for rescue on some nearby rocks. They were soon picked up by the schooner *Governor Ready*, which caught fire three hours later. Once again they abandoned ship, this time in lifeboats. Along came the cutter *Comet*, which had been blown off course by a storm. The crew of the *Comet* loaded the crews and passengers of all three vessels on board. Five days later a storm snapped the *Comet*'s mast, ripped her sails, and ruined her rudder. The *Comet*'s crew loaded into the longboat, leaving the passengers to cling to floating bits of wreckage. After 18 hours passed, the mail boat *Jupiter* came along and rescued everyone, only to hit a reef and sink two days later. Fortunately, the passenger vessel *City of Leeds* was nearby and picked up everyone, finally delivering them back to Sydney.

The entire incident resulted in five ships being sunk—but incredibly, not a single life was lost.

# FIVE FREAKY FACTS ABOUT...
# SPORTS

- Which basketball star fought Arnold Schwarzenegger in *Conan the Destroyer*? Wilt Chamberlain.

- During World War II, the Pittsburgh Steelers and Philadelphia Eagles combined as the "Steagles."

- In 1540 King Henry VIII banned soccer because of the riots that erupted after matches.

- Wakeboarding was originally called skurfing.

- The term "sports fan" was first used to insult baseball "fanatics" in the late 1800s.

# THE FIRST POLITICAL SEX SCANDAL

Well, the first *documented* sex scandal. In 1400 B.C. Kushshiharbe was the mayor of Nuzi, near modern-day Kirkuk, north of Baghdad. According to clay tablets unearthed in Iraq in the late 1920s, he went on trial for a variety of crimes, including theft, taking bribes, and kidnapping. The juiciest accusation: He committed adultery with a woman named Humerelli, a charge he vehemently denied. "No! Emphatically no! Not a word of it is true! I did not have sex with her!" the clay tablets quote him as saying.

Verdict: Unknown. Tablets describing the outcome haven't been found.

 3 "Facts" Aristotle Got Wrong

1. Bees come from rotting bull carcasses.
2. Flies have four legs.
3. The heart does all the thinking.

# Three Random Origins

**STRAWBERRY LEMONADE:** Pete Conklin worked as a lemonade vendor for the Mabie Circus in the 1850s. One hot day, business was so brisk he had to make a batch in a hurry and used a bucket of water from a nearby tent. When he poured his first glass, he noticed the lemonade was pink. Conklin began selling his mistake as "strawberry lemonade." So what made it pink? A circus performer's red tights had been soaking in the bucket of water that Conklin had used.

**THE MING DYNASTY:** *Ming* was not a man but an adjective—the Chinese word for "brilliant." In 1368 a Buddhist monk named Zhu Yuanzhang led a peasant rebellion that toppled the Mongol-ruled Yuan dynasty, which was oppressing and overtaxing the ethnic Han people. For the next three centuries, Yuanzhang's "brilliant" dynasty lived up to the name: Slavery was abolished, and peace, technology, wealth, and artistry flourished.

**THE WORD "PANTS":** It comes from a 16th-century Italian comic character known as Pantalone, who wore strange trousers. This gave us the word *pantaloon*, which first meant "clown," and then the plural *pantaloons*, or trousers. The word was shortened to "pants" when it reached America.

# Fly Away Home

The Roman poet Virgil (70–19 B.C.), best known for the *Aeneid*, once held a lavish funeral on his land. Senators and noblemen attended. The poet himself read a long eulogy for the deceased. An orchestra played solemn music as the tiny coffin was placed in its tomb. What was Virgil burying? His beloved pet...housefly.

But there was a method to the poet's madness: He actually did have a fondness for flies, but he also hated paying high taxes on his land. So, after noticing a loophole in the Roman tax code that excluded mausoleums from paying up, Virgil deemed his land a mausoleum. And he had the tomb of his beloved fly to prove it.

"All our sweetest hours fly fastest."
—**Virgil**

# Good Kitty

A severe drought hit Baltimore, Maryland, in the summer of 1930. Forecasters predicted an even longer dry spell, but Frances Shields called local newspapers and insisted they'd have rain in 24 hours. The reason: Her cat Napoleon was lying down with his "front paw extended and his head on the floor," and he only did that just before it rained. Reporters laughed...until there was a rainstorm the next day. Newspapers all over the country picked up the story, and Napoleon became a feline celebrity. He also became a professional weather-cat and newspaper columnist. His predictions were printed regularly—and he did pretty well. All told, he was about as accurate as human weather forecasters.

# More Kitty Cat Gods

**MATAGOT**. According to European folklore, matagots are magical cats. A French superstition says that a matagot can be lured home with a plump chicken. Once in the house, treat it well and it will bring good luck. For example, give it the first bite of every meal, and it will reward you with a gold coin each morning. In England, people whispered that Dick Whittington, a humble boy who grew up to become mayor of London in the 15th century, owed his good luck to his matagot.

**EL BROOSHA**. The ancient myths of the Sephardic Jews (ancient Hebrews who left Israel and went to what is now Spain and Portugal) tell of Lilith, Adam's first wife, created before Eve. According to the legend, when Lilith refused to submit to Adam, she was banished from paradise. Lilith still haunts the Earth as a demon in the shape of a huge black vampire-cat named El Broosha (or sometimes El Brooja—*bruja* means "witch" in Spanish), who sucks the blood of newborn babies.

**BASTET**. The ancient Egyptians worshipped this cat-headed goddess 5,000 years ago. Her name means "devouring lady" and she was celebrated on October 31, Bastet's feast day. The daughter of the sun god Ra, Bastet was associated with the moon, music, dancing, motherhood...and

vengeance. In the Egyptian Book of the Dead, she was said to have destroyed the bodies of the deceased with her "royal flame" if they failed entry tests for the underworld. Out of respect for Bastet, it became an honor to stage expensive funerals for cats, during which gold and gem-studded cat figurines were buried along with the mummified body of the deceased kitty.

**LI SHOU.** The ancient Chinese believed that at one time cats had the ability to speak, but they gave the gift to humans so that they could lay around all day. Li Shou was a fertility cat goddess who brought rain and protected crops. At harvest, peasants would hold an orgiastic festival in her honor, offering sacrifices to the cats that had protected the grain from rats and mice.

> "No matter how much the cats fight, there always seem to be plenty of kittens."
> —**Abraham Lincoln**

# Cocaine in Ancient Egypt?

How could Egyptian mummies—ranging from 800 to 3,000 years old—have traces of cocaine and tobacco in their hair, skin, and bones? Cocaine and tobacco come from plants that grew only in the still-undiscovered New World and weren't accessible to Egyptians. Tobacco wasn't introduced to the Old World until the Arawak tribe gave some to Columbus in 1492.

After scientist Svetlana Balabanova made the strange discovery at the Egyptian Museum in Munich, she tested hundreds more mummies from the Old World. Interestingly, cocaine was found only in the Munich museum's mummies. Some experts speculated that reckless, cocaine-using archaeologists there had contaminated the bodies. The tobacco, though, was a bigger mystery. A third of the mummies Balabanova studied contained nicotine, and evidence of tobacco had been found in the stomach of King Ramses II and in King Tut's tomb.

But no one can say for sure how it got there.

Henry David Thoreau once burned down 300 acres of forest trying to cook a fish.

# The First Thanksgiving Took Place in...

*...Plymouth, Massachusetts? Nope.*

The New World's real first Thanksgiving celebration took place in Texas. In 1540 Francisco Vázquez de Coronado of Spain was appointed to explore North America and seek out the Quivira, a legendary city of gold. The expedition turned out to be a disaster. The only gold Coronado found was in the west Texas sunset, and he lived the rest of his life as a desk jockey in Mexico City. (Yes, they had desks in the 16th century.)

On May 23, 1541, running low on both food and morale, Coronado and his men happened upon a band of Tejas Indians in Palo Duro Canyon (southeast of Amarillo), who gave them both grub and a good time. A grateful Coronado declared it a day of giving thanks for this bounty in the new country.

In 1959 the Texas Society Daughters of the American Colonists dedicated a plaque to the canyon, designating it as the place where the "first Thanksgiving feast" took place. And that makes it official.

# Die Hard: Czar Alexander II

In 1879 a violent anarchist group called Will of the People tried to bomb Alexander's train outside Moscow. It was common for the czar's entourage to consist of two trains—one in front to test the rails and a second in back to carry the czar. So when the first train rolled by, the attackers let it go and blew up the second train...only to learn later that Alexander had been riding on the first train. The second one was a decoy.

In 1881 Will of the People made another attempt, as Alexander was returning by carriage to the Winter Palace. They tunneled under a road along the czar's intended route and packed the space with explosives. But they were thwarted at the last minute when the czar's guards changed the route.

This time, however, there were backup bombers, and as the czar passed by, one of them tossed a bomb at the imperial carriage, blowing it apart and killing two of the czar's guards. Alexander somehow escaped unscathed and might well have survived the entire attack had he not lingered at the scene to tend to the wounded. But moments later a second bomb killed him.

So did the anarchists get the revolution they were hoping for? No—the czar, a reformer by czarist standards, was succeeded by his son Alexander III, considered one of the most repressive czars of the 19th century.

# More Boneheaded Blunders

**HORSE SENSE:** Horatio Bottomley (great name) was a convicted fraud artist and former member of the English Parliament. In 1914 he figured out what he thought was a foolproof way to rig a horse race: He bought all six horses in the race, hired his own jockeys to race them, and told them in which order he wanted them to cross the finish line.

Then he bet a fortune on the horses he'd picked to win, and also placed bets on the order of finish. Everything went according to plan...until a thick fog rolled in over the track in the middle of the race. It was so thick that the jockeys couldn't see each other well enough to cross the finish line in the proper order. Bottomley lost every bet he placed.

**A LACK OF DIRECTION:** In 1870 the French military made preparations to use its own new machine gun, called the *mitrailleuse*, in the imminent war against Prussia. Machine guns were new at the time, and the government wanted to keep the technology a secret. So it distributed the guns to military units...without instructions for how to use them; the instructions weren't sent until after the war had begun. But by then it was too late—France lost.

# FIVE FREAKY FACTS ABOUT...
## EXPLORERS

- First haircut in space: *Skylab 2* astronaut Paul Weitz got a trim from Pete Conrad in 1973.

- First person to make a solo flight from Hawaii to the U.S. mainland: Amelia Earhart.

- British explorer Robert Swan's claim to fame: First person to walk to the North and South Poles.

- Zebulon Pike never climbed Colorado's Pikes Peak—he claimed it was impossible.

- In 1642 Dutch explorer Abel Tasman sailed all the way around Australia and never saw it.

# Flesh-Brushing Apparatus

One of the weirdest fads of the 1880s was "flesh-brushing." It consisted of using a soft brush to carefully scrub your body from head to toe. It was so popular among the filthy rich that two New York inventors, Mary Stetson and William Bedell, patented a mechanical Flesh Brushing Apparatus—a large, coffinlike tube that covered your body from the neck down.

How it worked: You climb in—fully nude—and then crank a handle that's nestled amid the thousands of brush fibers made from "sea roots" (whatever those are). This rotated the bristles around your body, which, according to the patent, "effected a great saving of time and of exertion."

Or you could just have your servants wash you.

---

**WHY DO WE SAY "TIE THE KNOT"?**
The phrase comes from an ancient Irish tradition called "handfasting," in which a Druid priest tied the hands of the bride and groom together during the wedding ceremony.

---

# Kahoutek Goes Kaput!

A three-mile-wide, icy comet was discovered by German astronomer Lubos Kahoutek in 1973. Astronomers the world over said its flyby would be the "greatest sky show of the 20th century." One Harvard astronomer even predicted that the comet's tail length "might reach 36 times the apparent diameter of the full Moon."

On January 15, 1974, the comet came as close to our planet as it would get in 80,000 years...and no one could see it. One astronomer described the non-event as "a thrown egg that missed." Where was Dr. Kahoutek? He and 1,692 other passengers were on the *Queen Elizabeth 2*, which had been specially chartered for the once-in-a-lifetime event. As *Newsweek* magazine put it, "The weather turned out rough and overcast, and Dr. Kahoutek spent much of the voyage too seasick to leave his cabin."

Two weeks later, the comet did emit a burst of explosive color—but by then it was so close to the Sun that only three people saw it—the astronauts aboard the space station *Skylab*.

## Dumbest Dinosaur?

The stegosaurus had an elephant-sized body and a walnut-sized brain.

# Cheddar Man & Mr. Targett

Cheddar, England, is famous for its cheese, but it's also famous for the limestone caves that line Cheddar Gorge. In 1903 a Stone Age skeleton was discovered in one of the caves. He was called "Cheddar Man." Scientists believe he died 9,000 years ago. He was about 23 years old, stood 5'5", and had strong teeth.

An even more astonishing discovery was made in 1997 when Britain's HTV network produced a documentary about the cave. The filmmakers obtained a DNA sample from Cheddar Man's bones and wanted to compare it to DNA samples taken from Cheddar schoolchildren. To prove to the kids that it was safe, their history teacher, Adrian Targett, had his DNA swabbed as well.

When all the tests were completed, only one person tested was found to be related to Cheddar Man: Mr. Targett. All these years later, Mr. Targett still lives within walking distance of the cave. "We all have 9,000-year-old ancestors," he said, "I just happen to know who mine is."

# Bigfoot: A Star Is Born

One afternoon in October 1958, a logger named Jerry Crew was bulldozing a logging road in the woods of Humboldt County, California, when he discovered what he claimed was a set of enormous, humanlike footprints in the mud. He decided to make a plaster cast of one of the prints. Not knowing what kind of animal could have made it, Crew nicknamed the animal "Bigfoot."

It was an historic moment. A new creature was about to take its place alongside the Loch Ness monster and aliens from outer space in the pantheon of tabloid mythology. Not long after Crew's "sighting" was reported in newspapers around the United States, dozens more followed. It became such a craze that the local chamber of commerce started selling plaster replicas of Bigfoot footprints. Indeed, Humboldt County turned itself into the self-described "Bigfoot Capital of the World," complete with annual Bigfoot parades, Bigfoot softball tournaments, Bigfoot barbecues, a Bride of Bigfoot beauty contest, and a statue of Bigfoot located downtown in Bigfoot Square.

Conspicuously absent: Bigfoot himself.

# Calling All Occupants, Part I

*Here's the strange story of a strange man who inspired a strange band to write a strange song that later became a minor hit for the Carpenters.*

In the early 1970s, a Canadian "space rock" band called Klaatu formed (the name was inspired by the peaceful alien ambassador from the 1951 film *The Day the Earth Stood Still*). While working on their first album, Klaatu's fascination with aliens brought them in contact with a 1967 book called *The Flying Saucer Reader*. They learned about an odd man named Alfred K. Bender, a scissors salesman from Connecticut.

In 1952, amid reports of "flying saucers" coming in from all over Earth, Bender wanted to send the E.T.s a message that humans are friendly, so he formed the International Flying Saucer Bureau (IFSB). After recruiting thousands of members from several countries, Bender sent out a newsletter announcing "World Contact Day." The instructions: At 6 p.m. on March 15, 1953, every IFSB member was to "send out a message to visitors from space." How? Telepathically. Here's the message:

> Calling occupants of interplanetary craft! Calling occupants of interplanetary craft that have been observing our planet EARTH. We of IFSB wish to

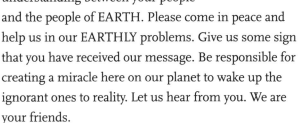

make contact with you. We are your friends, and would like you to make an appearance here on EARTH. Your presence before us will be welcomed with the utmost friendship. We will do all in our power to promote mutual understanding between your people and the people of EARTH. Please come in peace and help us in our EARTHLY problems. Give us some sign that you have received our message. Be responsible for creating a miracle here on our planet to wake up the ignorant ones to reality. Let us hear from you. We are your friends.

World Contact Day came and went—and the aliens didn't land. Shortly afterward, Bender claimed that he was visited by "Men in Black" who told him to stop looking for aliens... or else. So he retired from the E.T. business and disbanded the IFSB.

*But the story wasn't over...thanks to Klaatu. Beam yourself over to page 293 to see what happens next!*

# Notable Bulbs of History

### THE AWESOME ONION

• Onions have been cultivated for more than 5,000 years. The ancient Egyptians considered them sacred and believed that the round shape and concentric rings symbolized eternity. The slave laborers who built the Great Pyramid of Cheops at Giza 5,000 years ago were fed mainly chickpeas, onions, and garlic.

• Ancient Greek athletes ate onions to boost their energy. Roman gladiators were rubbed down with onion juice in the belief that it would make their muscles firm. By the Middle Ages, onions were common throughout Europe and were eaten by rich and poor alike (one of the few foods that were).

• Onion superstitions are common throughout history: They had the power to absorb poison (every onion was checked before cooking; bad onions were tossed out because it was assumed they'd absorbed poison); they cured colds, headaches, earaches, laryngitis, snakebites, and dog bites; they cleared warts and prevented baldness; if hung in the home, they warded off disease.

# The Myths and Legends of King Arthur

• The earliest known mention of Arthur is a reference to a mighty warrior in "Y Gododdin," a Welsh poem written circa 600.

• About 200 years later, the book *History of the Britons* credits Arthur with winning 12 battles against Saxon invaders.

• In 1135 Geoffrey of Monmouth popularized the tales of Arthur in his *History of the Kings of Britain.* He recorded Arthur's birth in the late fifth century, his marriage to Guinevere, and his relationship with his mentor Merlin.

• In 1155 Wace of Jersey introduced the concept of the Round Table.

• Five years later, the French poet Chrétien de Troyes wrote five Arthurian romances that are credited with introducing the Holy Grail and Sir Lancelot's love affair with Queen Guinevere.

• A 13th-century French poet, Robert de Boron, wrote that Arthur won his crown by removing a magic sword from a stone.

• In 1975 *Monty Python and the Holy Grail* added the Killer Rabbit of Caerbannog, the Holy Hand Grenade of Antioch, and much more silliness to the Arthurian legend.

# Who Was Merlin?

*Historians have tracked down four possibilities that may point to the inspiration for this strange wizard.*

• **THE BOY WHO SAW DRAGONS:** In the fifth century, when Britain's King Vortigern's tower kept falling down, his wise men told him to "kill a fatherless boy" and mix his blood into the cement to fix it. They found an orphan in a town and brought him to the king. The boy said there was a lake with dragons under the tower...and he was right (about the lake). So the king executed his not-so-wise men and gave their job to the orphan—named Merlin.

• **THE MADMAN OF THE FOREST:** A Scottish tale tells of a man named Lailoken who was the bard of King Gwenddoleu, who had two giant birds that wore golden collars and ate four men a day. Tragedy struck in 573 when Gwenddoleu lost a bloody battle in southern Scotland. Three hundred of his soldiers were killed. Lailoken blamed himself for the defeat and fled into the forest...for 50 years. He went mad in there, but gained the ability to see the future.

• **THE WARRIOR BARD:** A Roman noble named Ambrosius Aurelius stayed behind in Britain when the Roman legions left. A fierce warrior, Aurelius united the Britons and led them to victory against Anglo-Saxon invaders. And then, the story goes, he gave up his power to a young man named Arthur, who became king and made Aurelius his trusted adviser.

• **LOST IN TRANSLATION:** In Welsh writings, Merlin is called Myrddin. But some say Myrddin isn't a name at all. It's a job title for a bard. So Merlin Ambrosius, a name that shows up on a Welsh list of bards, means "the Bard Ambrosius." Others say the name Merlin isn't really the best translation of Myrddin. The word was first translated into Latin as Merdinus. Geoffrey of Monmouth changed the "d" to "l" and came up with Merlinus. Why the change? Geoffrey didn't want his wizard to have a name that sounds like the French word *merde*, which means "poop."

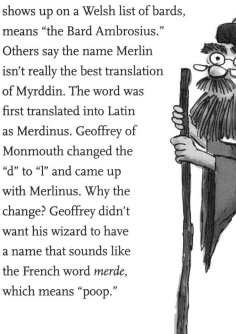

# Filles du Roi

*What do Madonna, Angelina Jolie, and Hillary Clinton have in common? Read on.*

In the 1600s, when Canada was known as New France, most of the early French settlers were men; few women were willing to make the journey. That gender imbalance concerned French officials because the settlers from England were rapidly outnumbering them. Solution: Recruit French women to come to the New World. Between 1663 and 1673, around 800 young women took up the challenge. They were known as the *Filles du Roi* ("Women of the King") because King Louis XIV's government sponsored their passage.

The women, most between 12 and 25, were chosen for their health and good character. Most were lower class, though there were a few impoverished nobility to pair off with officers and gentlemen. Thousands of present-day Canadians are descended from the "Daughters of the King." And many Americans, too—including Madonna, descendant of Fille du Roi Anne Seigneur; Angelina Jolie, descendant of Fille du Roi Denise Colin; and Hillary Clinton, descendant of Fille du Roi Jeanne Ducorps dite Leduc.

## BOTCHED HISTORY

"The Holocaust was an obscene period in our nation's history. I mean in this century's history. But I didn't live in this century."

—VICE PRESIDENT DAN QUAYLE

# Real-Life *WarGames*

The plot of the 1983 film *WarGames*: High school computer wiz David Lightman (Matthew Broderick) hacks into a military supercomputer and starts playing a game: Global Thermonuclear War. Defense commanders at NORAD think the game simulation is an actual attack by the Soviets...and prepare to retaliate in full. Sounds pretty far-fetched, right?

On November 9, 1979, computers at the Pentagon,  the Pentagon's emergency site in Maryland, and the Aerospace Defense Command in Colorado all displayed the same news: Soviet nuclear missiles were on their way. Officers immediately put missile launch sites on alert, and 10 fighter jets took off to patrol the skies and shoot down anything suspicious.

But just to be sure—before starting World War III—officers at the three bases decided to back up the information they'd received. Satellite data and radar across the country showed no signs of Soviet missiles in the air. It turns out that a training tape of attack scenarios had been placed into the computer running the military's early warning system.

171

# Myth-conceptions

**MYTH:** Vikings wore helmets with horns on them.
**TRUTH:** Vikings were buried with their helmets...and their drinking horns. When Victorians dug them up, they assumed the horns had fallen off the helmets.

**MYTH:** In Shakespeare's *Romeo and Juliet*, when Juliet stands on the balcony and asks, "Wherefore art thou, Romeo?" she is looking for him.
**TRUTH:** In Elizabethan times, "wherefore" meant "why," so Juliet was asking, "Why are you Romeo?" She was lamenting the fact that he came from a rival family, forcing them to keep their love a secret.

**MYTH:** St. Patrick was Irish.
**TRUTH:** The patron saint of Ireland was actually born in Scotland in the late fourth century. When he was a teenager, Palladius (his real name) was kidnapped and sold into slavery in Ireland. Six years later, he escaped and went back to Scotland, where he joined a monastery. As an adult, Palladius returned to Ireland as a missionary, where he lived for 40 years, dying in 461. (And he didn't drive away any snakes—there weren't any.)

# Upon Further Reflection

Famous for both his poetry and his love of liquor, the Chinese poet Li Po met his end in A.D. 762 while riding on a boat at night on the Yangtze River. Li was very drunk when he saw the moon's reflection in the water and decided to try to embrace it. He drowned.

---

### 8 WORDS AND PHRASES COINED DURING WORLD WAR I

1. Ace

2. Chow down

3. Trench coat

4. Red tape

5. Zero hour

6. Cooties

7. Cushy

8. Basket case

---

# Real-Life Frankensteins: Lazzaro Spallanzani

Spallanzani, a respected 18th-century Italian scientist, performed some very odd and gruesome experiments: He decapitated snails to see if their heads would grow back, and blinded bats to prove that they navigated by echolocation.

While he was a professor at Pavia University, Spallanzani reported to the Royal Society in London that he had attained "resurrection after death" by sprinkling water on seemingly dead microbes. The writer Voltaire agreed: "When a man like him announces that he has brought the dead back to life, we have to believe him."

But Voltaire was wrong—Spallanzani later realized the organisms were merely dehydrated, which led him to conduct further experiments proving that microbes could be killed by boiling (information that Louis Pasteur later put to great use). Italian researcher Paolo Mazzarello claims that Spallanzani was the inspiration for "Der Sandmann," a short story written in 1815 by E. T. A. Hoffman about a scientist who builds an artificial human. Written a year before Mary Shelley started *Frankenstein*, the story was a huge success in Europe and could well have planted the seed for Shelley's book.

# BAT BOMBS AWAY!

Not long after the Japanese bombed Pearl Harbor in 1941, a Pennsylvania dentist named Lytle S. Adams was visiting Carlsbad Caverns in New Mexico when inspiration struck: "Why not fit millions of bats with bombs and then drop them from planes!" The bats' instinct to find shelter would lead them to barns and buildings. And once they were settled…BOOM! A time-delayed fuse would ignite the bombs and start fires. Adams sent his idea to the Army Chemical Warfare Service, which actually tried attaching tiny thermite bombs to free-tailed bats.

But there were problems: Bats will resist having anything stuck to their skin, so they had to be refrigerated to force them into hibernation. Many didn't thaw out in time to fly; others fell to the ground because the bombs were too heavy. After two years of unsuccessful experiments, the project was canned. Cost to taxpayers: Around $2 million (and an untold number of bat lives).

# Meet Yin and Yang

*The ancient philosophy of Taoism teaches that harmony in the universe comes from balancing opposites such as good and evil, warm and cold, male and female, and darkness and light. This story, from the Chinese, tells how that balance created the world.*

**In the beginning of time,** there was only chaos, fighting, and churning inside an enormous egg. One day the egg broke and a giant called Pan Ku appeared. With him came the two basic forces: yin and yang. Yin, the dark energy, sank down and became the Earth. Yang, the light energy, floated up and became Heaven. Yin and yang, being complete opposites, always wanted to fight with each other.

But Pan Ku would not let them—he stood between them and pushed them apart. Every year Pan Ku grew taller and stronger, and Heaven and Earth were pushed farther and farther apart. At last, after 18,000 years, Pan Ku had grown so large and Heaven and Earth were so far apart that they could no longer hurt each other. When Pan Ku's work was finally finished, he was very, very old and very tired. So the giant lay down upon the Earth and prepared to die. As he died, a miracle happened: Pan Ku's hands and feet became the four quarters of the globe. His head turned into the mountains that rise up from the Earth. His right eye became the Sun and his left eye the Moon.

A thousand different plants and trees grew from his skin and hair. Pan Ku's blood made the rivers and the sea. His teeth, bones, and marrow became the metals, rocks, and precious stones within the Earth. From his breath came the winds and from his booming voice came thunder. Last of all came the people. They were created from the fleas and lice that crept all over Pan Ku's hairy body.

And that is how the world began.

# A Poor Excuse for a Pirate

In 1800 a pirate named Joseph Baker from Canada signed on to the merchant schooner *Eliza*. Not long after the ship set sail, Baker decided that he wanted to be the captain, so he, along with two other crewman, attacked the first mate during a night watch and tossed him overboard.

Then the three pirates went after the captain, William Wheland. They wounded him during a brief skirmish and took him hostage. But there was a problem: While discussing where to sell the ship's cargo, the mutineers realized that none of them actually knew how to navigate a ship. Sensing an opportunity, Wheland offered to sail them anywhere they wanted...if they spared his life.

Baker agreed to the deal, but he was a pirate after all, so he boasted to his fellow culprits that he'd kill Captain Wheland as soon as they sighted land. But Wheland overheard them and hatched a plan of his own: He locked the two other conspirators in the hold, caught Baker by surprise, and chased him up the mainmast.

Wheland kept Baker up there, lashed to the mast, until they landed on St. Kitts in the West Indies, and then turned him over to the authorities. After a four-day trial in April 1800, Baker and his pirate pals were hanged.

# Giving the Finger

• **HAROLD LLOYD**: Silent-film comedian Harold Lloyd was posing for a photograph in 1919 when he grabbed hold of a prop—a papier-mâché "bomb"—and lit it with his cigarette. Oops. The prop was a real bomb: It exploded, taking the thumb and index finger from Lloyd's right hand. Solution: Lloyd started wearing gloves. Along with his horn-rimmed glasses, they became part of his comic persona.

• **JERRY GARCIA**: When he was four years old, Jerry and his brother Tiff were splitting wood and playing "chicken" with the ax. Jerry was late removing his finger from the block, and Tiff chopped it off. (His dad drove him 30 miles to the nearest hospital.) In 1957, at the age of 15, Jerry discovered the guitar and went on to form the Grateful Dead.

• **JAMES DOOHAN**: During World War II, the Canadian soldier was shot six times by friendly fire; he took four bullets to his leg, one to his chest (he was saved by a cigarette case), and one to his right hand, causing him to lose the middle finger. Doohan survived and went on to play Mr. Scott on *Star Trek*. (Sharp-eyed viewers can spot his four-fingered hand.)

# More Movies You'll Never See

· *EL APOSTOL* [1917]. Made in Argentina by Italian film-maker Quirino Cristiani, this was the first-ever full-length animated movie. All copies were destroyed in a fire in 1926. Cristiani's other major work was *Peludópolis* (1931), the first animated feature with sound. All copies of that movie were lost in a 1961 fire.

· *HUMOR RISK* [1921]. The first Marx brothers movie. Harpo plays a detective chasing Groucho. It had a single screening, the audience hated it, and the Marx brothers themselves destroyed the only print.

· *THE GREAT GATSBY* [1926]. Only a trailer remains of the first film version of the classic novel.

· *HATS OFF* [1927]. Laurel and Hardy's first hit. There was only one print, and it was misplaced after the movie's theatrical run.

· *THE WAY OF ALL FLESH* [1927]. Emil Jennings won the first Oscar for Best Actor, but only five minutes of footage remains. It's the only Academy Award–winning performance that has been lost.

· *KING KONG APPEARS IN EDO* [1938]. One of the first Japanese "giant monster" movies, it was destroyed during World War II (not by Godzilla).

# The Riddle That Killed Homer

In the ninth century B.C., the Greek poet Homer wrote the *Odyssey*, a story about a king's long journey home after the Trojan War and his encounters with monsters, magic, and seductive enchantresses.

According to legend, Homer met his own end because he couldn't answer a "simple" riddle told by a fisherman:

*What we caught we threw away;*
*what we didn't catch, we kept.*

Homer was stumped; he tried and tried but couldn't figure it out. The account might not be true (whether or not there even was a Homer is still in debate), but the ancient Greeks really liked their riddles. The word comes from a Greek root meaning "to give advice."

So what did the fishermen keep? Lice, which they already had. Homer was so frustrated that he couldn't figure it out, so the story goes, that he committed suicide.

> "To say of what is that it is not, or of what is not that it is, is false, while to say of what is that it is, and of what is not that it is not, is true."
>
> —**Aristotle**

# Made-up Languages: Volapük

Invented in the 1870s by a Bavarian Catholic priest named Johann Martin Schleyer, Volapük (which means "World Language") was inspired by a dream in which God told Schleyer to invent a single, universal language that people of all nations could speak.

By the late 1880s, there were nearly 300 Volapük societies around the world. Three international Volapük conferences were held, in 1884, 1887, and 1889; the last one, in Paris, was conducted entirely in Volapük.

### SAMPLE WORDS:

*nenomik:* abnormal

*rolatridem:* escalator

*yebafel:* lawn

*sanavik:* medical

*niblit:* pants

*sasenan:* murderer

*delagased:* newspaper

*paänakek:* pancake

*geböfik:* ordinary

*släm:* mud

*jipal:* mother

*adyö!:* good-bye!

**Fatal Flaw:** Schleyer was so protective of Volapük that he blocked all attempts to "fix" the language. Speakers split into several factions, each of which created their own version of Volapük. The entire point of a universal language had been defeated. Today there are fewer than 30 Volapük speakers in the world.

# Slowpokes

• Antoin Miliordos of Greece is an Olympic record holder... for the slowest speed ever achieved in a ski slalom race. In the 1952 Winter Olympics in Oslo, Norway, Miliordos fell 18 times during his qualifying run, averaging a pathetic 6.33 miles per hour (not that much faster than a brisk walk). He crossed the finish line skiing backward.

• In the 50-kilometer cross-country ski race at the 1988 Winter Olympics, Mexican skier Roberto Alvarez lagged so far behind his fellow skiers that racing officials actually lost track of him and were forced to send out a search party. They found him, but he finished dead last—almost an hour behind the next-slowest skier.

• Runner Wallace Williams of the Virgin Islands ran the 1979 Pan-American Games marathon at such a slow pace that by the time he got to the stadium that housed the finish line, all the stadium doors were locked, and the crowd and race officials had already gone home.

"There are only three sports: bullfighting, motor racing, and mountaineering; all the rest are merely games."

—Ernest Hemingway

## FIVE FREAKY FACTS ABOUT...
# ANIMALS

- Salvador Dalí owned an anteater. He liked to take it for walks in Paris.

- Some early Antarctic explorers thought penguins were fish.

- According to the *Oxford English Dictionary*, the lawyer bird gets its name from its "large bill."

- They gave us the bird: Chickens were first domesticated in Vietnam about 10,000 years ago.

- Napoleon's wife Josephine had a pet orangutan that wore clothes and ate with utensils.

# Fight of the Gladiators

In A.D. 69, the Roman emperor Vespasian ordered the building of the Flavian Amphitheater. Today it's known as the Colosseum, and it allowed Vespasian to keep the more than one million Roman citizens under control by quenching their thirst for blood in a way that didn't threaten the empire.

• Festivities began at dawn and often lasted well into the night. "Second-rate" events were scheduled during mealtimes, however, so that spectators could return home for lunch without missing much. The feeding of Christians to the lions is believed by many historians to have been one of the mealtime events.

• On the mornings of the games, the gladiators rode by chariot from their barracks to the amphitheater and marched into the arena up to the emperor's box, where they saluted the emperor.

• The day often began with bloodless duels that mimicked the more violent events to come. Women, or sometimes dwarfs or cripples, battled one another using wooden swords that were made to look like metal.

• After this event ended, an attendant would blow a war trumpet to announce the beginning of the main event— most often a battle between gladiators. They usually fought to the death, although the loser had a chance of escaping with his life (but not his dignity) intact. When it became clear to a gladiator that he was going to be defeated, he could cast away his shield and raise a finger on his left hand—this was the gesture used to throw oneself upon the mercy of the emperor.

The emperor would then ask the crowd to help him decide the gladiator's fate. They would shout *Mitte!* ("Let him go free!") and give the emperor a thumbs-up, or *Iugula!* ("Pay the penalty!") and give a thumbs-down. The emperor would then give either a thumbs-up or a thumbs-down, and his orders would be carried out.

# The Princess and the Queen

Princess Diana was among the most famous people in the world, which meant that whenever she went out in public, she was mobbed. For someone who grew up as a commoner, that made her life difficult. But thanks to Queen lead singer Freddie Mercury, she got to see how the other half lived.

According to British comedian Cleo Rocos in her book *The Power of Positive Drinking*, one night in the late 1980s, she and Mercury disguised Diana as a male model, complete with an "army jacket, black cap, and sunglasses," and then took her to a gay bar in London. "When we walked in," wrote Rocos, "we felt she was obviously Princess Diana and would be discovered at any minute. But people just seemed to blank her. She sort of disappeared. But she loved it...She did look like a beautiful young man. She was always a very fit girl, so they might have thought, 'There's a nice young man with pert buttocks.'"

## HOLLYWOOD BOTCHES HISTORY
In the *Jurassic Park* movies, the fierce Velociraptors are about as tall as an adult. In real life, however, Velociraptors were about as tall as a turkey.

# TWO STRANGE COINCIDENCES

• **THE ROBERTS EXPRESS:** On October 15, 1952, a man named Robert Paterson was boarding a train from Phoenix to Los Angeles when the conductor told him that another man named Robert Paterson was already onboard. The two Robert Patersons had the same height, weight, and appearance. The train made an emergency stop in California and picked up *another* Robert Paterson. He looked like the other two. The three Robert Patersons disembarked in L.A.— when a *fourth* Robert Paterson got on board.

• **NEVER THE TWAIN SHALL MEET:** Mark Twain was born on November 30, 1835, shortly after an appearance of Halley's comet. The author thought that he and the comet were somehow connected. "I came in with Halley's comet in 1835. It is coming again next year (1910), and I expect to go out with it. The Almighty has said, no doubt: 'Now here are these two unaccountable freaks. They came in together; they must go out together.'" Twain died on April 21, 1910—the day after Halley's comet's return.

# Mary the Jewess

*Maria Hebraea, also known as Mary the Jewess, was not only the first Western alchemist but perhaps the most famous female alchemist in history. Although she lived in Alexandria circa A.D. 200, many of her inventions and ideas are still around today.*

• Hebraea is credited with discovering the formula for hydrochloric acid. She also experimented with sulfur vapor to synthesize a metal alloy compound, known to this day as Mary's Black.

• She invented the double boiler, in which a small pot is placed on top of a larger pot of boiling water to gently heat substances. It's called the *bain marie* in French and *Marienbad* in German.

• Hebraea also invented the *tribikos*, a complex distillation device that may have been the first of its kind.

• Even a saying she coined—"Join the male and the female, and you will find what is sought"—is still quoted today.

> "I have an idea that the phrase 'weaker sex' was coined by some woman to disarm some man she was preparing to overwhelm."
>
> **—Ogden Nash**

# Homer the Greek Poet Vs...

## The Poet

"It is the bold man who every time does his best."

"The charity that is a trifle to us can be precious to others."

"The fates have given mankind a patient soul."

"Nothing is so incontinent as a man's accursed appetite."

"I detest he who hides one thing in his heart and means another."

## The Simpson

"I don't know, Marge. Trying is the first step toward failure."

"You gave both dogs away? You know how I feel about giving!"

"Give me some peace of mind or I'll mop the floor with you!"

"Ahh, beer...I would kill everyone in this room for a drop of sweet beer."

"But, Marge, it takes two people to lie: one to lie, and one to listen."

# Homer the Simpson

## *The Poet*

"The man who acts the least, disrupts the most."

"A sympathetic friend can be quite as dear as a brother."

"A multitude of rulers is not a good thing. Let there be one ruler, one king."

"Never, never was a wicked man wise."

"How mortals take the gods to task! Yet their afflictions come from us."

## *The Simpson*

"It is better to watch things than to do them."

"Television—teacher, mother, secret lover!"

"I'd blow smoke in the president's stupid monkey face and all he'd do is grooooove on it!"

"I am so smart! S-M-R-T, I mean S-M-A-R-T."

"I'm not normally a religious man, but if you're up there, save me, Superman!"

# NOW THAT'S A SUPER VOLCANO!

The term "supervolcano" is something the media came up with to describe Yellowstone National Park. It has no exact scientific definition, but according to the United States Geological Survey, a supervolcano is capable of ejecting at least 240 cubic miles of scorching lava, ash, gases, and rock into the atmosphere. When a volcano erupts, the force is measured by the Volcanic Explosivity Index, or VEI. The scale is open-ended, but the highest magnitude ever measured is VEI 8, the size of a supervolcano.

To get an idea of how powerful a VEI 8 eruption is, consider this: The eruption of a supervolcano at La Garita (in present-day Colorado) 27.5 million years ago was approximately 105 times more powerful than the Tsar Bomba explosion, a nuclear bomb tested by the Soviets in 1961 and still considered to be the most powerful man-made explosive device ever detonated. La Garita spewed out enough ash and lava to cover the state of California 40 feet deep.

# Master of Puppet

John Hill of Hawkestone Park in Shropshire, England, had a puppet for a hermit—literally. That's because his real hermit, Father Francis, had died after living for 14 years in a cave at Hawkestone, sporting the requisite long beard and contemplating an hourglass to the delight of passersby.

After Hill's search for a suitable replacement failed, he instructed his servants to build him a life-size replica of Father Francis. The new "Francis" turned out to be distinctly less animated than his predecessor, but Hill had a solution for that as well: He hired a man to crouch behind the dummy and make it "stand up" whenever a visitor approached. The operator would then recite poetry while moving Francis's mouth with a string.

# Famous Last Stands

**ADMIRAL YI SUN-SIN:** On October 26, 1597, a Korean force of 13 ships met 133 Japanese warships and 200 more smaller ships in Myeongnyang Strait at the southwest tip of Korea. When the daylong battle was over, Korean admiral Yi Sun-sin had masterminded one of the most successful naval stands in history, losing no ships while sinking 31 Japanese ships and damaging 92 more.

**LOS NIÑOS HÉROES:** On September 12, 1847, an American force of 13,000 led by General Winfield Scott attacked Chapultepec Castle in Mexico City in one of the last battles of the Mexican-American War. Near the end of the following day, Mexican general Nicolás Bravo finally ordered retreat, but six military cadets—between 13 and 19 years old—refused. They stayed and faced the American onslaught, going down one by one to rifle fire or bayonet wounds. Legend says the last one wrapped himself in a Mexican flag and threw himself off the castle.

*Los Niños Héroes*—the Boy Heroes—are among Mexico's most admired historical figures.

# The First Korean in America

Seo Jae-pil was born in Korea in 1864. When he was a teenager, he joined a reform movement working for equality, and in 1884 he took part in the Kapsin Coup, a bloody attempt to take over the country. Seo's family was killed in the three-day melee, but he escaped and fled to Japan, where, in 1885, he boarded a ship for San Francisco, changing his name to Philip Jaisohn.

In 1890 he became a naturalized American citizen— the first Korean to do so. He was also the first Korean to receive a college degree in the United States (a medical degree from George Washington University in 1892). He also founded the *Independent*, the first Korean newspaper in America. And in 1945 he became the first Korean-born American to receive a medal from Congress, for his service as a physician during World War II.

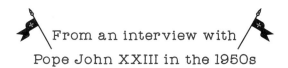

From an interview with
Pope John XXIII in the 1950s

REPORTER: "How many people work in the Vatican?"

POPE JOHN: "About half."

# The Great Bedzany Train Robbery

"I haven't got money, and I must have it for the ends I pursue." So wrote Józef Pilsudski in a letter to a friend on September 26, 1908...right before his team of Polish revolutionaries embarked on a daring train robbery.

Their target: a mail train carrying tax money from Warsaw to St. Petersburg, Russia. (Russia, Prussia, and Austria had conquered and divided up Poland in the late 1700s, and Pilsudski was leading a charge to free his people.) That evening, the 16 men and four women boarded the train in two waves.

When the train arrived at the tiny station in Bezdany, Lithuania, the robbers sprang into action: One group captured the station and cut telecommunications wires; the other attacked the train with guns and bombs. Using dynamite, they ripped open the fortified mail car and stuffed the money into cloth bags. Then they escaped in different directions and all got away. The haul was a spectacular 200,812 rubles, more than $4 million in today's dollars—a fortune in impoverished eastern Europe. It kept Pilsudski's paramilitary organization in good stead for many years.

In 1918 Poland became one country again, and Pilsudski became its first leader.

# What Goes Up...

Marie Blanchard was the first female aeronaut and the widow of Jean-Pierre Blanchard, the first person to cross the English Channel by balloon (he suffered a fatal heart attack after he fell out of his balloon).

But Mademoiselle Blanchard pressed on. To keep the crowds coming, she began flying at night so that she could shoot off fireworks in midflight. One problem: She preferred balloons filled with hydrogen gas...which happens to be explosive.

The end came on a night flight over Paris on July 7, 1819. The fireworks show got a little bigger than Blanchard had bargained for: One of her rockets ignited the hydrogen, and her balloon exploded. Blanchard managed to land on the roof of a building, but to the horror of the crowd below, she then slid off the roof to the street, breaking her neck.

History's first female aeronaut died just as the first male aeronaut had—in a balloon accident.

### ANCIENT SHREDDING

A carving from to A.D. 800 depicts the Norse hero Gunther playing a lute with his toes.

# Carriwitchet Quiz!

*What's a carriwitchet? One of the obsolete words in this quiz.*
*Try to match up each term with its definition.*

1. Thutter
2. Hierophant
3. Pettifogger
4. Cark
5. Sequacity
6. Elflocks
7. Abecedarian
8. Compossible
9. Gruntle
10. Desuetude
11. Epicene
12. Demulcent
13. Fichu
14. Carriwitchet
15. Wopsy
16. Dormition

A. Compatible
B. To burden someone
C. A priest
D. Hair matted from sleep
E. A triangular scarf
F. Of indeterminate gender
G. A dull, repetitive sound
H. A tendency to be servile
I. A beginner
J. Relating to a dead custom
K. A riddle or word puzzle
L. To soothe
M. A lozenge
N. An unscrupulous lawyer
O. Painless death
P. Tangled

**Answers:** 1–G, 2–C, 3–N, 4–B, 5–H, 6–D, 7–I, 8–A, 9–L, 10–J, 11–F, 12–M, 13–E, 14–K, 15–P, 16–O

# The Castrati

Ever heard of the castrati? They were boys who were castrated in an effort to fill the Catholic Church's need for singing talent.

The practice appeared in Europe as early as the 1500s, but historians estimate that between 1720 and 1730 (the height of the craze), 4,000 boys between the ages of nine and twelve who showed even vague musical promise were castrated each year. By that time, the practice was limited almost entirely to Italy, but its seeds had been planted years earlier when the Church, having banned women from singing in choirs (religious officials thought women's voices were too seductive) turned to young boys, whose sweet tones were preferable to the shrill soprano falsettists.

Castration prevented puberty, and without the male hormone testosterone, a castrato's vocal cords remained small and immature throughout his lifetime, which kept his voice high. And because his bone joints didn't harden, he also grew unusually tall and developed a large chest cavity, which gave him extra lung capacity.

With rigorous training, the combined effect was tremendous vocal flexibility, a high range, pure tone, and extraordinary endurance. The very best could hold a note for up to a minute without taking a breath.

# The Not-So-Mad Scientist

Arguably the most brilliant inventor of the 20th century, Nikola Tesla died broke and alone in 1943 after seeing so many of his greatest inventions passed off as other people's ideas; Marconi got the credit for the radio, and Edison passed off alternating current as the work of his engineers. When asked about his rivals late in his life, Tesla took the high road: "Let the future tell the truth and evaluate each one according to his work and accomplishments. The present is theirs; the future, for which I really worked, is mine."

And it turns out that Tesla really did know a thing or two about the future. In fact, he described a device in 1926 that sounds a lot like the smartphones of today:

> When wireless is perfectly applied the whole Earth will be converted into a huge brain, which in fact it is, all things being particles of a real and rhythmic whole. We shall be able to communicate with one another instantly, irrespective of distance. Not only this, but through television and telephony we shall see and hear one another as perfectly as though we were face to face, despite intervening distances of thousands of miles; and the instruments through which we shall be able to do his will be amazingly simple compared with our present telephone. A man will be able to carry one in his vest pocket.

**BOTCHED HISTORY**

"We're the country that built the Intercontinental Railroad."

—PRESIDENT BARACK OBAMA, TALKING ABOUT THE TRANSCONTINENTAL RAILROAD

# Napoleon's Botched Suicide Attempt

When Napoleon Bonaparte was about to be exiled to the island of Elba in 1814, the disgraced French emperor tried to commit suicide in order to spare himself and his family the humiliation. But unbeknown to Napoleon, the poison that he carried with him had lost its effectiveness, so it only paralyzed him temporarily. He recovered the next day and lived long enough to escape exile, rise back to power, and fight the British in the Battle of Waterloo. The fight involved 200,000 soldiers, 50,000 of whom were killed, injured, or captured. Napoleon lost, finally putting an end to his reign. He died in 1821 on the island of Saint Helena in the Atlantic Ocean.

> "I have come to realize that men are not born to be free."
> —**Napoleon Bonaparte**

# Vlad Be Impaling

Fifteenth-century Romanian ruler Vlad Dracula was better known as Vlad Tepes ("Vlad the Impaler") for his method of torturing and executing thousands of his enemies—and even his own countrymen—by impaling them upon wooden poles. A certifiable psycho, Vlad enjoyed watching people suffer, and made sure an impalement took several hours—sometimes even days. There were even various forms of impalement depending on age, rank, or gender.

Yet amazingly, in spite of his legendary cruelty, Vlad is often spoken of as a hero in Romanian history. Why? Because he used the terror of his reign to maintain public order and defend the country against foreign invasion. One time he scared off an advancing army by displaying the impaled remains of the previous invaders—20,000 Turks—outside his city.

But old habits die hard: When Dracula was later overthrown and imprisoned, he would catch insects and mice in his cell and impale them.

# The World's First Novel

In the history of the written word, the novel is a relatively recent addition, only dating back about 1,000 years or so. Before that, literary works were mainly collections of fables, legends, or poems. But then came *The Tale of Genji*, written by a Japanese widow named Murasaki Shikibu in 1002. Historians have deemed it the world's first true novel (though they debate whether it's the first modern psychological novel or the first classical novel).

Shikibu, a member of the emperor's royal entourage, penned her drama about the court life of a man named Hikaru Genji, the beloved son of Japan's emperor and the emperor's favorite (though lowly) concubine. Court intrigue leads to the death of Genji's mother, which keeps him from inheriting his father's throne. Nevertheless, Genji manages to have an influential and romantic life, and he eventually becomes the secret father of the heir to the throne. The end.

What was so influential about this "narrative prose"? It was among the first works to really explore the inner lives of human characters. Rather than relating a series of supernatural epic adventures, it followed a small group of people through time, showing how they changed as they grew older. When novelist Yasunari Kawabata accepted the 1968 Nobel Prize for Literature, he described *The Tale of Genji* as "the highest pinnacle of Japanese literature."

# Two Illegal Word Origins

• In 1849 a criminal named William Thompson would walk up to strangers in New York City and, after making friends with them, ask, "Have you confidence in me to trust me with your watch until tomorrow?" If they said yes, Thompson would gratefully borrow the watch...and then keep it. When he was caught, the prosecutors referred to him as a "confidence man." That didn't fit on headlines, so newspapers shortened it to "con man."

• Another trickster in 1840s New York was Alec Hoag. He used prostitutes to lure men into hotel rooms. When the men's clothes were on the floor, Hoag lifted money from the pockets via a hole in the wall. He was known for his ability to stay one step ahead of the police...and brag about it all over the city. The nickname the cops gave to Hoag survives as a slang term used to describe an intelligent, cocky person: "smart aleck."

 Six Things Invented by Accident

| | |
|---|---|
| **1.** Velcro | **4.** Superglue |
| **2.** The Slinky | **5.** Teflon |
| **3.** Microwave oven | **6.** The X-ray machine |

# Magnum P.U.

*On page 82, you read about "privvy diggers," people who dig up old outhouses looking for treasures that were thrown in the hole. Oftentimes the items they find can reveal a lot about the daily lives of times gone by. It's time for another "Outhouse Detectives" mystery!*

**DISCOVERY:** Bottles, tin cans, and other brand-name items recovered from the hole underneath a 19th-century outhouse on Franklin Street in downtown Annapolis, Maryland. That area was part of the African American community.

**MYSTERY:** A surprisingly high percentage of the items recovered were national brands instead of local products. These findings correspond to other excavations of outhouses in the area, which suggests that African Americans used more national brands and fewer local brands than did white communities. Why?

**THEORY:** Anthropology professor Mark P. Leone, who directed the excavation, speculates that African Americans preferred national brands because the prices were set at the national level instead of by neighborhood grocers. By purchasing these brands, he explains, "They could avoid racism at the local grocery store, where shopkeepers might inflate prices or sell them substandard goods."

## FIVE FREAKY FACTS ABOUT...
# CHINA

- Chinese people have been painting their fingernails for more than 5,000 years.

- Confucius has more than three million living descendants.

- Why did people in ancient China scatter firecrackers around the house? They made great fire alarms.

- The Chinese once called eggplants "mad apples," believing they caused insanity.

- One of the ingredients in the Great Wall of China: rice flour. (It made the bricks stronger.)

# Real-Life Frankensteins: Giovanni Aldini

At the turn of the 19th century, scientists experimented with a process called *galvanism*—using electrical currents to stimulate nerves and muscles. The pioneer was Luigi Galvani, who discovered that a dead frog's legs would kick when zapped with electricity.

His nephew, Giovanni Aldini, galvanized much larger creatures. Huge crowds turned out to see the mad puppeteer manipulate the dead. According to a witness account:

> Aldini, after having cut off the head of a dog, makes the current of a strong battery go through it: The mere contact triggers terrible convulsions. The jaws open, the teeth chatter, the eyes roll in their sockets; and if reason did not stop the fired imagination, one would almost believe that the animal is suffering and alive again!

In 1803 Aldini published a book called *An Account of the Late Improvements in Galvanism*, full of illustrations showing the results of his experiments in graphic detail. He was also the first person to apply the use of electrical impulses to treat the mentally ill—a procedure later known as electroshock therapy.

# The Astronaut's Blank Stare

On March 9, 1961, Ivan Ivanovich became the first person to fly into space. Well, the first personlike thing to fly into space. Ivan Ivanovich (the Russian equivalent of "John Johnson") was a life-size test-flight mannequin, and he and his companion, a (live) dog named Chernushka ("Blackie"), were rocketed into space weeks before Yuri Gagarin was to take his historic flight.

Ivanovich's mission: to test the *Vostok* spacecraft and the SK-1 pressure suit. After completing a single orbit in 89 minutes, Ivanovich and the dog returned safely to Earth. He was so lifelike—with eyes, eyelashes, eyebrows, lips, and all—that the word *maket*, or "dummy," was written on his forehead so nobody would think he was a dead cosmonaut. **Update:** Ivan the Space Mannequin was sold at Sotheby's auction house in 1993. He was purchased by Texas billionaire (and onetime presidential candidate) H. Ross Perot for $189,500.

## HORSING AROUND

In the 2003 movie *Seabiscuit*, most of the crowd at the 1938 Pimlico horse race were blow-up sex dolls with masks over their faces and painted-on suits.

# The Big Dipper & the Pointer Stars

At the tip of the handle of the Little Dipper is the most celebrated star in the sky, Polaris, the North Star. While not the brightest star in the heavens, Polaris has provided directions to countless travelers for thousands of years. The two stars at the end of the bowl of the Big Dipper, called the "Pointers," point to the North Star.

The Greeks used the Greater Bear and the Phoenicians used the Lesser Bear to find north. American slaves called the Big Dipper the "Drinking Gourd" and followed it northward to freedom.

Seen from the spinning Earth, the sky appears to move during the night, carrying all the stars along with it. Only the North Star stands in the same spot at the hub of the dome of the sky. The Greeks called this star Cynosure, a word that has found its way into our language, meaning "the center of attraction or interest." Want to find the North Star yourself? Head out on a starry night, look up at the Big Dipper, and follow the Pointers to Polaris. Here's Alaska's state flag to help you out:

# How a Piece of Tape Changed History

In the early morning of June 17, 1972, an $80-a-week security guard named Frank Wills was patrolling the parking garage of an office complex in Washington, D.C., when he noticed that someone had used adhesive tape to prevent a stairwell door from latching. Wills removed the tape and continued on his rounds, but when he returned to the same door at 2:00 a.m., he saw it had been taped again. So he called the police, who discovered a team of burglars planting bugs in an office leased by the Democratic National Committee.

This "third-rate burglary"—and the cover-up that followed—grew into the Watergate scandal that forced President Richard M. Nixon to resign from office in 1974.

> "I would have made a good pope."
> —**Richard Nixon**

# The Birth of Political Correctness

It seems like everyone is talking about "political correct-
ness" these days, so you'd think that this method of using
language that seemingly goes out of its way to not offend
anyone is a relatively modern term, like maybe from the
1980s or 1990s. It actually dates way further back than
that—all the way back to the founding of the United States.

During a 1793 U.S. Supreme Court case called *Chisholm
v. Georgia*, Justice James Wilson argued that it is the people,
not the states, who held the real power in the country. He
wrote: "To 'the United States' instead of to the 'People of
the United States' is the toast given. This is not politically
correct."

The phrase was used sparingly in politics after that.
It didn't hit the mainstream until the 1960s when pinko
hippie commies, er...socially minded, progressive activists
revived the term.

# KENTUCKY FRIED HOBBIT

Nowadays, people eat birds. But around 13,000 years ago, on an island in Indonesia, the opposite was true. *Homo floresiensis*, an ancient humanlike species referred to by scientists as "hobbit people," shared the island with an ancient species of stork called *Leptoptilos robustus*. "Robustus" is putting it mildly—the birds stood more than six feet tall, towering over the three-foot-tall people. Scientists theorize that the birds fed on the hobbits.

## Politician Incorrect

Francis Scott Key wrote "The Star Spangled Banner," but his son Philip Barton Key also made a name for himself—he was shot and killed in 1859 by New York congressman Daniel Sickles for having an affair with Sickles's wife, Teresa.

# The Mysterious Theremin

If this book had a soundtrack, the theremin would be the lead instrument. The weirdest thing about it is that to play the theremin, you cannot touch the theremin. Two antenna-like capacitors—one controlling pitch, the other volume—protrude from a box that houses radio frequency oscillators. The resulting signal is fed out through a speaker. The device is played with delicate, precise motions of the hands in the air around the antennae. The effect is eerie, as if the player is conjuring music from the ether. In fact, inventor Léon Theremin's original name for it was the "etherphone."

A physicist and cellist, Theremin invented it in 1919 by accident while working for the Soviets on a device to detect objects through the air (like radar). Even though the spying device didn't work out, Soviet leaders were so impressed with Theremin that they sent him on a European tour to demonstrate the instrument—and Soviet ingenuity. The maestro played to packed concert halls across the continent.

In 1928 Theremin defected to the United States and set up a lab in New York City to sell his namesake to the public. From there, his instrument became a staple in 1950s science-fiction movies, and is still quite popular today.

# Dinner Music

In 1870 the James Robinson & Co. Circus and Animal Show wanted to drum up some publicity for its touring cavalcade prior to a performance in Middletown, Missouri. As the clowns, circus performers, and animals paraded through town, the circus band played along while standing on the roof of a cage...that held two hungry lions. Despite concerns that the roof wasn't strong enough to support ten grown men, circus bosses ordered the band to keep on playing.

So they did...right up until the moment the roof caved in.

The musicians plunged into the den of hungry lions, who tore them limb from limb and ate most of their bodies. Ten band members started the parade; only three survived the mauling.

### MY BIG FAT GREEK LANDFILL

The first known official landfill opened in Athens, Greece, around 500 B.C. A law was passed requiring garbage to be disposed of two miles outside of the city limits. Reason: defense. The garbage had previously been thrown right outside the city walls, which allowed invaders to climb up the pile and over the walls.

# The Year Without a Summer

On April 10, 1815, Mount Tambora blew its top. The massive eruption lasted 10 days and completely ravaged the Indonesian island of Sumbawa. The ash from Tambora combined with the dust and debris from several other eruptions...and blocked out the sun. The effects were devastating to agriculture across the globe. It got really bad the following year, in 1816, which has been called "the year without a summer."

In the United States, New England was beset with a "dry fog" that would not dissipate. The lingering fog dimmed and refracted the sunlight, creating a constant eerie red glow in the sky. Even heavy rainfall failed to disperse it. Temperatures routinely fell below freezing throughout the spring.

The situation in Europe was even worse. Abnormal rainfall caused rivers to rise, while many areas endured frost in mid-August. People reported snowfall throughout the summer months. Even stranger: The dust in the atmosphere turned the white snowflakes red. The ensuing famine was the worst the continent would experience in the 19th century. By the time that "summer" was over, nearly 200,000 Europeans had perished.

# The Poem About the Year Without a Summer

You just read about the year without a summer. (If you didn't, go back to the previous page.) A Vermont woman named Eileen Marguet captured the misery of that dark summer in this poem:

> *It didn't matter whether your farm was large or small.*
> *It didn't matter if you had a farm at all.*
> *'Cause everyone was affected when water didn't run.*
> *The snow and frost continued without the warming sun.*
> *One day in June it got real hot and leaves began to show.*
> *But after that it snowed again and wind and cold did blow.*
> *The cows and horses had no grass; no grain to feed the chicks.*
> *No hay to put aside that time, just dry and shriveled sticks.*
> *The sheep were cold and hungry and many starved to death,*
> *Still waiting for the warming sun to save their labored breath.*
> *The kids were disappointed, no swimming, such a shame.*
> *It was in 1816 that summer never came.*

# Almost Assassinated

On August 16, 1972, King Hassan of Morocco was flying home from France aboard his Boeing 727 when it was attacked by four jet fighters from the Royal Moroccan Air Force. During the attack, someone claiming to be a mechanic on the royal plane radioed to the attackers, "Stop firing! The tyrant is dead!" The 727 was allowed to land.

The "mechanic," it turned out, was the king himself. He participated in the welcoming ceremonies as if nothing had happened. Realizing they'd been fooled, the plotters sent eight more fighter planes to attack the ceremonies. They killed eight people, but not the king—he hid under some trees. Later that day, the plotters attacked a guest house next to the royal palace, where it was thought the king was hiding. Hassan survived all three attempts, executed the general behind the plot, and remained on the throne until 1999.

# "Turn Away When Spitting"

*In 1530 a philosopher named Erasmus of Rotterdam wrote a book on manners called* On Civility in Children. *It was so popular that it became a best-seller. Here are a few choice excerpts.*

• "If you cannot swallow a piece of food, turn 'round discreetly and throw it somewhere."

• "Retain wind by compressing your belly."

• "Do not be afraid of vomiting if you must; for it is not vomiting but holding the vomit in your throat that is foul."

• "Turn away when spitting lest your saliva fall on someone. If anything disgusting falls on the ground, it should be trodden upon, lest it nauseate someone."

• "Some people put their hands in the dishes the moment they have sat down. Wolves do that!"

• "To lick greasy fingers or to wipe them on your coat is impolite. It is better to use the tablecloth."

• "Do not move back and forth on your chair. Whoever does that gives the impression of constantly breaking or trying to break wind."

# BOTCHED HISTORY

"It's like the Roman Empire. Wasn't everybody running around covered with syphilis? And then it was destroyed by the volcano."

—Actress Joan Collins, discussing the AIDS epidemic

# Tapeworm Trap

Tapeworms are vile little creatures. They take up residence in your intestines, feed on the food you ingest, and then steal all the nutrients for themselves. These days, they're not so much of a problem (at least in the First World, except when people misuse them as part of a fad diet), but throughout history tapeworms have wreaked havoc on the human body.

In 1854 an Indiana doctor named Alpheus Myers invented a tapeworm-removal device that didn't "employ medicines" or "cause much injury." Myers's gadget was a cross between a plumbing snake and a fishing pole. After fasting for a day to make your tapeworm hungry, you swallowed the device—a three-inch-long metal trap on the end of a metal chain. The trap went into the stomach; the other end hung out of the person's mouth. The trap, outfitted with "any nutritious material," would lure the worm and grasp its head, at which point you would pull out the trap, and the tapeworm along with it.

# The Beast Slayers

*Are you not entertained?*

• Roman sports fans loved to watch professional *bestiarii* ("beast slayers" who weren't considered gladiators) kill fierce animals in the Colosseum—including lions, tigers, bulls, bears, or just about anything that could bleed to death. Many of the events involved the killing of ostriches, deer, and even giraffes.

• Some of the animal events involved audience participation. Spectators were invited to throw spears from their seats or to use bows and arrows. At other events, skilled hunters entered the arena and chased down the animals with hounds. At still other events, it was the wild animals who hunted people, when condemned criminals (or regular criminals, if condemned criminals were in short supply) would be thrown to them completely defenseless.

• The Romans scoured the empire and its provinces looking for things to kill; by the time the animal hunts were abolished in the sixth century, several species of animals—including the elephants of North Africa, the hippopotamuses of Nubia, the lions of Mesopotamia, and the tigers of Hyrcania—had been driven to extinction.

# A Tale from the Crypt

In August 1943, a group of Freemasons unsealed a crypt containing the body of Alexander Irvine, the founder of freemasonry on Barbados. (Irvine's remains were interred in the 1830s in the same crypt as Sir Even McGregor, the owner of the crypt, who was laid to rest in 1841.)

The inner door of the crypt had been locked tight and cemented with bricks and mortar, which itself was covered with a huge stone slab. When the Freemasons unsealed the crypt, the inner door wouldn't open. Peeking in through a hole, they saw that a heavy lead coffin was standing on its head, leaning against the inner door. The masons carefully moved it and opened the door—only to discover that Irvine's coffin was missing; McGregor's was the one up against the door.

The mystery was never solved; the island's burial records confirmed that both men had been interred in the crypt nearly 100 years before, but no evidence was ever found to explain the missing coffin.

# STICK + BALL = FUN!

*People have been competing at sports for all of recorded history, and a lot of the games our ancestors played bear a striking resemblance to games we still play today.*

• **PUKKU–MIKKU.** As far back as 3000 B.C. in the city-states of the Sumerians in Mesopotamia (present-day Iraq), the Sumerians played *pukku-mikku*, a ritualistic religious-themed game that was representational of their creation myth. It was played with a stick, the *mikku*, and a hoop or ball, the *pukku*. The object: Hit the pikku with the mukku. (The pukku and the mikku are mentioned in the *Epic of Gilgamesh*, the world's oldest known written story, from about 2100 B.C.)

• **CHOGAN.** This game was played on horseback and is believed to be polo's precursor. It was developed by Persian tribes around the sixth century B.C. and was probably first played without horses. An inscription on a stone tablet found in the Persian city of Gilgit (in modern-day Iran) describes the importance of chogan:

> *Let other people play at other things.*
> *The king of games is still the game of kings.*

# The Halifax Explosion

In December 1917, during the height of World War I, the French cargo ship *Mont Blanc* was transporting 5,000 tons of explosives through Halifax Harbor in Nova Scotia on its way to reinforce the war effort in England. But it never made it out of Halifax. Due to a navigation error, the *Mont Blanc* collided with another ship, caught fire, and the crew abandoned it. In a tragic turn of events, thousands of people gathered at the shore to watch the floating, burning ship...unaware of the cargo it held.

Then, shortly before 9:05 a.m., a blinding white flash filled the harbor. The *Mont Blanc* exploded into bits and a giant mushroom cloud rose up over the town. More than 1,600 people were killed instantly. Thousands more were injured, many blinded from the glass and shrapnel that rained down on Halifax and Dartmouth. Schools, homes, factories, and churches were leveled by the ensuing shock wave.

A 30-foot tidal wave swept away what was left of the waterfront, drowning many of the initial survivors and sinking dozens of ships in the harbor. Shattered pieces of the *Mont Blanc* were hurled as far as three miles away. A tugboat was thrown from the middle of the harbor onto the Dartmouth shore. The wave also rushed over the shores of Dartmouth and up Tufts Cove, where it completely washed

away the settlement of an indigenous tribe called the Micmac. The blast was so strong that windows were broken in Charlottetown—120 miles away. It was the largest man-made explosion in history up until that point. Its size and devastation wouldn't be eclipsed until the atomic bomb was dropped on Hiroshima in 1945.

On January 22, 1918, the Canadian government appointed the Halifax Relief Commission to handle pensions, insurance claims, rehousing, and rebuilding, as well as the rehabilitation of survivors. The extent of the damage was so great that the commission would remain open until 1976.

### That Explains the Strange Paintings

Pablo Picasso, the influential Spanish cubist, wasn't breathing when he was born in 1881. His face was so blue that the midwife left him for dead. An uncle revived him by blowing cigar smoke up his nose.

# FIVE FREAKY FACTS ABOUT...
# ROYALTY

- Elizabethan women used toxic white paint to imitate Queen Elizabeth's elegant pallor.

- During one insanity attack, King George III of England ended every sentence with "peacock."

- In 1953 future Rolling Stones guitarist Keith Richards sang in the choir at Queen Elizabeth II's coronation.

- Hair to the throne: Louis XIV of France had 40 wigmakers...and approximately 1,000 wigs.

- Queen Victoria smoked marijuana to treat her cramps.

# Outdated Concepts:
# HUMORISM

Humorism dates back to 400 B.C. and persisted well into the 1800s, when advances in medical research led to a more accurate understanding of human physical and mental health.

The concept went like this: A person's health and personality are determined by the proportions of four basic substances—blood, phlegm, yellow bile, and black bile—in the body. When the four humors were in balance, the person was healthy; when they were out of balance, the person was sick. Diet and physical activity of various kinds affected the balance and could make it better or worse; treatments such as bloodletting, inducing vomiting, and purging the bowels were administered to sick people to restore proper balance of the humors.

> "The abdomen, the chest, and the brain will forever be shut from the intrusion of the wise and humane surgeon."
> **—Sir John Eric Erichsen, British surgeon, appointed Surgeon-Extraordinary to Queen Victoria 1873**

# Mer-monstrosity

The "Feejee Mermaid"—displayed by circus mogul P. T. Barnum in the 1840s—did mermaids everywhere injustice. The thing was hideous: The three-foot-long carcass was brown and shriveled; it had coarse hair and its open mouth was full of jagged teeth. Yet for several years, the Feejee Mermaid was the star of Barnum's American Museum in New York.

Most scientists dismissed the specimen as a hoax, but Barnum fooled the public into believing it was real. How? Using pseudonyms, he wrote to newspapers about an amazing discovery in Fiji (which gave the mermaid its name) and had one of his employees pose as a naturalist named Dr. Griffin to authenticate it. Then he distributed 10,000 pamphlets to local hotels, stores, and businesses with "facts" about the existence of mermaids.

Sadly, the scientists were right—it wasn't a mermaid. So what was the thing? The head of a mummified baby monkey sewed onto a fish body. It probably came from Asia, where fake animal hybrids were often sold to gullible tourists.

# India's "Nine Unknown Men"

Whispers about the Nine Unknown Men bring the Illuminati to mind, but this secret society is much older, dating back to 270 B.C. It began with Emperor Ashoka, an Indian emperor of the Maurya dynasty, who led a war that killed 100,000 men.

According to legend, he regretted the bloodshed and vowed to protect humanity from further damage caused by science and technology in the hands of evildoers. So he chose nine superintelligent men to write, and then guard, nine books full of dangerous knowledge—about energy, gravity, radiation, and the structure of matter—that was way ahead of its time. Each of the Nine Unknown Men has been responsible for protecting the information in one book as well as expanding on it (and passing it on to his successor).

Is this just the stuff of myth, or are there still nine men in India guarding nine books today? No one knows for sure. Their identities and the books are so well hidden that there's no evidence that they even exist. But some people believe that prominent men from history have served as the guardians—or were given secrets by them—including Pope Sylvester II, who in the 900s supposedly built a robotic head that could answer questions.

# The Reagan Joke That Bombed

In 1984, during the height of the Cold War, President Ronald Reagan took a break from his reelection campaign to do a radio interview. He thought he was doing a sound check for the crew, but was actually being broadcast live over the airwaves. Here's what he said:

> "My fellow Americans, I'm pleased to tell you today that I've signed legislation that will outlaw Russia forever." [Laughter.] "We begin bombing in five minutes." [More laughter.]

Neither Reagan nor his supporters thought it was a big deal—it just proved that the president had a sense of humor. (Reagan's staff took steps to ensure that in the future the Great Communicator would know unequivocally whether he was being broadcast.) But Democrats blasted the president as a trigger-happy madman out of touch with the severity of his "joke."

The Soviets weren't amused, either. One Moscow television station wondered how much Reagan was joking, claiming that bombing Russia was his "sacred dream." The joke didn't hurt Reagan politically, though—he won that year's election by a landslide (and he never did bomb Russia).

# Antiques Roadshow: More Top Finds

**BLING IT ON:** In 1998 a Virginia woman appeared on PBS's *Antiques Roadshow* with a collection of gaudy rings, bracelets, and pendants dating to the Jazz Age of the 1920s. Her friends told her it was just costume jewelry, but she wasn't convinced.

She was right: The large "fake" gems were not only real rubies (2.5–3 carats each) but rare Burmese ones…and diamonds. Total worth: $257,000.

**DON'T BE SO JADED:** At a 2009 taping in Raleigh, North Carolina, a woman brought in two bowls and two sculptures made from carved jade and celadon, a type of Chinese pottery, that her father had bought while stationed in China in the 1940s. It turns out they were crafted in the 18th century for Emperor Qianlong (ruler during the Qing dynasty). "I would doubt if he paid more than a hundred dollars for any one of these," appraiser James Callahan said. "It's the best thing I have ever seen on the *Roadshow*." The collection's worth: $1.07 million.

# The Ball of the Burning Men

King Charles VI of France (1368–1422) spent much of his reign struggling to maintain his sanity. Sometimes he was convinced that he was made of glass. He even had steel rods placed inside his robe so he wouldn't "break."

But he wasn't always that way. When he was crowned in 1380, the young king was known as "Charles the Beloved." Then everything changed on January 28, 1393.

A wild party was held at the royal residence to celebrate the third wedding of a widow named Catherine de Fastaverin. Back then, widow weddings involved loud music, lavish costumes, and silly shenanigans. So for this occasion, Huguet de Guisay, a nobleman with a reputation for being a jerk, came up with a plan to prank Catherine. Huguet convinced King Charles and five of his knights to dress up as masked "wild men" in disguises made out of wood, resin, and weeds. Because the costumes were highly flammable, plans were made ahead of time to extinguish all the torches in the party hall.

At the designated moment, the fires went out and the pranksters burst in, shouting obscenities, howling, and dancing frantically. Five of the wild men were chained together. That proved to be a very bad idea.

All was going well until the Duke of Orléans, Charles's brother, showed up late, drunk as a skunk...carrying a lit

torch. He held his torch over one of the chained pranksters' heads to see who it was...and then a spark fell, setting the man's costume ablaze. Chaos ensued as the fire spread from one wild man to another. They cried out in pain as the costumes of other partygoers burst into flames. People frantically stormed the exits, screaming and running for their lives. Several didn't make it out alive.

The king barely escaped, and he spent the rest of his life battling to stay sane. No longer called "Charles the Beloved," his new nickname was Charles la Fou, or "Charles the Mad." By the end of the 14th century, he wasn't even fit to rule anymore, and his role as king had become purely ceremonial.

Were they high? Every member of Teddy Roosevelt's family owned a pair of stilts, including the First Lady.

# The Secret Hitler Files

*What did Adolf Hitler like to do for fun? Here are excerpts from a 1942 secret profile of the Führer compiled by the Office of Strategic Services.*

• "Hitler loves the circus. He takes real pleasure in the idea that underpaid performers are risking their lives to please him. He sent extremely expensive chocolates and flowers to the female performers. Hitler even remembered their names and would worry about them and their families in the event of an accident. He isn't interested in wild animal acts, unless there is a woman in danger."

• "He will often laugh merrily at Jewish comedians. He even likes a few Jewish singers, but after hearing them he would remark that it was too bad he or she wasn't an Aryan."

• "Hitler's staff secretly made films for him of the torture and execution of political prisoners, which he very much enjoyed viewing. His executive assistants also secure pornographic pictures and movies for him."

• "He adores gypsy music, Wagner's operas, and especially American college football marches and alma maters."

• "To excite the masses, he uses American college football–style music during his speeches. His rallying cry—'Sieg heil!'—was even modeled after the cheering techniques used by American football cheerleaders."

# Merry Chris-myth

**MYTH:** The popular Christmas carol contains the yuletide phrase "God rest you, merry gentlemen."

**TRUTH:** The comma is in the wrong place. The original phrase, which dates to the 1400s, was "God rest you merry, gentlemen." The phrase "God rest you merry" uses "rest" not in the sense of "relaxing," but more like "rest assured." So in essence, the song says, "May God keep you merry, gentlemen."

**MYTH:** According to the Bible, three wise men, or "Magi," riding camels from the east, brought gifts to baby Jesus on the night he was born.

**TRUTH:** Nowhere does it say there were three of them or how they got there—only that they brought three gifts. The plural "Magi" means that there could have been two or even ten. Their names—Caspar, Melchior, and Balthasar—did not appear until the sixth century in Greek writings.

**MYTH:** "Xmas" is a secular attempt to take Christ out of Christmas.

**TRUTH:** "X" is the Greek letter *chi*, which is short for the Greek word that means "Christ." So "Xmas" means "Christ's Mass." It's been in widespread use since the 16th century, but it didn't become controversial until the 20th century.

# REAL-LIFE FRANKENSTEINS: ANDREW URE

This Scottish scientist was convinced that electrical stimulation of the phrenic nerve, which runs between the neck and the abdomen, could restore the dead to life. In 1818 he caused quite a sensation in Glasgow when he attempted to prove his theory by zapping the body of murderer John Clydesdale shortly after he was hanged.

Although Ure was able to make the dead man appear to breathe and kick his legs, as well as open his eyes and make horrific faces, he was unable to resuscitate the corpse. However, the event is notable for what Ure suggested afterward: Successful resuscitation might have been achieved, he said, if the body had been shocked by two "moistened brass knobs" placed over the phrenic nerve and diaphragm—an early description of what we now call a defibrillator.

# Meeting of Tears

It was one of the darkest chapters in modern history, and a harsh lesson about the dangers of biological warfare. In the 18th century, Native Americans were giving the British all sorts of trouble during the French and Indian Wars, so in 1763 Sir Jeffrey Amherst, commander of the British forces in North America, came up with a plan that would make any supervillain proud. "We must on this occasion use every stratagem in our power to reduce them."

Usually, after smallpox patients died, their blankets were burned. But Amherst ordered his men to save the blankets for an upcoming meeting with the Delaware Indians. The tribe leaders were called to discuss terms of the war, and as a show of "good faith," the British gave them several blankets and a scarf...all of which were ridden with the disease. The Delaware had no natural antibodies to protect them from smallpox, and as a result, they were decimated by the disease.

Amherst expected to be hailed as a hero when he returned to England, but instead he was reprimanded...and then promoted to lieutenant-general.

# FIVE FREAKY FACTS ABOUT...
# INDIGENOUS PEOPLES

- The Uape Indians of Brazil mix the ashes of their dead with their alcohol.

- Sioux chief Sitting Bull's name in his own language: Tatanka Yotanka.

- The Apaches referred to horses as "god dogs."

- Polynesian explorers used stars, wind, wave patterns, and gulls to navigate their way across the Pacific.

- The Aztecs sacrificed up to 15,000 people a year to their sun god.

# The Iron Lady Gets Bombed

In 1984, four weeks before a scheduled meeting of British prime minister Margaret Thatcher's Conservative Party in Brighton, an Irish Republican Army bomber named Patrick Magee checked into the Grand Hotel, where he knew Thatcher would be staying. He then rented a room five stories above Thatcher's and planted 30 pounds of explosives.

The bomb was programmed to explode at 3:00 a.m. on the last night of the conference. Thatcher should have been asleep...had her speechwriters done a better job preparing the speech she was to deliver the next day. But she was still working on it. Just moments after she left of her room, the powerful bomb destroyed much of the hotel...including Thatcher's suite. By then, however, she was in another part of the hotel, unharmed.

Five people, including a member of Parliament, were killed in the blast and 30 more were injured. Authorities speculated that the death toll would have been much higher if so many officials had not been downstairs in the hotel bar.

# Father of the Paranormal: Charles Fort

UFOs. ESP. Spontaneous combustion. We've all been hearing about these things for our entire lives, and we have one man to thank for that: Charles Fort (1874–1932). Fort was a British author and inspiration for the paranormal magazine *Fortean Times*, which chronicles strange occurrences all over Earth.

In his time, Fort was a human search engine—a living, breathing Google. It wasn't until someone like him came along—who spent more than 20 years sifting through books, journals, magazines, and newspapers, taking copious notes, and sorting the information—that anyone realized that strange, unexplained events around the world might be connected. For example, when he read of the case of 77-year-old Barbara Bell of Blyth, England, whose badly burned remains were found in a room where nothing else had burned, he filed it with other cases he'd heard about. All of a sudden, "spontaneous combustion" was a thing.

And after Fort read an account from 1887 about a "large ball of fire" that rose out of the sea off the eastern coast of Canada, he filed it in the shoe box that contained his notes on similar incidents, such as the account of three "luminous bodies" that rose out of the Mediterranean in 1845.

And then, more than 10 years after Fort's death, on June 24, 1947, a pilot named Kenneth Arnold saw some mysterious flying objects over Mt. Rainier in Washington State. People who wanted to know more about similar sightings went to Fort's books, where they read about reports of several sightings of a cigar-shaped craft with butterfly wings in the skies over Colorado, Texas, Nebraska, Iowa, Missouri, Wisconsin, Illinois, and Indiana during the first three weeks of April 1897. The objects Kenneth Arnold saw over Mt. Rainier weren't shaped like cigars. They were shaped like flat disks—his was the first modern sighting of "flying saucers." Regardless, the public paid attention. Fort had laid the groundwork for Arnold's sighting to be taken seriously. The modern UFO craze had begun.

# The Aliens Are Already Here!

*It seems like only weirdos and conspiracy nuts see UFOs, but sometimes respected people have had encounters. Does that mean that aliens exist on Earth? Yes, it does. Here's proof.*

• **Commander Malcolm Scott Carpenter, USN, *Mercury 7* astronaut:** "At no time when the astronauts were in space were they alone: There was a constant surveillance by UFOs." (Carpenter reportedly photographed a UFO while in orbit on May 24, 1962. NASA has never released it.)

• **Captain Robert Salas, USAF missile launch officer, describing events from March 16, 1967:** "The security guard called and said, 'Sir, there's a glowing red object hovering right outside the front gate. I've got all the men out here with their weapons drawn.' We lost between 16 and 18 ICBMs at the same time UFOs were in the area."

• **Astronaut Donald "Deke" Slayton:** "In 1951 I was testing a P-51 fighter in Minneapolis when I spotted this object... it looked like a weather balloon, gray and about three feet in diameter. But as soon as I got behind the darn thing, it... looked like a saucer. I realized that it was suddenly going away...and there I was, running at about 300 miles per hour. I tracked it for a little way, and then all of a sudden the (expletive) thing just took off. It pulled about a 45-degree climbing turn and accelerated and just flat disappeared."

# Spinal Tap Moments

*Proving the 1984 rock 'n' roll mockumentary* This Is Spinal Tap *was based more on fact than on fiction.*

**THE BIG BANG:** The High Numbers were just another English club band until one night in 1964 when Pete Townshend raised his brand-new Rickenbacker 12-string guitar above his head. "The neck poked through the ceiling," he recalled. "When I pulled it out, the top of the head was left behind." Townshend's friends were all laughing at his predicament, so he pretended he'd done it on purpose and smashed the rest of the guitar. Not to be outdone, drummer Keith Moon then kicked over his bass drum. The crowd went wild. After that, they changed their name to the Who and went on to smash hundreds more instruments over the next five years.

**MEAT SABBATH:** The giant hand (a stage prop) was supposed to fling a bunch of meat into the first few rows of the crowd at a 1981 Ozzy Osbourne concert, but it fell a little short. "The stage crew had been trying it out all day," recalled Osbourne, "so the elastic wasn't quite as springy during the show. So I'm standing there, I put my foot on this lever and several @*&%$ pounds of offal slowly come up and splat all over the back of my head!"

# EINSTEIN'S EYES

Did you knows that Albert Einstein's eyes are sitting in a bank vault in New Jersey? About the same time that pathologist Thomas Stoltz Harvey absconded with the brain mere hours after the famed physicist's death in New Jersey in 1955, Einstein's ophthalmologist, Dr. Henry Abrams, removed the eyes. Abrams placed them in a jar and locked them away in a bank vault. Although rumors pop up from time to time that the eyes will be put on the auction block, Abrams maintains that he has no plans to sell them. "When you look into his eyes, you're looking into the beauties and mysteries of the world," he said. "They are clear as crystal; they seem to have such depth."

**Bonus Fact:** *Star Wars* creature designers based Yoda's eyes on Albert Einstein's eyes.

"I love Humanity, but I hate humans."
—**Albert Einstein**

# Sir Walter Raleigh's Head

Before losing his head, Sir Walter Raleigh (1554–1618) was a well-to-do English admiral, politician, explorer, and aristocrat. Most famously, he brought tobacco back from an expedition to the New World and popularized it among London's elite. At age 28, Raleigh became a favorite courtier of Queen Elizabeth I and later named the colony of Virginia after her (Elizabeth was known as "the Virgin Queen").

But Raleigh's true love was the queen's handmaiden, Elizabeth Throckmorton. The two secretly married in 1592. When the queen found out, she was devastated and briefly imprisoned the couple. After their release, Raleigh tried to win back Her Majesty's favor by leading an expedition to find a legendary gold-rich land known as El Dorado in Venezuela. He failed. The queen's successor, King James I, disliked Raleigh, and in 1618 had him beheaded. Throckmorton was inconsolable: She kept her dead husband's embalmed head in her satchel for three decades until she died in 1647.

# Notable Bulbs of History

### GARLIC BREATH

• If you were a bald man in ancient Egypt, or if you had tuberculosis, backaches, gas, or low sex drive, garlic would have been the medication of choice. Garlic has also been used to treat arthritis and rheumatism, dysentery, chicken pox, measles, malaria, typhoid, dandruff, constipation, and the common cold. Eighteenth-century doctors thought it could cure the plague. (It can't.)

• In the early 20th century, garlic was considered low-class in the United States. Immigrant, working-class people from the south of Italy received most of the scorn: Garlic was called "Italian perfume" and "Bronx vanilla" (because of the large Italian community in the Bronx in New York City). That may seem unthinkable today, when Americans of every income level, religion, background, and ethnicity eat nearly three pounds of garlic per person annually.

• When did garlic start repelling vampires? In Bram Stoker's 1897 novel *Dracula*. This superstition most likely came from the fact that garlic in the blood was a common way to fend off another bloodsucker: the mosquito.

# The Fartiste

Joseph Pujol (1857–1945) could control the pitch and timbre of his farts to create beautiful melodies and imitate people and animals. Known as Le Petomane ("the Fartiste"), aka "the Elastic Anus"—Pujol was one of the most popular acts in Paris. Here's a review of one of his shows at the Moulin Rouge:

> He took the stage in a costume of red coat, a red silk collar, and black satin breeches. He began by explaining each impersonation that was to follow. This is a little girl…(poot). This is a bride on her wedding night (another poot). The morning after (loud rasping noise). A dressmaker tearing calico (ten seconds of ripping cloth). And this a cannon (loud thunder). The audience were at first astounded. Then there would be an uncontrollable laugh, followed by more until the whole audience was wriggling in their seats, convulsed. Women, bound rigid in corsets, were escorted from the hall by nurses, cleverly placed by the manager so that they could be seen in their bright white uniforms.

# A Mozart Fart

The Urban Dictionary describes a "Mozart fart" thusly: "To cut the cheese in a particularly tuneful way." It turns out that Wolfgang Amadeus Mozart (1756–91) would have been very proud of that "honor." Why? Because the famous Austrian composer appreciated farts so much that he wrote poems about the best ones he encountered. He (de)composed this masterpiece in a letter to his mother: "Yesterday, though, we heard the king of farts / It smelled as sweet as honey tarts / While it wasn't in the strongest of voice / It still came on as a powerful noise."

---

**A PAUSE FOR POETRY**

*A profound poem by Sir John Suckling, 17th-century cavalier poet.*

> Love is the fart
>
> Of every heart.
>
> For when held in,
>
> Doth pain the host,
>
> But when released,
>
> Pains others most.

# Magnum P.U.

*Hey, privy diggers, it's time for another "Outhouse Detectives" mystery! (See page 82.)*

**DISCOVERY:** A "multitude" of Lydia Pinkham brand patent-medicine bottles, plus an entire set of gold-trimmed china dishes

**MYSTERY:** These items were recovered from an outhouse behind the 19th-century home of a wealthy Michigan family that was excavated by John Ozoga in the 1990s. The bottles were clustered in a single layer, and the china dishes were found right on top of them. Why?

**THEORY:** The wife had fallen ill at a young age and died. Ozoga speculates that she was treated with the patent medicine. After she died, her family threw all of her belongings down the outhouse hole— including the entire set of china—to avoid catching whatever it was that killed her.

"One-quarter of what you eat keeps you alive. The other three-quarters keeps your doctor alive."
   **—Hieroglyph found in an ancient Egyptian tomb**

# A Brief History of the Mullet

*Hair cut short in the front and left long in the back didn't start in the United States in the 1980s, or even with the 1994 Beastie Boys hip-hop hit "Mullet Head."*

• Historians say the mullet goes all the way back to Neanderthal times. Cave-dwelling humanoids probably just wanted to cut some hair out of their eyes.

• Ancient Egyptians, however, turned the mullet into a fashion statement. Egyptian mullets were wigs made of black wool or flax. Women—as well as men—wore them.

• With the rise of the Roman Empire, mullets went out of favor. Long hair was considered "barbaric," and the mullet was banned in the Roman military. Why? Because long locks in the back made it easy for an enemy to grab a soldier's hair, pull back his head, and cut his throat.

# Words of the Gods

**CEREAL:** Named after Ceres, the Roman goddess of grain and agriculture.

**ATLAS:** One of the Greek Titans banished by Zeus when they sided with his son against him. Atlas was condemned to carry the world on his shoulders. That scene was popular with early mapmakers, who regularly put it on the covers of their books of maps. The books themselves eventually became known as atlases.

**PANIC:** Named after the Greek god Pan, who was believed to howl and shriek in the middle of the night. Greeks who heard these noises often panicked.

**HYGIENE:** Inspired by Hygeia, the Greek goddess of good health.

**PANACEA:** The Roman goddess who cures diseases.

**TANTALIZE:** Tantalus was a Greek king who was punished by the other gods for trying to deceive them. He was forced to stand in a pool of water up to his chin, but when he lowered his head to drink, the water receded just out of reach. The same was true with food: Whenever he reached to pick a piece of fruit from a tree, the wind blew it just out of his reach. The tantalizing food filled him with desire... but was unobtainable.

# Breaking and Entering

*Why does Santa Claus break into your house via the chimney?*
*It's an odd tradition that goes back nearly two millennia.*

In his day, St. Nicholas was known as Nikolaos of Myra.
He was born in Patara, Lycia (now a part of Turkey) around
A.D. 270 when the area was ruled by the Greeks. According
to legend, Nicholas inherited a large fortune from his father
and decided to give it away to the poor children.

One night, Nicholas encountered a nobleman and three
daughters, who had all fallen on hard times. Because their
father couldn't provide dowries, the girls had no shot at
marriage. One night Nicholas intervened and tossed a sack
of gold coins through their window for the first daughter.
He returned the following night and tossed in another sack
for the second daughter. On the third night, the window
was closed. Undaunted, Nicholas climbed onto the roof and
dropped more gold down the chimney. The next morning,
the daughters found the coins in the stockings they had
hung to dry over the fireplace. (Sound familiar?)

# The Famous Bigfoot Film

In 1967 a Sasquatch enthusiast named Roger Patterson was searching for Bigfoot in Bluff Creek Valley in Northern California when he filmed a remarkable encounter: The grainy footage appears to be a female Bigfoot walking in the distance. Suddenly the creature turns toward the camera, then turns away, and strides into the forest. In his book *Bigfoot: The Yeti and Sasquatch in Myth and Reality*, anthropologist John Napier describes its appearance:

> The creature was heavily built, particularly around the chest and shoulders; the trunk was chunky with hardly a change in width from shoulders to hips. The body was covered in short, dark reddish-brown hair. The top of the head was somewhat conical and flowed into the trunk without the interruption of a neck. The face was bare and, as far as could be seen, dark in color.

"The Film," as serious enthusiasts call it, became the backbone of the Bigfoot movement, which true believers claim is a real piece of physical evidence. (Deniers maintain that the film was faked.)

# BOTCHED HISTORY

"Paul Revere warned the British that they weren't going to be taking away our arms, by ringing those bells and making sure as he was riding his horse through town to send those warning shots that we were going to be free."

—Former Alaska governor Sarah Palin, while touring Boston. (Revere didn't ring bells or fire shots, and he was warning American rebels, not the Brits.)

# DIVINE INTERVENTION?

On March 1, 1950, choir practice was due to begin at the Westside Baptist Church in Beatrice, Nebraska, at 7:20 p.m. It didn't. Why not? Not a single choir member had shown up. One person was late because she needed to iron her daughter's dress. Two wanted to hear the end of an exciting radio program. One mom couldn't wake her daughter from a nap. Fifteen people were supposed to be there, but they had ten different excuses for why they were late.

And then, at 7:27 p.m.—seven minutes after choir practice should have begun—an explosion blew apart the church, completely destroying the building. Fire inspectors attributed the blast to a natural gas leak. Was it just a coincidence that no one was in the building? Rowena Vandegrift, one of the tardy choir members, thinks there was something more at work that night: "It was an absolute miracle."

> "I do not know whether there are gods, but there ought to be."
> —Diogenes

# What a Dummy

In 1912 an Austrian tailor named Franz Reichelt invented an overcoat that was supposed to double as a parachute. He needed to give it a field test, so he asked for permission to try it from the first deck of the Eiffel Tower, almost 200 feet off the ground. Authorities gave Reichelt the go-ahead...as long as he used a dummy.

When Reichelt arrived, he proudly announced to the gathered crowd that *he* would be the dummy. Onlookers tried to dissuade the "Flying Tailor" (as he called himself), but Reichelt was adamant. He carried his bulky contraption up to a platform nearly 200 feet above the ground, stepped up onto a chair next to the railing, peered out over the edge, and stood there. He looked down again, and stood there some more. And then some more.

Finally, Reichelt took a deep breath (his last) and stepped off. His parachute did not open, and he slammed face-first into the ground at 130 feet per second. He left a crater nearly six inches deep.

# Museum of Horrors

There's a museum in Philadelphia that is not for the faint of heart, but it's worth a visit if you think you have the stomach. And if you don't, don't worry—they've got plenty of stomachs in the collection.

Founded in 1856 by a Philadelphia surgeon named Thomas Dent Mütter, the Mütter Museum was a place to display his bizarre medical collection—more than 1,700 items—including deformed skulls, tumors, hernias, blood clots, appendages, bony growths, and more gross stuff.

Doctors throughout the United States sent more oddities: giant hairballs swallowed by mental patients, shrunken heads collected from natives in Peru, brains of several prominent surgeons and at least one executed murderer, deformed fetuses floating in formaldehyde-filled jars—as well as syphilitic skulls, gangrenous lungs, cirrhotic livers, and other diseased organs, appendages, growths, limbs, and a plaster cast of Chang and Eng, the original "Siamese" twins.

And guess what? The museum is still open today! (One of the weirdest items they have on display is featured on the next page.)

# Glover Cleveland's Secret Tumor

Early in his second term as president (1893–97), Grover Cleveland was given a grim diagnosis from his doctor: cancer of the mouth. At the time, the country was mired in one of the worst economic depressions in American history, and Cleveland feared the situation would get even worse if the public learned of his life-threatening illness. So on July 1, 1893, he slipped aboard a friend's yacht and surgeons cut out a large part of his upper jaw as the boat steamed up New York's East River.

The secret surgery was a success—Cleveland was fitted with a rubber partial jaw that gave him a normal appearance and did not impair his speech, and he was able to serve out the remainder of his term without the public realizing what had happened. The full story did not emerge until 1917, when one of the attending surgeons, Dr. William W. Keen, donated the tumor and some of the surgical equipment used in the procedure to the Mütter Museum in Philadelphia.

> "Sensible and responsible women do not want to vote."
> —**President Grover Cleveland**

# The Head-Shaped Pumpkin Mold

"Considerable skill is required to produce a good likeness."
Of what? The human head. Evidently, John Czeszcziczki
was not a skilled carver of jack-o'-lanterns, so in 1937
the Ohio inventor patented "Forming Configurations on
Natural Growths." It was a head-shaped mold that you
were supposed to place around immature pumpkins; as
they grew and ripened, they would take the shape of the
mold. Result: precarved jack-o'-lanterns! As clever as it was,
Czeszcziczki's idea failed to catch on.

## 6 Baseball Players with Weird Nicknames

1. Putsy Caballero
2. Togie Pittinger
3. Bots Nekola
4. Pid Purdy
5. Twink Twining
6. Waddy MacPhee

# Terrance & the Mayans

The ancient Mayans, a civilization in Mexico and Central America that reached its zenith from A.D. 250 to 900, created a "long count" calendar that divides enormous lengths of time into "eras," each roughly 5,125 years. The era we just finished began on the Mayan creation day, a date astronomers and other scientists have translated to our calendar as August 11, 3114 B.C.; the era ended on December 21, 2012. But despite all of the doomsayer prophecies, the world didn't end.

So why all the hype? Blame Terrance McKenna. In the mid-1970s, the California writer used a complex system of mathematics, Chinese philosophy, and psychedelic drugs to develop his "Timewave Zero" system, which he claimed could predict when significant events will occur around the world. He claimed that his analysis pointed to a profound "cosmic awakening" in 2012...on the exact same date the Mayan calendar ended. "You may not believe that I didn't know about the Mayan date when I made this prediction," he said, "but I didn't."

# Your Guess Is as Good as Mayan

*As you read on the previous page, Terrance McKenna's prediction of a "cosmic awakening" on December 21, 2012, never came true. Nor did these other prophecies.*

• In the 1980s, José Argüelles, in his book *The Mayan Factor*, described a 25-year "harmonic convergence" leading up to December 21, 2012, at which time "humanity will experience an evolutionary upgrade from human to super-human," marking the end of a Mayan World Age and the beginning of a New Age. People will become more intui-tive—and even telepathic. However, only the enlightened ones will be able to adapt. Everyone else, Argüelles said, will be taken away on "silver ships."

• In 1995 a Wisconsin woman named Nancy Lieder—who claimed to communicate with ancient aliens from a world called Zeta Reticuli—said that an enormous "Planet X" was going to enter Earth's "orbital zone" and knock the planet off its axis, causing an apocalypse. When? May 27, 2003. When that didn't happen, she changed the date to December 21, 2012. It didn't happen then, either.

• Richard C. Hoagland, known mostly for talking about con-spiracies and UFOs on late-night radio, claimed that Earth's "torsion fields" were out of balance. And if we couldn't fix them, life as we know it would end on December 21, 2012.

He claimed the Mayan long count calendar also contained instructions on how to survive the coming disaster, and that the government had been misleading the public about it since the 1940s. According to Hoagland, several so-called natural events—the 2004 tsunami in Indonesia, Hurricane Katrina in 2005, and the 2010 earthquakes in Haiti and Chile—were actually botched attempts to fix the torsion fields.

• Authors Patrick Geryl and Robert Bast claimed that both the Mayans and the ancient Egyptians actually came from the lost continent of Atlantis. After a catastrophe sank the mythical country, the survivors spread out across the planet to preserve their knowledge for future generations, including how to survive the 2012 disaster. Unfortunately, that particular bit of information is written in an unknown language, and as of yet, it hasn't been deciphered.

In the Mayan civilization, cacao beans were used as currency. Painted-clay counterfeit beans were common.

## FIVE FREAKY FACTS ABOUT...
# MEDICINE

- In the Middle Ages, Europeans attempted to cure muscle pain by drinking powdered gold.

- Sixteenth-century French doctors prescribed chocolate as a treatment for venereal disease.

- Crocodile-dung suppositories were used as contraceptives in ancient Egypt.

- Between 1873 and 1880, some U.S. doctors gave patients transfusions of milk instead of blood.

- The Greek physician Hippocrates, the "father of medicine," tried to cure baldness with pigeon poop.

# THE GREAT PIG WAR

San Juan Island in Puget Sound separates Washington State and Canada. In 1859 it was inhabited by both the British and the Americans. Due to some vague wording, the Oregon Treaty did not specify who owned the island, so both sides claimed San Juan as their own. One morning, an American farmer named Lyman Cutlar caught his British neighbor's pig eating his potatoes, so he shot it. That would be the only fatality in a tense standoff that nearly brought the United States and England into a full-scale war.

Unhappy with the upstart Americans living on "his" island, a British governor named James Douglas ordered Cutlar to pay $100 for the pig. He refused, and the big guns were called in: U.S. Army General William S. Harney, a known hothead, sent Captain George Pickett, another hothead who earlier had been cited for "reckless bravery" in the Mexican War, to San Juan Island.

The British sent five warships and 2,000 soldiers. Undeterred, Harney ordered Pickett to stop the British from landing, and if they tried, to open fire. Pickett pledged that if he had to, he would "make a Bunker Hill out of it" and fight to the last man. Governor Douglas ordered his navy

to take San Juan by force, but British Rear Admiral Robert L. Baynes, who commanded the fleet, was the only one of the bunch with a knack for diplomacy. "I refuse to involve two great nations in a war over a squabble about a pig!" So Baynes kept his men on the ships, their guns pointed at the American fort. Both sides were ready to fight, but neither wanted to fire the first shot. So there they stayed, facing each other's guns, waiting.

Thirteen years passed before the matter was finally settled. Kaiser Wilhelm I of Germany arbitrated the matter...and gave San Juan Island to the United States. As for the wayward pig that started the whole fiasco...it's assumed he ended up on Cutlar's kitchen table.

### MY UNFAIR LADY

From the 1300s to the 1600s, the heads of England's slain enemies—including William Wallace and Thomas More—were displayed on London Bridge.

# The Black Rock That Changed History

In 1799 soldiers in Napoleon Bonaparte's army in Egypt were digging a trench near the town of Rosetta when they uncovered a smooth, black lump of basalt with inscriptions carved into it. Scholars knew immediately that it was a significant find. The inscriptions were in three different languages—Greek, hieroglyphics, and demotic script (a writing system derived from hieroglyphics).

In 1802 the Greek was translated as a decree by priests praising the pharaoh Ptolemy V, who reigned from 205 to 180 B.C., but the other markings were a mystery. Hieroglyphics hadn't been used since the fourth century A.D., and no one knew how to read them until they were deciphered by French linguist Jean-François Champollion. Working independently, Thomas Young, an English physicist, determined that the names of pharaohs were circled, and he was able to translate the name "Ptolemy" phonetically. Later, Champollion determined that some signs were alphabetic, some phonetic, and some symbols were translated as whole ideas. The rock was named the Rosetta Stone, and without it, much of what we now know about ancient Egypt's history and culture would have remained unknown.

# The World's Worst Novelist?

In 1895 an Irish schoolteacher named Amanda McKittrick Ros wrote the novel *Irene Iddesleigh*. Two years later, her husband paid to have it published as a gift for their 10th wedding anniversary. Literary critics were not kind, noting that her prose is wordy and alliterative ("frivolous, frittery fraternity of fragiles flitting round and about" reads one passage), her grammar is quirky, and she embellishes insignificant details for no particular purpose. Mark Twain called the book one of the "great works of Hogwash Literature."

But the terrible reviews only made Ros more popular... and she kept on writing. Here are some choice excerpts:

> "Her superbly-formed eyes of greyblue, with lightly-arched eyebrows and long lashes of that brownish tint, which only the lightly-tinted skin of an Arctic seal exhibits, looked divine."
>
> —*DELINA DELANEY*

> "Leave me now deceptive demon of deluded mockery: lurk no more around the vale of vanity, like a vindictive viper: strike the lyre of living deception to the strains of dull deadness, despair and doubt..."
>
> —*IRENE IDDESLEIGH*

"Have you ever visited that portion of Erin's plot that offers its sympathetic soil for the minute survey and scrutinous examination of those in political power, whose decision has wisely been the means before now of converting the stern and prejudiced, and reaching the hand of slight aid to share its strength in augmenting its agricultural richness?"

—OPENING LINES OF *DELINA DELANEY*

"They reached Canada after a very pleasant trip across the useful pond that stimulates the backbone of commerce more than any other known element since Noah, captain of the flood, kicked the bucket."

—*HELEN HUDDLESON*

## THE WORLD'S MOST STOLEN PAINTING

The Ghent Altarpiece is a Dutch panel painting known as *Het Lam Gods* ("The Lamb of God") that was completed in 1432. It weighs two tons, measures 14 feet by 11 feet, and has been stolen 13 times, the most of any famous piece of artwork.

# When the Cat's Away... Millions Die

When the Black Plague devastated Europe in the 14th century, many people assumed it was caused by witchcraft. And cats, with their glowing eyes and night-prowling habits, were thought to be tools of witches. Result: Thousands of cats (and several women thought to be witches) were slaughtered.

Irony alert: Scientists later determined that the plague was transmitted by fleas that lived on rats. Had all those cats not been slaughtered, they might have been alive to kill all those rats, which could have vastly reduced the death toll of approximately 30 million people.

# KINGS WHO ATE THEMSELVES TO DEATH

- **KING HENRY I OF ENGLAND** was a man of indulgence. Crowned in 1100, he was popular with the people, especially the ladies, fathering at least 20 illegitimate children through his many mistresses. He found food hard to resist, too. Even though his doctors warned him not to consume one of his favorite foods, sea lampreys, which can be toxic if they're not cleaned properly, the king wolfed down a large meal of the fatty fish one evening in 1135. Result: He got food poisoning and died.

- **KING ADOLF FREDERICK**, who ruled over Sweden in the 18th century, is known today as "the king who ate himself to death." On February 12, 1771, Frederick devoured a feast fit for a dozen kings: multiple helpings of lobster, caviar, sauerkraut, cabbage soup, smoked herring, and champagne. Frederick may have survived dinner, but his intestines couldn't take what he ate for dessert: 14 servings of *semla*, a bun filled with hot milk and marzipan, a rich mixture of sugar and ground almonds. He died a painful death.

# A Strange Musical

*1776:* You recognize the year—but how about the Broadway musical? Debuting in 1969, *1776* was a musical comedy about the Second Continental Congress and the writing of the Declaration of Independence.

That improbable combination somehow worked: *1776* ran for three years (1,217 performances) and won three Tony Awards (Best Musical, Best Featured Actor in a Musical for Ronald Holgate, and Best Director).

Highlight: Thomas Jefferson, Benjamin Franklin, and two cohorts perform a high-stepping song and dance called "But Mr. Adams" in which they each try to get out of writing the Declaration of Independence. Sample lyric:

> *"I cannot write with any style or proper etiquette/*
> *I don't know a participle from a predicate/*
> *I am just a simple cobbler from Connecticut."*

"Anything too stupid to be said is sung."
—**Voltaire**

# Socrates' Swan Song

Socrates was arguably the most celebrated philosopher who ever lived. And we have Plato to thank for that. In his work *Phaedo*, Plato transcripted conversations between Socrates and his students (including Plato himself) during Socrates' final days—just before he was executed in 399 B.C. for "corrupting Greek youth."

*Phaedo* also introduced a popular phrase that's still in use today. In one section, Socrates declares that he has to come to terms with his impending death and is at peace with it to such a degree that he can actually enjoy his final days. He tells his friends that he has "as much of the spirit of prophecy as do the swans. For they, when they perceive that they must die, having sung all their life long, do then sing more, and more sweetly, than ever, rejoicing in the thought that they are about to go away."

Socrates was so revered that after he died, the quote was frequently repeated in documents by philosophers and writers such as Aeschylus, Aristotle, Cicero, Chaucer, and Shakespeare. That's why we still say "swan song" today. It basically means "a triumphant final performance before death or retirement."

Only problem: Swans don't sing—they honk.

# VELCOME TO DRACULALAND!

In 2001 the Romanian Ministry of Tourism proposed opening a theme park based upon Romania's most famous historical figure: Vlad the Impaler, the murderous lord who served as the inspiration for Count Dracula. At a cost of $35 million, the park would have been built in the Transylvanian village of Sighisoara, where Vlad was born in 1431. The ministry drew up plans for attractions, including underground tunnels, castles, man-made caves full of live bats, a replica medieval town, an "International Dracula Center," a golf course, and—for the kids—a demonstration of how Vlad cut people's heads off.

Despite the allure of 3,000 new jobs, the Sighisoara citizens fought the construction of the park. Led by a local minister, the townspeople claimed that glamorizing Vlad, who is believed to have killed more than 80,000 people, was "an attack on Christian values." Not only that, but the environmental impact on the proposed site would have been significant. In 2002 the Dracula theme park idea was laid to rest.

# Snake Attack!

• In the fifth century B.C., Scythian archers (in what is now the Crimea near the Black Sea) had pinpoint accuracy and could shoot more than 20 arrows per minute. Making them even more lethal: The arrow tips were dipped in viper venom mixed with blood and animal dung. The venom contained toxins that destroy red blood cells and cause excruciating pain; a wounded soldier would suffer greatly until dying of heart failure or respiratory paralysis. If the venom didn't work, the infection caused by the blood/feces combination would do the job.

• Hannibal—best known for leading an army of elephants over the Alps to attack Rome—also dabbled in venomous vipers. In 190 B.C., when his navy fought against King Eumenes of Pergamon (Turkey), Hannibal stocked his ships with clay pots filled with venomous snakes. When the ships came within range of Eumenes's navy, Hannibal's men hurled the pots at their enemies. The pots smashed on the decks, and the snakes slithered out, throwing Eumenes's sailors into a panic. Hannibal won the battle.

# REAL-LIFE FRANKENSTEINS: ROBERT E. CORNISH

In 1932 this scientific wunderkind (he graduated from the University of California at age 18 and earned his Ph.D. by 22) became obsessed with the idea that he could bring the dead back to life, not by electricity but through the use of a teeter-totter, or seesaw.

Inspired by the work of George Washington Crile on blood transfusion, Cornish believed that placing a recently deceased person on a seesaw and moving the body up and down rapidly, combined with an injection of epinephrine and oxygen, would get the blood circulating again. He spent more than a year attempting to revive victims of heart attack, drowning, and other sudden deaths with his seesaw therapy. His success rate: zero. Then, in 1934, Cornish was able to resurrect two dogs, Lazarus IV and V, for a short time (no word on the fates of Lazauruses I through III). He later played himself in the 1935 movie *Life Returns*, about a doctor who attempts to revive the dead.

# Two Strange Coincidences

**THE KING AND I:** On July 28, 1900, King Umberto I of Italy and his wife, Margherita, visited a restaurant and found that the owner, also named Umberto, bore a striking resemblance to the king. It gets even weirder: The two men were both born on March 14, 1844. The restaurant owner's wife's name was also Margherita, and the restaurant's opening and the king's inauguration had both occurred on the same day. The day after that strange dinner, the restaurant owner was shot dead. So was Umberto I.

**THE LONG WAY HOME:** Charles Coghlan was born on Prince Edward Island, Canada, in 1841. He became a successful stage actor and toured the world, but he always considered Prince Edward Island his home. In 1899, during an appearance on Galveston Island, Texas, he fell ill and died, and was buried in a Galveston cemetery. On September 8, 1900, a hurricane struck Galveston, washing away most of the town and swamping all the cemeteries.

Seven years later, a fisherman from Prince Edward Island noticed a large box in the water. He towed it to shore, chipped off the barnacles, and discovered the coffin of Charles Coghlan, beloved native son. It had floated into the Gulf of Mexico, been caught by the West Indian current, carried into the Gulf Stream, and deposited on the shore only a few miles from his birthplace.

# Toba Party

The Toba volcano in Sumatra, Indonesia, erupted in massive fashion about 75,000 years ago. Volcanists estimate that it ejected an incredible 670 cubic miles of lava, rock, and ash into the atmosphere. By comparison, the Mount St. Helens eruption that killed 57 people in 1980 released just 0.25 cubic miles of volcanic material.

The Toba eruption sent volcanic ash several miles into the atmosphere. But the real damage was caused by an avalanche of lava and rock that traveled hundreds of miles an hour and covered 7,700 square miles—an area about the size of New Jersey. In some places the molten rock and ash was 2,000 feet thick. The ash contained sharp particles of pulverized lava, rock, and volcanic glass shards that killed most—if not all—of the plants and animals in its path. Land more than 1,000 miles away was buried in ash, including India and much of Southeast Asia.

But the most widespread effect of Toba's eruption was the global climate. Nobody knows exactly how severe Toba's volcanic winter was, but geological records show that temperatures suddenly dropped in some areas by at least 18°F—and it's possible that the volcanic winter lasted as long as 10 years. The climate change killed off 80 to 90 percent of the humans on the planet, leaving only a few thousand in Africa who survived to become our ancestors.

# Go as the Romans Go

- For ancient Romans, going to the bathroom was a social occasion, and they brought their customs to the far corners of their empire. In North Africa, for example, a large privy dating from the Roman era had 25 seats arranged around three sides of a room. There was no privacy: only a carved dolphin separated each seat.

- Public urinals were a source of income for Emperor Vespasian, who had the urine collected; the ammonia in it was used to make fabric dyes.

- Romans developed the art of plumbing and built their sewer system to last. The Cloaca Maxima ("big sewer"), which connected the Forum to the Tiber River, is still in use today, 2,500 years later.

- After using the public latrines, a citizen of Rome looked for the bucket, which held salt water and a long stick with a sponge attached to one end. The user wiped his posterior with the sponge and then returned it to the water bucket for the next patron to use. Careless use of this device has been said to be the origin of the expression "getting the wrong end of the stick."

# Dino-Bird

In 1999 *National Geographic* made a shocking announcement: A Chinese farmer had discovered the missing link between dinosaurs and birds. Paleontologists had long suspected that dinosaurs evolved into birds, and this fossil—supposedly found in the Liaoning Province—revealed a new species named *Archaeoraptor*, which the press called "the turkey with teeth." It was a feathered theropod (a two-legged, meat-eating dinosaur) that could fly. "This is the true missing link in the complex chain that connects dinosaurs to birds," wrote *National Geographic*.

A few months later, the truth came out: The artifact was a fake, made solely so it could be sold on China's black market (it fetched $80,000 in the U.S.). The fraudsters attached the tail of a small dinosaur to the skeleton of an ancient bird, and then filled it in with bones from other species.

Although the actual artifacts were nearly destroyed by the ruse, both the dinosaur, now called *Microraptor*, and the bird, *Yanornis*, had been previously unknown. So in the end, it was a significant discovery of two species…just not the dinosaur-bird as they had initially believed. Storrs L. Olson, the eminent curator of birds at the Smithsonian Institution, wrote that *National Geographic* "reached an all-time low for engaging in sensationalistic, unsubstantiated, tabloid journalism." P. T. Barnum would have been proud.

# Roll the Dice

Dice go back to before recorded history. The first ones were the anklebones of hoofed animals. These bones—later called *astragali* by the Greeks—were roughly cube-shaped, with two rounded sides that couldn't be landed on, and four flat ones that could. The first dice throwers weren't gamers, though—they were religious shamans who used astragali (as well as sticks, rocks, and animal entrails) for divination, the practice of telling the future by interpreting signs from the gods. How did these early dice make their way from the shaman to the layman? David Schwartz writes in *Roll the Bones: The History of Gambling*:

> The line between divination and gambling is blurred. One hunter, for example, might say to another, "If the bones land short side up, we will search for game to the south; if not, we look north," thus using the astragali to plumb the future. But after the hunt, the hunters might cast bones to determine who would go home with the most desirable cuts.

And with that, gambling—and dice gaming—was born.

# Dicey History

- Around 7,000 years ago, ancient Mesopotamians carved down the rounded sides of sheep anklebones to make them even more cubelike. Now they could land on one of six sides, allowing the outcome to become more complex.

- As technology advanced, materials such as ivory, wood, and whalebone were used to make dice. It's believed that the shamans were the first to put marks on the sides of the dice.

- Dice first appeared in board games in Ur, a city in southern Mesopotamia. Now referred to as the "Royal Game of Ur," this early version of backgammon (circa 3000 B.C.) used four-sided, pyramidal dice.

- The six-sided cubic *hexahedrons* with little dots, or *pips*, to denote their values—one opposite six, two opposite five, and four opposite three—first appeared in Mesopotamia circa 1300 B.C.

- When Julius Caesar led his army across the Rubicon River to attack Rome in 49 B.C.—which set in motion his rise to power—he knew that there was no turning back, proclaiming, *"Alea iacta est."* Translation: "The die is cast."

# The King's Edict: Eat It

For at least 4,000 years, potatoes have been cultivated in the Peruvian Andes. Called *papas* by the Incas, they were so integral to local culture that the Incas buried their dead with potatoes (for food in the afterlife) and measured time based on how long it took a potato to cook.

But the potato was not so revered in the Old World. It arrived in Europe in 1565 via English and Spanish explorers. They called it the "edible stone" because it was dirty and tasted horrible when eaten raw. As a result, spuds weren't popular, and most Europeans still hadn't heard of them by the 1600s. If farmers grew them at all, it was for pig feed.

That's why the Prussians refused to eat potatoes. But during a war against Austria in the 1740s, King Frederick the Great urged his subjects to grow potatoes for food. Why? Because the edible part— the tuber—grows underground and could survive if invading armies marched over or burned the fields. Even so, the Prussian people refused to eat what they considered animal fodder. So Frederick issued an edict that anyone who didn't eat potatoes would have their ears cut off.

Potatoes caught on quickly after that.

# Miracle Mike:
# the Headless Chicken

On September 10, 1945, a farmer in Fruita, Colorado, named Lloyd Olsen grabbed a rooster named Mike and put it on the chopping block. Remembering that his mother-in-law (who was coming to dinner) loved chicken necks, Lloyd took special care to position the ax so a generous portion of neck would remain. He gave the rooster one strong whack and cut off his head. But then the headless bird did something strange: He ran around in circles, flapping his wings. At this point, most chickens would have dropped dead. Instead, Mike raced back to the coop, where he joined the rest of the chickens as they pecked for food.

The odd bird actually lived without his head for 18 more months. Olsen used an eyedropper to drip food and water into Mike's gullet. (Scientists at the University of Utah determined that the ax had missed the jugular vein, and a clot had kept Mike from bleeding to death. Although his head was gone, his brain stem and one ear were left on his body. Since a chicken's reflex actions are controlled by the brain stem, Mike's body was able to keep on ticking.)

Seeing dollar signs, Olsen took his chicken on the road. Audiences all over the United States paid a quarter each to see "Miracle Mike" with their own eyes. *Time* and *Life*

magazines ran feature articles on the amazing fowl. Mike even made it into the *Guinness Book of World Records*.

Sadly, in March 1947, after living for 18 months without a head, Mike choked on some food at a motel in Arizona and died.

To honor his memory, every third weekend in May, the town of Fruita holds the Mike the Headless Chicken Festival. The two-day celebration features the 5K Run Like a Chicken race, egg tosses, Pin the Head on the Chicken, a Cluck Off, Rubber Chicken Juggling, and the Chicken Dance. Of course, great quantities of chicken—fried or barbecued—are enjoyed by all. (Heads not included.)

**BOTCHED HISTORY**

## History Teacher:

"Who was Joan of Arc?"

**Ted:** "Noah's wife?"

—*BILL AND TED'S EXCELLENT ADVENTURE*

# Hearing Voices: Joan of Arc

Born in France in 1412, Joan of Arc started hearing voices in her head when she was a little girl. When she was 16 years old, the voices told her to go to war against the ruling British. Joan appealed to the dauphin prince (the future French king Charles VII) for soldiers and equipment, claiming that God was talking to her. "I heard this Voice to my right," she later explained, "towards the Church; rarely do I hear it without its being accompanied also by a light."

Although Charles was concerned that Joan might be a witch, he didn't want to tempt fate, so he gave the teenager what she asked for. It turned out to be a good move.

Joan led her army offensively, attacking the British at unexpected places and times, a contrast to the typically cautious French army. She won several battles and rallied the French army.

But then tragedy struck: After ordering her outnumbered soldiers to attack a force from Burgundy that was sympathetic to the British, she was captured and sold to England...where she was sentenced to death. Right before Joan was burned at the stake for heresy, she blamed the voices in her head for misleading her. After her death, an English soldier was quoted as saying, "God forgive us, for we have burned a saint."

# The Wrath of Dalí

In 1939 the New York department store Bonwit Teller commissioned Spanish surrealist painter Salvador Dalí to create a window display. Dalí called it "Day and Night." On the "day" side was a female mannequin with red hair dressed in green feathers. Behind her was a clawfoot bathtub lined with Persian lambskin, and filled with water and floating narcissi. Three mannequin arms reached out of the bath water, each holding a mirror. On the "night" side, a male mannequin was lying on a bed of glowing coals under the body of a bizarre beast, which Dalí described as "the decapitated head and the savage hooves of a great somnambulist buffalo extenuated by a thousand years of sleep."

Stuffy New Yorkers complained that the display was "too extreme," so Bonwit Teller's staff took it upon themselves to alter the scene...without asking the artist. Bad idea: That afternoon, Dalí walked by the window and flew into a rage. He stormed into the store, screamed at the managers, and picked the bathtub and spilled the water all over the floor. Then he threw the tub through the plate-glass window. Dalí was thrown in jail, but he was released that evening by a judge who remarked, "These are some of the privileges that an artist with temperament seems to enjoy."

And Dalí's one-man show, which just happened to be opening that night, was a huge hit.

# It's a Trap!

It's generally agreed upon these days that Bigfoot is not a real animal (despite what you may see on sensationalized basic cable shows), but back in the 1970s, the search for Sasquatch was a serious undertaking for many scientists. In 1974, after hearing about a sighting near southern Oregon's Applegate River, a Bigfoot researcher named Ron Olson used grant money to build a trap on a wooded hillside above Grouse Creek.

It was supposed to work like this: The creature comes strolling through the forest minding his own business when he gets a whiff of a rabbit carcass hanging inside the 10-foot-tall metal cage. He ventures in, takes the bait, and then a massive steel door drops like a guillotine— locking the big guy in there until researchers come in and tag, photograph, and release him. However, in the six years that the Bigfoot Trap was in use (1974–80), it only caught (depending on which account you read) two bears, or a bear and a hunter, or a bear and a hippie.

The trap is still there today, but the steel door has been removed for safety. Now we'll never know if Bigfoot was there...unless he happened to leave some tracks.

# The Rodent Controller

The Old West was the heyday of the handgun. Revolvers had catchy nicknames such as the Civilian, the Sheriff's Model, and the Storekeeper. Less known: the Rodent Controller.

In 1882 an inventive gunsmith patented this spring-loaded contraption—it consisted of a wooden stand that held a trusty six-shooter at a downward angle, locked and loaded, pointed at a metal plate where the bait was placed. A metal arm ran from the front of the device to the trigger. Result: Any varmint that tried to make off with the vittles would trip the switch and meet its maker (and make a mess).

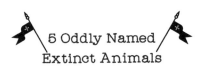

### 5 Oddly Named Extinct Animals

1. Gilbert's potoroo
2. Pig-footed bandicoot
3. Bubal hartebeest
4. Syrian onager
5. Slender-billed grackle

# Darwin in the Bathroom

In 1859 British naturalist Charles Darwin, after decades of research into evolution and natural selection, published his groundbreaking book *On the Origin of Species*. His publisher, John Murray III, cautiously printed only 1,250 copies. Although understandable considering that the cover price was 15 shillings (the equivalent of $83 in today's money), Murray's reticence was unwarranted: Buyers depleted the publisher's entire stock within a few days.

Fast-forward to 2009. A man, fresh from a commemorative exhibit of the book's 150th anniversary, stepped into his father-in-law's bathroom in Oxford, England, and perused a shelf stocked with bathroom reading. His heart nearly stopped when he saw a familiar cover and discovered that his wife's dad owned one of Darwin's first editions. He asked how his father-in-law had gotten it and why it was in the loo. The man shrugged, saying he bought it for a few shillings in a used bookstore back in the 1950s.

Christie's auction house said the book was worth "maybe as much as £60,000" (about $100,000). But even the experts at Christie's were stunned when the bathroom book brought in an astonishing $182,000.

**One more surprise:** The word "evolution" never appears in the first edition. Darwin didn't use the term until he revised the text for its sixth printing, in 1872.

# Eye Can See You

The star Sirius was worshipped by a whole range of ancient peoples. The Arabs and some tribes in Mali believed that Sirius had a companion called the Eye Star, which was supposed to have supernatural qualities. Sirius really does have a companion: a small white dwarf called Sirius B, which is not visible to the naked eye. So how did these primitive peoples know about it?

The Dogon people of Mali have precise astronomical information about its movements, which they celebrate with rituals, even though they admit that it's invisible. They even have a story about a third star, the Star of Women, which is also invisible.

In 1995 astronomers discovered this "invisible" third star, a red dwarf that's been named Sirius C. So how did ancient people know about stars that can only be seen by powerful modern telescopes?

Maybe it did have supernatural qualities.

# Calling All Occupants, Part II

After Alfred K. Bender (see page 163) left the International Flying Saucer Bureau, the movement might have faded into obscurity. Then in 1976, the Canadian "space rock" band Klaatu recorded "Calling Occupants of Interplanetary Craft (Recognized Anthem of World Contact Day)." An excerpt:

*In your mind you have abilities you know*
*To telepath messages through the vast unknown...*
*Calling occupants of interplanetary craft*
*Calling occupants of interplanetary, quite extraordinary craft!*

The song opened Klaatu's debut album, *3:47 EST* (the time of day in *The Day the Earth Stood Still* that Klaatu landed on Earth). It was a minor hit in Canada and the U.S., but not enough to convince the aliens to land.

The song did, however, reach the ears of one the most famous groups of the day, the Carpenters. In the summer of 1977, as another space movie, *Star Wars*, was breaking box-office records, the Carpenters' cover version of "Calling Occupants of Interplanetary Craft (Recognized Anthem of World Contact Day)" reached #32 on the pop chart. It even spawned a 1978 TV special: *The Carpenters...Space Encounters.* But still, the aliens didn't respond.

In March 2013, on the 60th anniversary of the first World Contact Day, the event was stretched out to an entire week. Again, the aliens failed to show up.

# First Jobs of World Leaders

- **ADOLF HITLER** sold paintings to Viennese tourists. (He copied the scenes from postcards.)

- **JOSEPH STALIN** led the Communist Party from the mid-1920s until 1953. Before that he was a seminary student.

- South Africa president **NELSON MANDELA** was once a night watchman at a gold mine.

- **TONY BLAIR** wanted to be a rock star like his idol Mick Jagger, so he worked as a music promoter and formed his own band, the Ugly Rumours. He became England's prime minister instead.

- **HARRY TRUMAN**, the only 20th-century president without a college degree, worked as a mail boy for the *Kansas City Star*, a timekeeper on the Santa Fe Railroad, and a sales clerk in his own men's clothing store.

- Mexican president **VICENTE FOX** (2000–6) started his career as a delivery driver for Coca-Cola.

- **HO CHI MINH**, president of Vietnam during the war against the U.S., had traveled to America as a young man. Living in Harlem and Boston, he worked as a baker at the Parker House Hotel. He later moved to London and Paris, and worked as a pastry chef and waiter before eventually returning to his home country to lead the nationalist movement.

# Horrible, Horrible History

*Some facts to put things into perspective the next time you're depressed about modern life...*

- In 1014 Byzantine emperor Basil II (nicknamed "Slayer of the Bulgars") captured 15,000 Bulgarian soldiers. He blinded 99 of every 100 prisoners and let the 100th keep one eye to lead the others home.

- King Goujian of China placed sacrificial soldiers on the front lines of his army. Their sole purpose: to slit their own throats at the start of battles to terrify enemy soldiers.

- After the Mongols killed their enemies, they'd boil the bodies to liquefy their fat, set the fat on fire, and catapult it into enemy territory along with severed heads and limbs.

- A medieval torture/execution device called the "breaking wheel" was well named. The condemned prisoner was tied to a large wheel, which turned slowly, breaking his or her bones one by one...in full view of the public.

- One out of every 25 coffins from the 16th century has been found to have scratch marks on the inside.

- In 1838 General Antonio López de Santa Anna, president of Mexico, was hit by cannon fire while fighting France in the Pastry War (yes, really). His leg was amputated, and he ordered a full military burial for it.

- The ancient Mayans turned the sap of several plants into rubber—which they made into balls for their ritualistic games. But when balls weren't available, or they wanted to prove a point, they played their games with severed human heads.

- Prisoners condemned to death in ancient Greece were placed in a "brazen bull." Made of bronze, this life-size bull was hollow. A fire was lit underneath it, and the prisoner was roasted alive. Special acoustics were built into the bull to amplify the screams so they would sound like a bellowing bull.

- During World War II, nine U.S. airmen were shot down over a Pacific island held by the Japanese. Eight were executed, some by swords. Then Japanese officers held a dinner party but ran out of meat. So they cooked and served the livers from the prisoners' bodies. The one soldier who escaped was future U.S. president George H. W. Bush.

> "Life itself is the most wonderful fairy tale!"
> **—Hans Christian Andersen**

# The "Okay" Corral

Whether you spell it "okay," "o.k.," or "OK," it is so universal that linguists say it's the most recognized word on the planet. (Second-most recognized: Coke.) But where the word actually came from is a bit of a mystery.

According to Columbia University linguistics professor Allen Walker Read, the word originated in Boston in the 1830s. Back then, comical abbreviations and silly misspellings were a fad among writers in New England. Boston newspapers typically featured satirical abbreviations like OFM ("our first men") to describe local hooligans, SP ("small potatoes") for matters of little importance, and NS (" 'nuff said"). Besides being funny, the abbreviations took up far less precious newspaper space than complete words. (Modern equivalent: texting the phrase "OMG.")

And then there was OW, which stood for "oll wright," a 19th-century equivalent to "all right." *Oll wright* didn't make it to the modern day. And neither did *OW*, because it was used interchangeably with another abbreviation—*OK*, which meant the same thing but was short for "oll korrect." The first known use of *OK* in print in this way dates to a March 1838 *Boston Morning Post* article by journalist Charles Gordon Greene (about a group called the Anti-Bell-Ringing Society).

And ever since then, life has been pretty okay.

# Greco-Roman Myth-conceptions

**MYTH:** Vomitoriums were places that Romans went to vomit.

**TRUTH:** No such specialized rooms existed. The Latin verb *vomitum* means "to spew forth," which is what ancient Romans did when they entered the Colosseum and other arenas through large arched passageways. It was the passageways that were called *vomitoria*.

**MYTH:** Greco-Roman architecture and statues were white.

**TRUTH:** They may look white now, but ancient traces of pigment have been detected on many of these structures, leading archaeologists to believe that buildings like the Parthenon were very colorfully and elaborately painted.

**MYTH:** Nero fiddled while Rome burned.

**TRUTH:** Nero was emperor during the fire that destroyed half of Rome in A.D. 64, but he never owned a fiddle (which wouldn't be invented for 1,000 years). He played the lyre. And he was 50 miles away when the fire began. It was the heavy taxes he imposed after the fire—while living in luxury—that did him in.

# When in Rome...
# Don't Go Swimming

These days, sportscasters might describe a particularly rough football game as a "bloodbath." Back in ancient Rome, that's a literal description of what went on in the Colosseum.

For special occasions at Rome's Colosseum, the heavy wooden planks that served as the floor of the arena were removed, and the stadium was flooded with water so that mock sea battles could be staged. The Colosseum's opening-day celebrations in A.D. 80 had just such a sea battle; it involved hundreds of boats, more than 3,000 participants, and was watched by an estimated 50,000 spectators.

It was just as bloody as the regular gladiator fights; the only difference was that the gladiators were in boats. The sea battle was followed by an animal hunt, in which more than 5,000 animals were killed.

**"Some people talk to animals.
Not many listen though.
That's the problem."
—A. A. Milne**

# FIVE FREAKY FACTS ABOUT...
# INVENTORS

- Leonardo da Vinci invented an alarm clock that woke him by rubbing his feet.

- Countess DuBarry, mistress of King Louis XV, invented the fish bowl.

- In 1935 inventor Israel Pilot coined the name "Wonder-Bra."

- According to the Bible, Noah invented wine and was the first meat eater. (He also had a son named Ham.)

- In the 1860s, Thomas Edison developed a device to electrocute cockroaches.

# Throwing Up Down Under

What do you call a boomerang that doesn't come back?
A stick. Or, in the case of the Australian weapon, a *kylie*.
Unlike boomerangs, kylies are not designed to return to the
thrower. Like boomerangs, kylies are curved, but the curve
is less pronounced. (They look sort of like a Nike swoosh.)
These lethal hunting sticks actually predate boomerangs;
Australian Aborigines used throwing sticks for hunting at
least as early as 15,000 years ago.

Originally made out of wood or bone, the kylie was
thrown parallel to the ground; it spun quickly as it traveled
toward its target. A skilled hunter could kill his prey from
a distance of 50 to 80 yards, but if he missed, it was a long
walk to pick it up; a well-thrown kylie could travel the length
of nearly two football fields.

Although the kylie was the Aborigines' main hunting
weapon, it's the boomerang that has become famous.
That's because for most of its existence, it was used primarily for competition. But it did have one use in hunting, and
it's quite ingenious: Aborigines placed large nets not far
off the ground and then waited for a flock of birds to fly
overhead. When they did, the hunter threw his boomerang
high in the air so that it swooped back toward the flock,
resembling a bird of prey. The birds would dive to avoid the
boomerang...and some would get caught in the nets.

# Tesla and the Runaway Twain

Born in 1856 during a lightning storm, Nikola Tesla was a strange man. According to Tesla biographer W. Bernard Carlson, the brilliant inventor once "shook the poop out of Mark Twain." The two men were friends, and one night Tesla invited Twain to check out his laboratory. At one point he told Twain to step up onto the high-frequency oscillator, also known as Tesla's "earthquake machine."

Unbeknownst to Tesla at the time, Twain had an upset stomach and wasn't feeling his best. But Twain was game, so he stepped up onto the platform and Tesla flipped the switch.

The famous author actually lasted about 90 seconds of severe shaking before jumping to the floor and running as fast as he could to the nearest bathroom.

First recorded mastectomy: performed in A.D. 548 on Theodora, Empress of Byzantium.

# Died on the John

• *The Wizard of Oz* actress **Judy Garland** had a fight with her fifth husband, Mickey Deans, in 1969. The next morning, she was found dead of a barbiturate overdose; according to one obituary, she was "perched like a little bird" on her toilet.

• In 1016, 27-year-old **King Edmund II of England** was murdered in the bathroom. An assassin hid behind the toilet and, as Edmund sat, the murderer stepped out and quickly shoved his sword twice "into the king's bowels."

• **Claude François** was a French singer/businessman who made a fortune translating English-language hits into French, including Beatles songs and early Michael Jackson. Ironically, one of his few original songs, "Comme d'Habitude" ("As Usual"), was rewritten into English by Paul Anka and recorded by Frank Sinatra as "My Way." One day in 1978, the 39-year-old was showering in his Paris apartment when he noticed an electric light had burned out above the shower. He probably should've turned off the shower and dried himself before trying to change the bulb.

• Perhaps the most famous death-by-toilet is **Elvis Presley's.** A combination of weight gain and too many prescription drugs gave the 42-year-old singer a heart attack while he was "takin' care of business." At the time, he was reading a book titled *The Scientific Search for the Face of Jesus.*

# The Lost Tomb of Queen Hetepheres

In 1925 a photographer traveling with an American Egyptologist was setting up his tripod in Giza, Egypt, near the Great Pyramid of Khufu when the legs of the tripod sank into a crevice. It turned out to be a hidden shaft to an underground staircase that led to another vertical shaft that had been filled with limestone to protect the tomb beneath it from grave robbers. It took archaeologists 10 years to excavate the shaft.

When they entered the tomb, they found it filled with gilded wooden furniture and 20 silver bracelets inlaid with turquoise, lapis lazuli, and carnelian—some of the finest examples of ancient Egyptian jewelry and furniture ever found. Inscriptions showed that the tomb was built for Queen Hetepheres, mother of the pharaoh Khufu, and although it was filled with treasure, the sarcophagus was empty, a mystery that archaeologists have so far not been able to explain. King Khufu's mommy's mummy was gone.

# I Challenge You to a Duel!

In 1859 Senator David Broderick of California, a power broker in the Democratic Party's antislavery faction, was challenged to a duel by political enemy and proslavery activist David Terry, California's chief justice.

The two men agreed to meet at dawn at Lake Merced, south of San Francisco. With a crowd gathered, the men faced each other. Broderick had the first shot, but when his gun misfired, Terry calmly put a bullet through Broderick's chest. That gives Broderick the unique distinction of being the only U.S. senator to be killed in a duel while in office. Terry was tried for murder and acquitted, and three years later he joined the Confederate army.

In 1889 the elderly Terry came to a fitting end. He was in a train station restaurant when he saw one of his rivals, Supreme Court Justice Stephen Fields. Terry walked up to Fields and slapped him. In response, the justice's bodyguard gunned Terry down...never to duel again.

Random Fact: License plates came before cars—they were used on horse-drawn carriages in 1884.

# The Ghost Bus of Ladbroke Grove

In London during the mid-1930s, motorists near the junction of St. Mark's Road and Cambridge Gardens in Kensington made some chilling reports to the police. Here's one of them:

> I was turning the corner and saw a bus tearing toward me. The lights of the top and bottom decks were full on but I could see no crew or passengers. I yanked my steering wheel hard and mounted the pavement, scraping the roadside wall. The bus just vanished.

The phantom vehicle was described as a red double-decker bus emblazoned with route number 7. The strange occurrences all took place at night, after regular bus service had ended for the day. When eyewitnesses blamed the phantom bus on a fatal crash in June 1934, the coroner expressed his skepticism, prompting hundreds of people to send him and the local newspapers their own accounts of what was by then known as the "Ghost Bus." When a transport worker claimed to see the bus pull up to a depot and then disappear into thin air, officials decided to take action. They ordered the blind corner at St. Mark's and Cambridge Gardens straightened to provide better visibility for drivers. The move had a dual effect: Accidents were greatly reduced, and the Ghost Bus of Ladbroke Grove was never seen again.

# Lost in Translation

In the winter of 1776, colonial commander George Washington led his troops to Trenton, New Jersey, to launch a surprise attack on the redcoats. A farmer spotted the army, and he rushed to warn the Brits, who were commanded by Hessian colonel Johann Rall. It was Christmas, though, and the colonel was too busy drinking wine and playing cards to talk to anyone. So the farmer left a note... in English. Unfortunately, the colonel spoke German and didn't bother to have the message translated.

Result: The colonists won that battle as well as the next one in Princeton, and historians say those were both crucial battles in the war. It gave the soon-to-be Americans the morale boost they needed to ultimately win the Revolutionary War.

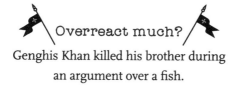

Overreact much?

Genghis Khan killed his brother during an argument over a fish.

# Lost and Found:
# The Dead Sea Scrolls

The western shore of the Dead Sea is desolate and remote, just the sort of area a goat smuggler needed to avoid customs officers. In 1947 a Bedouin boy herding contraband goats lost one and scrambled up a cliff to search for it. Instead, he discovered a long-lost cave. Hidden in the cave in ancient pottery jars were texts written on papyrus and animal hides that experts determined dated back to between 200 B.C. and A.D. 100. Eventually, over 800 scrolls were found in 11 caves in the area of Qumran, now part of Palestine's West Bank. They contained nearly all the books of the Bible, the only known surviving biblical documents written before A.D. 100. The find confirmed the accuracy of the transmission of the biblical texts over thousands of years. The caves had once been a base for Jewish resistance against the Romans, and the Dead Sea Scrolls, preserved by the extremely dry conditions, had remained hidden there for around 2,000 years.

> "Everything has a natural explanation. The moon is not a god, but a great rock, and the sun a hot rock."
> —**Anaxagoras, Greek philosopher (510–428 B.C.)**

# Two Ancient Riddles

- The Babylonians used riddles to teach students about the world. In fact, the oldest riddles we know of were preserved on an ancient Babylonian clay tablet that probably served as a schoolbook. Here's one:

> *Who becomes pregnant without conceiving?*
> *Who becomes fat without eating?*

Are you smarter than a Babylonian fifth-grader? If not, here's the answer: A rain cloud.

- Here's another riddle that was found inscripted on a stone slab about 3,500 years ago. The translation is a bit uncertain, but here is what linguists think that it was trying to say:

> *In your mouth and your urine, constantly stared at you,*
> *the measuring vessel of your lord.*
> *What is it?*

The answer is beer.

# Real-Life Frankensteins: Vladimir Demikhov

Russian physician Demikhov (1916–98) was a pioneer of organ transplant surgery. But he's notorious for his grotesque experiments with dogs. A surgeon in the Red Army in World War II, Demikhov honed his surgical technique while amputating the shattered limbs of wounded soldiers, skills he put to use later when he grafted the head of one dog onto the body of another.

Demikhov made 20 two-headed dogs, none of which survived more than a month after surgery. His work was reported by *National Geographic* and *Time* magazine in the 1950s as part of a bizarre Cold War race between the United States and the USSR to be the first to successfully transplant a human brain. So far, no one has been able to accomplish that feat.

Random Fact: Influenza means "influence" in Italian. The illness was so named because doctors in 1743 believed its spread was under the influence of certain "evil" stars and constellations.

# DON'T BLAME THE ICEBERG

There were several mitigating circumstances that led to the sinking of the *Titanic* after it sideswiped an iceberg in 1912. The going theory is that the rivets used to hold the hull together were made from cheap steel, so they weren't able to hold the ship together after the accident.

But were it not for one man's absentmindedness, the *Titanic* would have never hit that iceberg in the first place. Second Officer David Blair was transferred just before the doomed ship set off for New York on April 10, 1912. In his haste, Blair either forgot or neglected to turn over all of his equipment to his replacement. Two of the forgotten items: the crow's nest binoculars and the key to the crow's nest telephone.

According to crew survivor testimony, if the lookouts had been given the binoculars, they would have seen the iceberg sooner. And if they'd had access to the phone, they could have alerted the bridge sooner. Either one of those two scenarios might have given the *Titanic* enough time to get out of the way, thereby saving 1,522 lives.

# STICK + BALL = FUN!

- Hurling is an ancient Celtic game: Hit a small ball with a curved stick down a field and into a goal. According to Irish mythology, in 1272 B.C. the Battle of Moytura—between the native Fir Bolg peoples and the invading Tuatha De Danann—was fought not with weapons but with a hurling match. The Fir Bolg won a bloody and bone-breaking game...and then killed their opponents.

- Cambuca became popular in Britain starting around the 12th century, and is similar to modern golf. The object: Hit a wooden ball with a curved stick toward a mark in the ground. In 1363 King Edward III made cambuca illegal because men were playing the game instead of practicing their archery.

- Carved into a wall in the burial chamber of ancient Egypt's Prince Kheti, two men are facing each other, bent at the waist and poised over a ball, holding long sticks with curved ends. Put gloves, helmets, and skates on them and it looks just like a picture of a hockey face-off...from 4,000 years ago.

# An Army of Flying Saucers

Thomas Townsend Brown began studying the use of gravitational fields as a means of propulsion in the 1920s. He found that when he charged a capacitor to a high voltage, it moved toward its positive pole, creating an "ion wind." This effect, he claimed, proved a link between electrical charge and gravitational mass could be harnessed to create flight, seemingly free of both the strictures of mainstream physics and the need for gasoline.

In 1953 Brown demonstrated his "electrogravitic" propulsion for the U.S. Army at Pearl Harbor by flying a pair of metal disks around a 50-foot course. Energized by 150,000 volts, the disks, which were three feet in diameter, reached speeds of several hundred miles per hour. According to Brown, the military immediately classified the project and no more was heard about it. But throughout the 1950s, Brown's work was cited as a possible explanation for how UFOs might be able to fly.

# The Aliens Are Already Here!

*More close encounters of the credible kind.*

• *Apollo 14* **astronaut Captain Edgar Mitchell, USN:** "The evidence points to the fact that Roswell was a real incident and that indeed an alien craft did crash, and that material was recovered from that site. We all know that UFOs are real. All we need to ask is where do they come from, and what do they want?"

• **Air Chief Marshal Lord Dowding, commanding officer, RAF, in World War II:** "More than 10,000 sightings have been reported, the majority of which cannot be accounted for by any 'scientific' explanation...They have been tracked on radar screens and the observed speeds have been as great as 9,000 mph. I am convinced that these objects do exist and they are not manufactured by any nation on Earth. I can therefore see no alternative to accepting the theory that they come from an extraterrestrial source."

• **Dr. James McDonald, senior physicist, Institute for Atmospheric Physics, University of Arizona, testifying before Congress in 1968:** "My own present opinion, based on two years of careful study, is that UFOs are probably extraterrestrial devices engaged in something that might very tentatively be termed 'surveillance.'"

• **Colonel Philip Corso, head of foreign technology, U.S. Army Research and Development Department, 1961:** "Let there be no doubt. Alien technology harvested from the infamous saucer crash in Roswell, New Mexico, in July 1947 led directly to the development of the integrated circuit chip, laser and fiber-optic technologies, particle beams, electromagnetic propulsion systems, depleted uranium projectiles, stealth capabilities, and many others. How do I know? I was in charge! I think the kids on this planet are wise to the truth, and I think we ought to give it to them. I think they deserve it."

• **President Jimmy Carter, 1976:** "I don't laugh at people anymore when they say they've seen UFOs. I've seen one myself."

# War Is Hellebore

- When the Greeks besieged the town of Krissa in the sixth century B.C., they poisoned the local wells with the toxic hellebore plant, a flowering perennial. The enemy was knocked out with extreme stomach distress, diarrhea, and—in strong enough doses—death.

- Another case of mass poisoning took place in the first century B.C. The Heptakomotes (who lived in what is now Turkey) knew that rhododendrons were poisonous. They also knew that when bees made honey from rhodo-dendron nectar, the honey contained alkaloids that could severely sicken humans. So the Heptakomotes used the plant to defend themselves against Roman legions led by Pompey the Great. How? The Heptakomotes left batches of the toxic honey along the path of Pompey's advancing troops. The soldiers, who thought they'd found abandoned spoils of war, ate it all. The strong Roman soldiers—now suffering from delirium, vomiting, and diarrhea—were easily defeated by the weaker Heptakomotes.

# Sexist Ads from the *Mad Men* Era

"The Chef does everything but cook—that's what wives are for!"

—Kenwood Chef mixer

"Do you still beat your wife? Maybe you should never have stopped."

—Ad for the booklet
*Why You Should Beat Your Wife*

*A woman with an animal-rug body lies on the floor as a man steps on her head:* "After one look at his Mr. Leggs slacks, she was ready to have him walk all over her."

—Dacron Leggs

"Most men ask 'Is she pretty?' not 'Is she clever?'"

—Palmolive soap

*A man holds his wife over his lap, spanking her:* "If your husband finds out you're not 'store-testing' for fresher coffee..."

—Chase & Sanborn coffee

"Blow in her face and she'll follow you anywhere."

—TIPALET CIGARETTES

*A woman cries over the stove as her husband comforts her:* "Don't worry, darling, you didn't burn the beer!"

—SCHLITZ BEER

*A man reclines in bed as his kneeling wife serves him his meal:* "Show her it's a man's world."

—VAN HUESEN TIES

*A man on a mountaintop dangles a woman over the cliff by a rope:* "Indoors, women are useful—even pleasant. On a mountain they are something of a drag."

—DRUMMOND SWEATERS

*A female astronaut (wearing gobs of makeup) holds cleaning solution:* "Women of the future will make the Moon a cleaner place to live."

—TOMORROW'S LESTOIL

**BOTCHED HISTORY**

"Throughout our history, the words of the Declaration of Independence have inspired immigrants from around the world to set sail to our shores. These immigrants have helped transform 13 small colonies into a great and growing nation of more than 300 people."

—President George W. Bush

# A Biblical Tablet in New Mexico?

According to the Bible, Moses climbed Mt. Sinai in Egypt, where God gave him the Ten Commandments. But was Moses ever in New Mexico?

That's where, in the 1930s, a 90-ton rock carved with the Ten Commandments in ancient Hebrew was discovered near Los Lunas. The find baffled archaeologists and historians alike. The Hebrew inscription also contains Greek letters, which led some to conclude that ancient Samaritans wrote it. One problem: Samaritans lived on the other side of the planet; some characters on the rock had been used as far back as the seventh century B.C., long before explorers set foot in the New World.

It may seem like a hoax, but geologists have dated the rock and the carvings at 500 to 2,000 years old. That puts it in pre-Columbian times, when the only people known to live in that region were Native Americans...who had no way of knowing ancient Hebrew or Greek.

So who did carve the rock? And who put it there? It remains a mystery.

# The Fairy Tale That Fooled the World

Sir Arthur Conan Doyle created Sherlock Holmes, a master detective with an uncanny knack for uncovering the truth. Unfortunately for the British author, he wasn't quite so astute in real life.

In 1917 Doyle, an ardent believer in the occult, announced that, just as he'd always believed, sprites, gnomes, and other types of fairies really did exist. His proof: photographs of fairies taken by 16-year-old Elsie Wright and her 10-year-old cousin Frances Griffiths. In the photos, the little girls are posing next to a stream in the woods, and they're surrounded by flying fairies and dancing gnomes. Doyle assured a skeptical public that photography experts had deemed the pictures to be authentic; there was no retouching or superimposition or other trickery. The photos, backed by Doyle's testament to their authenticity, launched an international fairy craze.

More than 60 years later, in 1983, Wright and Griffiths, now elderly women, came clean. The cousins simply posed alongside paper cutouts of fairies and gnomes that were held up by hatpins. They said that they didn't confess back then because they didn't want to embarrass Doyle, who was so sure the pictures were authentic. "I never even thought of it as being a fraud," said Griffiths, "it was just Elsie and I having a bit of fun."

# Outdated Concepts: Diluvialism

Diluvialism was the belief that many geological features—such as fossils of sea creatures found on mountaintops and deposits of boulders, sand, and clay found in the valley floors of many parts of Europe—can be attributed to the great flood described in the Bible. Diluvialism was popular in the 18th and 19th centuries but was displaced by the theory of uniformitarianism, which held that rock formations could be explained by natural forces such as erosion and volcanic activity rather than supernatural forces like biblical floods. (Science may have discarded diluvialism, but some religious groups still accept it as true.)

> "Nuclear-powered vacuum cleaners will probably be a reality within ten years."
> —**Alex Lewyt, vacuum cleaner company executive, 1955**

# FIVE FREAKY FACTS ABOUT...
## DENTISTRY

- Dr. Alphonse Rockwell, a dentist, invented the electric chair.

- In medieval Japan, dentists extracted teeth with their hands.

- Peter the Great, tsar of Russia, practiced dentistry on some of his subjects.

- The ancient Greeks thought that telling lies caused toothaches.

- The world's first recorded tonsillectomy was performed in the year 1000 B.C. It was most likely very painful.

# ¡VOTO CACARECO!

Politicians need to be thick-skinned, right? That may explain why, in 1958, a rhinoceros was elected to serve on São Paulo, Brazil's, city council. With a population of three million, the city was suffering from unpaved streets, open sewers, food shortages, and rampant inflation, but officials had ignored these issues for years.

So when the city council elections were held, a group of fed-up college students decided to nominate Cacareco, a female rhino living at the São Paulo Zoo. (Part of the attraction might have been that her name means "garbage" in Portuguese.)

In all, 540 candidates—including many well-known incumbents—participated in the election, but voters were so eager to embarrass the failed city government that Cacareco won easily with a spectacular 100,000 votes. And even though she was disqualified from serving, the rhino's big win made news around the world. "Better a rhinoceros than an ass," a voter explained, and the quote made *Time* magazine.

Cacareco's election left a legacy: Today in Brazil, a protest vote is known as a *voto Cacareco*.

# The Warship That Got Too Big

In 1628 Sweden's King Gustav II ordered his Royal Navy to build him a warship that would strike fear into the hearts of their enemies. Called the *Vasa*, it was a 111-foot-long ship with one gun deck. But when Gustav found out that Denmark was building a ship with two gun decks, he had to have one, too. That, however, would require a 135-foot-long ship. There was no time to start over, so workers simply expanded the upper decks. Then the king decided he wanted more guns; the first version was designed to carry 32 cannons; by the end he had doubled that amount. Gustav wasn't done yet: He ordered his men to cover the ship with ornate oak carvings of biblical scenes.

On August 10, 1628, a huge crowd cheered as the *Vasa* left Stockholm Harbor on its maiden voyage. A few minutes later, a gust of wind capsized the top-heavy warship. It sank to the bottom of the harbor.

# Three Things Named for Caesar

*Some namesakes of the Roman general Julius Caesar (100–44 B.C.)—or GAIVS IVLIVS CÆSAR, as it was spelled in his day.*

**JULY**: Before Caesar, the Roman calendar year was too short and no longer synced with the seasons, so the Roman leader implemented the Julian calendar: For the first time, every year had 365 days (plus a leap day every four years). His birth month was renamed *Julius*, or July, after him.

**KAISER & CZAR**: Caesar's five successors were related to him and thus included "Caesar" as part of their names. The Caesars ruled Rome for the next 120 years. Over time, the term *caesar* came to mean "ruler." Pronounced in Latin with a hard "c," caesar spread to the Germanic languages—it was pronounced the same way but spelled kaiser. Caesar was also adopted into Russian, becoming the Old Slavic word *tsesari*, or *tsar*. It came to English as *czar*, meaning any person in power (like a drug czar).

# Three Things *Not Named* for Caesar

**CESAREAN SECTION:** Contrary to popular belief, the Roman general was not born via the procedure. We know this because Caesar's mother, Aurelia Cotta, survived to see her son rise to prominence. (Until the late 19th century, mothers did not live through the operation.) Roman philosopher Pliny the Elder (A.D. 23–79) claimed that the Caesar family name came from an ancestor of the general who was born by being "cut" from his mother's womb. The Latin word for "cut" is *caedere*; the past tense is *caesus*. So Caesar may have been named after the term that gave us *cesarean section*, not vice versa.

**CAESAR SALAD:** It was invented in the 1920s by Italian-born restaurateur Caesar Cardini in San Diego during a busy Fourth of July celebration when kitchen supplies were running low.

**ORANGE JULIUS:** Also from the 1920s, the Orange Julius is a sweetened, icy orange drink. It was first sold by Julius Freed. Customers would line up and shout, "Give me an orange, Julius!"

# BLAGIN'S BLAGINISM

In 1934 the Soviet Union scored a propaganda coup when it rolled out the *Maxim Gorky*, then the world's largest airplane. Larger than a Boeing 747, the *Maxim Gorky* had a movie theater, newspaper office, darkroom, laundry, pharmacy, and café. On some flights the *Maxim Gorky* was accompanied by a single-engine plane, so that onlookers could see just how big the *Maxim Gorky* really was. On May 18, 1935, Ivan Blagin was piloting the smaller craft. He was supposed to fly in tandem with the large plane…but he decided to perform aerobatic stunts to impress the crowd below. When Comrade Blagin tried to loop his plane around the *Maxim Gorky*, he miscalculated and slammed into one of its wings, causing both planes to break apart. Blagin died in the crash, as did all 43 people aboard the *Maxim Gorky*. Soviet officials were so furious with Blagin that they coined a new word—*blaginism*—which means "selfish exhibitionism and lack of proper Socialist discipline."

# How to Speak Hobo

Hobos were American migratory workers from a century ago. They were resourceful, self-reliant vagabonds who took on temporary work to earn a few dollars before moving on. Some experts think the word *hobo* comes from "hoe boys," what farmers in the 1880s called their seasonal migrant workers. It may also be shorthand for the phrase "homeward bound," used to describe destitute Civil War veterans who took years to work their way home.

If you ever hop on a rail car and find a hobo to converse with, here's a quick primer (so you don't sound like a yegg).

**Accommodation car:** The caboose of a train

**Banjo:** A portable frying pan

**Big house:** Prison

**Bindle stick:** A small bundle of belongings tied up in a scarf, handkerchief, or blanket hanging from a walking stick

**Bull:** A railroad cop (also called a "cinder dick")

**Cannonball:** A fast train

**Chuck a dummy:** Pretend to faint

**Cover with the moon:** Sleep out in the open

**Cow crate:** A railroad stock car

**Crums:** Lice (also called "gray backs" and "seam squirrels")

**Doggin' it:** Traveling by bus

**Easy mark:** A hobo sign, or "mark," that identifies a person or place where one can get food and a place to stay overnight

**Honey dipping:** Working with a shovel in a sewer

**Hot:** A hobo wanted by the law

**Knowledge box:** A schoolhouse, where hobos sometimes sleep

**Moniker:** Nickname

**Road kid:** A young hobo who apprentices himself to an older hobo in order to learn the ways of the road

**Rum dum:** A drunkard

**Snipes:** Other people's cigarette butts (O.P.C.B.); "snipe hunting" is to go looking for butts

**Spear biscuits:** To look for food in garbage cans

**Yegg:** The lowest form of hobo—he steals from other hobos

# Puppy Love

The maharajah of Junagadh, India—Muhammad Mahabat Khanji III Rasul Khanji—owned a lot of dogs. How many? Upwards of 300. He liked to dress them up in fancy clothes and then hire chauffeurs to give them rickshaw rides around town. Each dog even had its own private room in his lavish mansion, complete with a personal servant and a telephone (though it's unclear why a dog would need to have a phone).

In 1922 Khanji's most beloved canine, Roshanara, married a Golden Retriever named Bobby. The celebration lasted three days. Several other heads of state attended. Author Kathleen Walker-Meikle describes the nutty nuptials in *The Dog Book: Dogs of Historical Distinction*:

> Perfumed and in brocade and pearls, Roshanara was brought to the Dubar Hall in a palnquin while Bobby was greeted at the train station by a military band and the maharajah on an elephant with 250 brocade-dressed dogs (also on elephants). The breakfast was attended by 700 guests from Indian princely families, who were entertained by dancing girls singing for the dogs and Mendelsohn's "Wedding March." Alas, the wedding night was interrupted by the maharajah himself, who sent Bobby to the kennels so he could have his beloved Roshanara on his bed as usual.

# The Criminal Truth Extractor

What's the scariest thing in the world? According to this strange invention from the 1930s, a "skeleton ghost." Called the Criminal Truth Extractor, it was designed to coerce suspects into confessing.

Here's how it was supposed to work: The accused sat in a chair in a small room. An officer in another room asked questions while viewing the suspect through a small window. The wall that separated the rooms looked like a regular wall, but it was extra thin. If the suspect refused to talk, the interrogator would fire up the Truth Extractor. The lights went out and the wall lit up with the image of a ghostly skeleton with rapidly blinking eyes. The theory went that the criminal would get so scared that he would confess. How well did it work? Considering how little information there is about the Criminal Truth Extractor, not too well.

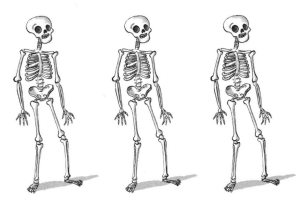

# Carters and Kelloggs and Shreks

- A "carter" was a delivery person who drove a cart from town to town.

- If you're a Cooper, one of your ancestors made wooden barrels. (From the old Dutch word *kupe*, meaning "tub.")

- The name Kellogg literally means a hog-killer, a nickname for pork butchers, derived from "kill hog." (Irony alert: The Kellogg brothers, who invented Corn Flakes, were vegetarians.)

- A "parker" was the groundskeeper of a park surrounding a nobleman's estate.

- A "kemp" was a wrestler—from *cempa*, the Old English word for "champion" or "warrior."

- In the Middle Ages, "leach" was a word for "doctor." It came from the Old English word *laece*, which meant "leech"—because medieval doctors used bloodsucking leeches on their patients.

- A "black" was a cloth dyer whose specialty was shades of black.

- A "chamberlain" was a personal servant who cleaned the chambers (rooms) of a nobleman's home.

- The name Shrek comes from the German word *schreck*, which means "fear" or "terror."

# Symbols of Love

**I ♥ YOU:** The Romans were the first to propose that the heart was a person's emotional center. The physical reactions we have when we fall in love—that heady rush, the flip-flop in the midsection, the increase in pulse—probably led to that belief. The ancients also thought that there was a vein that ran from the fourth finger of the left hand directly to the heart (there isn't), which is how the heart became a symbol of love. (It also explains why we wear wedding rings on the left ring finger.)

 **OSRAM NE NSOROMMA:** In Ghana and the Ivory Coast, this stenciled moon-and-star symbol represents love and faithfulness; the feminine North Star awaits the return of the masculine moon, her partner. The symbol traditionally decorated textiles that priests used in religious ceremonies. Today, the osram ne nsoromma most often appears on cloths used during wedding ceremonies.

**LOVE SPOONS:** Romantic Welshmen profess their love by offering hand-carved wooden spoons. The spoons originated in the 1500s among illiterate farmers who used the carvings—instead of words—to express their affection. They usually used sycamore for the spoons and then carved ornate, symbolic designs: Chained links symbolized loyalty and friendship, a diamond symbolized wealth, and an anchor meant that the carver had found a place where he wanted to settle with his beloved. Back then, the man gave a love spoon to the woman he wanted to marry. Today, the spoons have general appeal and can be gifts at weddings, birthdays, or between friends.

 **CLADDAGH**: This Irish symbol typically appears on a ring. The hands represent friendship; the crown, loyalty; and the heart, everlasting love. According to legend, the first claddagh rings appeared in the 17th century when pirates captured Richard Joyce (a fisherman from Claddagh, Ireland), leaving Joyce's true love all alone. When he was freed years later, he returned to Ireland and married her. They opened a goldsmith's shop. There, Joyce made the first claddagh ring for his wife. Soon after, the rings became popular with royalty in Great Britain; everyone from King Edward VII to Queen Victoria wore them.

**LYCHEE FRUIT**: According to legend, an ancient Chinese emperor married a woman who loved lychees, a sweet fruit that looks like a raspberry. Because it grows in tropical areas and the royals lived in northern China, the empress had trouble keeping fresh lychees on hand. So her husband sent his fastest horsemen to southern China and had them bring back the fruit. Inspired by the emperor's devotion for his wife, lychees came to represent love for the Chinese, and today the fruit is a popular gift between partners.

# Notable Bulbs of History

### TAKE A LEEK

- More popular in Europe than in the United States, leeks have been cultivated in the Mediterranean region for over 4,000 years. Ancient Egyptians grew them, and they were a favorite vegetable of the Greeks and Romans. The emperor Nero believed that leeks would improve his singing voice, and he ate so many of them that he was nicknamed Porrophagus—"Leek Eater."

- The Welsh have adopted the leek as a national symbol. Legend says that in a seventh-century battle against the Saxons, Welsh warriors wore leeks on their hats to identify themselves to each other and prevent friendly fire. Even now, Welsh people wear leeks on March 1, St. David's Day (he's their patron saint), and celebrate by eating leek broth and chicken-and-leek pie.

- French aristocrats used to hate leeks. They called them the "asparagus of the poor." But that all changed in 1917 thanks to the famous French chef Louis Diat. While working at New York's Ritz Carlton Hotel, he fancied up a traditional recipe his mother and grandmother used to make and called it vichyssoise, named after his hometown of Vichy. What is it? A cold soup made of cream, leeks, and potatoes. Today it can be ordered at most fancy restaurants—even in France.

# "The Blast Blasted Blubber Beyond All Believable Bounds"

An eight-ton sperm whale carcass washed ashore on a Florence, Oregon, beach in November 1970. And it really stank. It fell upon George Thornton of the Oregon State Highway Division to figure out how to remove it. He couldn't bury the decomposing corpse on site because the tides would uncover it. And because of the stench, his workers refused to cut it up and transport it elsewhere. He also couldn't burn it. Solution: Blow up the whale with dynamite. Thornton figured that the whale's body would be nearly disintegrated by the explosion; gulls would scavenge the small chunks that landed on the beach.

As workers piled 20 cases—half a ton—of dynamite on the carcass, a crowd of onlookers and reporters gathered at (what they thought) was a safe distance. And then...BOOM! The whale suddenly erupted into a giant plume of sand and blubber. "Oohs" and "aahs" are heard from the bystanders as whale fragments flew through the air. Then a woman screamed, "Here come pieces of...*whale*!" Splattering noises of whale chunks hitting the ground grew louder as onlookers tried to dodge the onslaught. In the words of Paul Linnman, a Portland TV reporter on the scene, "The humor of the entire situation suddenly gave way to a run for

survival as huge chunks of whale blubber fell everywhere."

For several minutes after the blast, it rained blubber particles. Fortunately, no one was hurt by the chunks, but everyone—and everything—on the scene was coated with foul-smelling whale bits. The worst casualty: An Oldsmobile parked a quarter of a mile away was crushed by a large slab of blubber.

The beach was littered with huge chunks of ripe whale, including its entire tail and a slab of mangled whale meat that never left the blast site. And the smell was actually worse than before. The townspeople (and all the gulls) stayed far away. Thornton and his workers spent the rest of the day burying their mistake. His blunder drew the attention of news stations all over the country, but amazingly, he was promoted just six months later.

Nearly 50 years later, the Oregon Highway Division still gets asked about the exploding whale—many callers hoping to get their hands on the video. The whale is still dead, but the story took on a life of its own.

"From hell's heart I stab at thee; for hate's sake I spit my last breath at thee."
—**Captain Ahab, from Herman Melville's *Moby Dick***

# The Not Mahal

The Taj Mahal was built by Mughal emperor Shah Jahan for his wife, who died in 1631. That's what the history books say, anyway.

But P. N. Oak, author of *Taj Mahal: The True Story*, claims that the world-famous palace is actually three centuries older than everyone thinks it is. According to Oak, the Taj Mahal is actually the Tejo Mahalaya, an ancient Hindu temple to the Lord Shiva that was later converted into the queen's tomb by Shah Jahan. Oak points to evidence from Shah Jahan's own writings, eyewitness statements, and carbon-dating tests of a Taj Mahal door that's supposedly 300 years older than thought. Most scientists and historians refute Oak's claims...which his supporters say is all part of a massive cover-up.

> Random Fact: The word "hooch" comes from the Hoochinoo Indians of Alaska. They made liquor so strong it could knock someone out.

## BOTCHED
## HISTORY

"Adolf Hitler lost the war and was painted out to be a monster after his death. This is what breaks my heart. Hitler was a good man."

—Reality show star Tila Tequila

# Broken Bodies

In 1942 an unlucky Brit exploring the Roopkund area of the Himalayas discovered a lake full of human skeletons. There were bones floating in the water; others were piled up along the banks. Some of them still had hair and soft tissue attached. Investigators discovered the remains of more than 200 people.

But how did they die? And when?

The mystery was solved in 2002 thanks to modern forensics. Researchers determined that the people died circa A.D. 850 (ice had preserved them). Cause of death: blunt force trauma to their heads. But not by weapons— these people were done in by a violent thunderstorm that rained down hailstones the size of baseballs.

---

**5 ROMAN DELICACIES, CIRCA A.D. 200**

1. Parrot tongue
2. Ostrich brain
3. Thrush tongue
4. Peacock comb
5. Nightingale tongue

# Epitaphs de la Strange

### In England:

*In Memory of Charles Ward*
This stone was not erected by Susan his wife.
She erected a stone to John Salter her second husband
forgetting the affection of Charles Ward, her husband.

### In Massachusetts:

Nearby these grayrocks
Enclosed in a box
Lies Hatter Cox
Who died of smallpox.

### In Scotland:

Here lies the body of Sarah,
Wife of John Hayes.
The Lord giveth
And the Lord taketh away
Blessed be the name of the Lord.

### In Illinois:

*Anonymous*
Cold is my bed,
but ah I love it,
For colder are my friends above it.

**In Rhode Island:**
*Thomas Coffin*
He's done a-catching cod
And gone to meet his God.

**In Scotland:**
Here lies John Macpherson
Who was a very peculiar person
He stood six foot two without his shoe
And was slew at Waterloo.

**In New York:**
*John Phillips*
Accidentally shot as a mark of affection by his brother.

**In Colorado:**
*Anonymous*
He called Bill Smith a liar.

**In Georgia:**
*Dr. J.J. Subers*
Been Here
And Gone
Had a Good Time

# MORE MYTH-CONCEPTIONS

**MYTH:** Buddha was fat.

**TRUTH:** He was thin. The man who we know today as Buddha, Siddhartha Gautama, lived 2,500 years ago in India. No pictures of him exist, but he was said to be "tall and slender." Other men after him have also been given the title Buddha, which means "one who has achieved a state of perfect enlightenment." The portlier version, known as the "laughing Buddha," was a 10th-century Chinese folk hero known as Budai.

**MYTH:** The armor worn by medieval knights was so heavy that the knights had to be hoisted onto their horses with cranes.

**TRUTH:** Designed for battle, armor was made as lightweight and flexible as possible. A knight might use a stool to mount his horse, but otherwise he could get up there just fine. The myth was popularized by the 1944 film *Henry V*, in which an armor-clad Laurence Olivier is hoisted onto his horse via a "medieval" crane. Olivier, who also directed the film, included the crane over the objections of the film's historical advisers.

# The Bard's Best Barbs

"Go, prick thy face, and over-red thy fear,
Thou lilyliver'd boy."

—*MACBETH*

"Thou art like a toad; ugly and venomous."

—*AS YOU LIKE IT*

"He's a disease that must be cut away."

—*CORIOLANUS*

"Thou art a flesh-monger, a fool and a
coward."

—*MEASURE FOR MEASURE*

"Thy tongue outvenoms all the worms of
Nile."

—*CYMBELINE*

"You scullion! You rampallian! You
fustilarian! I'll tickle your catastrophe!"

—*HENRY IV, PART 2*

"Methink'st thou art a general offence and
every man should beat thee."

—*ALL'S WELL THAT ENDS WELL*

"Thou clay-brained guts, thou knotty-pated fool, thou whoreson obscene greasy tallow-catch!"
—*HENRY IV, PART 1*

"You are as a candle, the better burnt out."
—*HENRY IV, PART 2*

"I scorn you, scurvy companion. What, you poor, base, rascally, cheating, lack-linen mate! Away, you mouldy rogue!"
—*HENRY IV, PART 2*

"Thou art unfit for any place but hell."
—*RICHARD III*

"Thine face is not worth sunburning."
—*HENRY V*

"It is certain that when he makes water, his urine is congealed ice."
—*MEASURE FOR MEASURE*

"I do wish thou wert a dog,
That I might love thee something."
—*TIMON OF ATHENS*

# DIED ON THE JOB

**THE LAWYER WHO WAS RIGHT:** Clement Vallandigham was an attorney and former U.S. congressman. In 1871, while defending a murder suspect in court, he argued that the alleged victim hadn't been murdered; he could have accidentally shot himself. To prove his point, Vallandigham took out a gun, held it as it was held at the scene of the crime, and—thinking it was unloaded—he pulled the trigger.

Good news: He proved his point and his client was acquitted. Bad news: Vallandigham died from an accidental gunshot to the head.

**A REAL CROWD-PLEASER:** On March 5, 1923, a daredevil named Harry F. Young climbed the facade of New York City's Martinique Hotel. It was a paid gig: Young received $100 to wear a placard advertising a new silent movie as he climbed up the building without ropes, a harness, or a safety net. "Frequently, in order to give the crowd an extra thrill, Young seemed purposely to let his foot slip," the *New York Times* reported. When Young reached the 11th story, his foot did slip—this time for real. The crowd gasped as he plunged to the street below. He died on impact. The name of the movie Young was promoting: *Safety Last*.

# Made-up Languages: Láadan

Meaning "Perception Language," Láadan is the world's first feminist language. It was invented in 1982 by science-fiction author Suzette Haden Elgin as an experimental language in order to test a theory that was popular with feminists: namely, that modern languages had a male bias that restricted feminine thought and perception.

Remember the old saying that Eskimos have a hundred different words for "snow" while English has only "snow"? If having only one word for "snow" limits how English speakers think about snow, the feminist theory went, then a male bias in modern languages, if it existed, would similarly restrict the perceptions of women. Elgin theorized that if women embraced Láadan within 10 years, or were at least inspired by it to create a better feminist language, that would support the theory of a male bias in modern languages. If Láadan flopped, that was evidence of little or no bias: Women had no need for Láadan because they were well served by the languages they already spoke.

Láadan had five words for "joy," five words for "anger," four words for "it" (three female and one male), and six words for "alone." It also had 13 words for "love," including *ab*, "love for one liked but not respected"; *ad*, "love for one

respected but not liked"; and *éeme,* "love for one neither liked nor respected." (Curiously, Láadan also has a word for "sewage plant"—*waludal.*)

## SAMPLE WORDS:

| | |
|---|---|
| *with:* adult (female) | *miwith:* city |
| *withid:* adult (male) | *miwithá:* city dweller |
| *héeya:* fear | *yob:* coffee |
| *lub:* chicken | *oma:* hand |
| *oba:* body | *wíi:* alive |
| *sheb:* change | *óol:* moon |

**Outcome:** Láadan never attracted more than a handful of enthusiasts, some of whom are still contributing new words and grammar to this day. But as Arika Okrent writes in *In the Land of Invented Languages,* "After 10 years passed, and women still had not embraced Láadan or come up with another language to replace it, Elgin declared the experiment a failure, noting, with some bitterness, that Klingon (a hyper-male 'warrior' language) was thriving."

"A man who teaches a woman to write should know that he is providing poison to an asp."
—**Menander, Greek dramatist (342–290 B.C.)**

# Bad Trips

- In the sixth century B.C., the Assyrians poisoned the wells of the Israelites and other enemies with a fungus—rye ergot—that caused hallucinations and, in strong enough doses, death.

- During World War I, the British military started dropping cigarettes and propaganda leaflets from planes to try to persuade the Ottoman Turks to drop their alliance with the Germans, but the Turks would smoke the cigarettes and throw away the propaganda. Just before the Battle of Beersheba, a British intelligence officer decided to drop cigarettes laced with opium. When the British attacked the next day, the Turks were so high that they had trouble standing, let alone fighting. Needless to say, the British were victorious.

> "The illegal we do immediately. The unconstitutional takes a little longer."
>
> **—Henry Kissinger**

# Edison Shmedison

Thomas Edison invented the lightbulb, right? Wrong! The first incandescent bulb was patented by Joseph Swan, an English inventor, in 1845. By the time Edison began experimenting with lightbulbs in 1878, his goal was to find a long-lasting filament that would make the lightbulb practical for the first time. So he did that all by himself, right? Wrong!

More a tinkerer than a scientist, Edison's strategy had been to blindly build prototype after prototype. He ignored the work of other researchers, often unwittingly repeating their failed experiments. That's what happened with the lightbulb. After a month of getting nowhere, he hired Francis Upton, a Princeton physicist, to help him.

Upton had the lab's researchers study old patents, electrical journals, and the work of competing inventors to see what progress they had made. He also shifted the focus of the work from testing prototypes to methodically experimenting with raw materials (in order to understand their scientific properties and see which ones made the best filaments). Without this important shift in strategy, Edison's lab might never have developed a practical bulb at all—and certainly would have fallen behind competing labs.

"I have not failed," Edison once said, "I have just found 10,000 ways that won't work." (Until someone helped him, that is.)

# Spooner and His "Isms"

William Archibald Spooner (1844–1930) was at Oxford
University for 70 years as a student, professor, and then
president. Today, however, he's known for his "spooner-
isms"—the unusual habit he had of mistakenly wurning
his turds around, er...turning his words around.

For example, Spooner would say "well-boiled icicle"
when he meant a "well-oiled bicycle," or "cattle ships and
bruisers" when he was trying to get his mouth around
"battleships and cruisers." He toasted Queen Victoria with
"Here's to our queer old dean!" At chapel he prayed, "Our
Lord is a shoving leopard." Then there was the occasion
when he officiated at a wedding; he asked if it was
"kisstomary to cuss the bride."

There's no doubt that Spooner was prone to spooner-
isms, but historians believe that most of the ones attributed
to him were apocryphal. Does it matter if he said "pat my
hiccup" instead of "pick my hat up"? Or imagine camping
with a "scoop of boy trouts." Either way, Spooner lives on in
quountless cotations, whether he ned them or snot.

# The Aliens Inside Mt. Shasta

Towering 14,179 feet above sea level, Mt. Shasta is a dormant volcano in the Cascade Range in Northern California. Its snowcapped peak has been surrounded by mystery and legend since indigenous people first encountered it thousands of years ago.

But things got really strange in 1884 when a teenager named Frederick Oliver, from the nearby town of Yreka, first saw the mountain. He immediately fell into a trance. And then, under the control of what he claimed were "other forces," Oliver wrote a book called *A Dweller on Two Planets*. It tells the history of Mt. Shasta, which Oliver claimed was channeled directly to his mind by an immortal creature named Phylos, whose race, the Lemurians, once lived on a Pacific Ocean continent called Mu. Like Atlantis, Mu was a "lost continent" that modern scientists say never existed.

Lemurians, Oliver wrote, talk to each other telepathically in a language called Solara Maru, but Phylos spoke English to Oliver (curiously, with an English accent). Oliver described the Lemurians as physically stunning—more than seven feet tall with long, flowing hair and lean, graceful bodies. They wore white robes lined with sacred stones.

Technologically advanced even by today's standards, the ancient Lemurians developed water generators, antigravity machines, high-speed trains, and devices comparable to cellular phones and televisions. But then, one night about 12,000 years ago, Mu began shaking and sinking into the sea. The 25,000 Lemurians boarded tall ships bound for the uninhabited land of what is now Northern California. They chose Shasta because it's "the earthly incarnation of the Great Central Sun, the source of all physical and spiritual energy in the universe."

Once there, their engineers hollowed out the mountain and constructed a subterranean city called Telos. According to Oliver/Phylos, floating in the sky directly above Mt. Shasta is yet another Lemurian city: "The Crystal City of the Light of the Seven Rays." It's visible only to the most tuned-in human psychics, who describe it as a huge, floating, purple pyramid, the point of which extends into space. From within the Crystal City, the Lemurians operate interplanetary, interdimensional spaceships called the "Silver Fleet" (which would seem to explain all of the UFO sightings near Mt. Shasta). The Lemurians represent our galaxy in the intergalactic "Confederation of Planets."

Today, Mt. Shasta, and the town that shares its name, is a hot spot for the New Age movement. To thousands of people, *A Dweller on Two Planets*—which is still in print today—is not a science fiction book...but the source material for their belief system.

# FIVE FREAKY FACTS ABOUT...
## SCIENTISTS

- Albert Einstein once used a $1,500 check from the Rockefeller Foundation as a bookmark...and then lost the book.

- The notebooks that Marie and Pierre Curie used to record their radium experiments are still radioactive.

- Who's John Tyndall? The Irish scientist who answered the question "Why is the sky blue?"

- Italian astronomer Galileo went blind studying the sun through telescopes.

- Galileo died on January 8, 1642. Exactly 300 years later, on January 8, 1942, Stephen Hawking was born.

# Bunnies in the Oven

In 1726 an English housewife named Mary Toft told an unbelievable tale: She convinced doctors that she'd given birth to a litter of stillborn rabbits—in front of a midwife and a doctor, no less!

An investigation was conducted by the surgeon to King George I. His conclusion: Toft was telling the truth. The surgeon even went so far as to publish a medical report about her, and people all over the United Kingdom were so sympathetic to her case that they stopped eating rabbit stew.

Toft's explanation: While she was pregnant, she got startled by a rabbit and thereafter dreamed of rabbits. She craved rabbit meat and was tempted to chase them around. It wasn't such a far-fetched story in the 1700s—people believed that a pregnant woman's thoughts and actions could directly affect her baby's characteristics.

Sadly, Toft was lying, and it eventually came to light that, in a bid for fame and fortune, she had bribed people to bring her dead rabbits, which she actually hid *inside* her body and then pretended to deliver. The public was reportedly furious at the ruse, the medical community was embarrassed, and authorities were eager to punish her. Result: Toft went to prison for four months after a court exposed her as a "cheat."

# ALLIGATORS IN THE SEWERS

Why are they called "urban legends"? In the 1940s, folklorists started collecting modern American legends and noticed that they had different characteristics than older, rural-based legends did. They called these legends "urban belief tales" or "city tales," the words *urban* and *city* indicating their darker, more modern themes, even though the stories weren't necessarily based in cities. The term evolved to become "urban legend" in the 1960s.

The most famous example of an urban legend tells of a race of giant alligators living in the sewers beneath New York City. Like a lot of urban legends, there's a grain of truth to this tall tale: An alligator actually was found in a Harlem sewer in 1935. It didn't live there, though. (Probably just visiting from Florida.) But the legend was born, and even though scientists have completely discredited the notion that warm-blooded, sun-loving reptiles could survive in cold, dark sewers, there are still people today who will try to convince you that there really are alligators living in the Big Apple's sewers. Their best friend's brother's teacher's accountant's aunt said so, and she *swears* it's true!

# Weird Ways to Die

### THE LONGEST KILL SHOT IN HISTORY

In 1893 Henry Ziegland of Texas jilted his fiancée, and she killed herself over it. Her brother swore revenge. He got his gun and confronted Ziegland; he shot him in the face and then turned the gun on himself. But the bullet only grazed Ziegland and then got lodged in a tree.

Twenty years later, Ziegland was removing the same tree that had the bullet buried in it. He decided to use dynamite to make the job easier. Bad idea: The explosion blasted the bullet out of the tree, striking Ziegland in the head and killing him...two decades after it left the barrel of the gun.

### WINNING AT ALL COSTS

In the 564 B.C. Olympic games, the Greek athlete Arrachion of Phigalia won the pankration event, a mix of boxing and wrestling where virtually anything was permitted. After a very tough fight, his opponent conceded the bout as Arrachion lay on the ground. Unbeknownst to his rival, Arrachion had expired from the duel, becoming the only dead person to win an Olympic event.

# The Stanleys and Their Steamers

In 1899 the Stanley Steamer was hailed as the "car of the future." Easily the fastest machine on the road (of which there were very few back then), it could hit 70 mph with ease while getting up to 10 miles per gallon...of water.

Built by twin brother geniuses Francis E. and Freelan O. Stanley from Maine, these steam-powered vehicles were as powerful as a small locomotive—they could accelerate from 0 to 60 mph in 11 seconds. And unlike the racket made by noisy gas-powered cars, the Stanley steam engine ran almost silently with only the occasional hiss of steam. Turn-of-the-century hot-rodders liked to startle other drivers by passing them backward!

So how come the roads aren't filled with steam-powered cars today? The Stanley Steamer—or Flying Teapot, as it was affectionately called—had two fatal flaws: It took 30 minutes for its boiler to build up enough steam to operate, and it cost a very expensive $3,950 (about $49,000 today). Unwilling to make their cars less expensive, the Stanleys were quickly overtaken by Henry Ford and his gasoline-powered Model T.

# Human Hailstones

*Hailstones are formed when ice crystals in a thunderhead are tossed around, gathering successive coats of ice until they become heavy enough to fall to the ground. It turns out that ice crystals aren't the only things that can get tossed around in a thunderhead.*

• In 1930 a German glider society held an exhibition. Five glider pilots flew into a towering thunderhead hoping to set new altitude records by using the updrafts. But the updrafts were more than they had counted on—the gliders were torn to pieces by the violent winds. The pilots bailed out but were carried to the upper regions of the cloud, where they were coated by ice. All but one froze to death before finally falling to the ground.

• Lt. Col. William Rankin bailed out of his single-engine plane in 1959 when the engine failed at 47,000 feet above Virginia. A storm was in progress, and he fell right through the middle of it. It would normally take a man 13 minutes to fall 47,000 feet, but Rankin got caught in the updrafts and remained aloft for 45 minutes. He tumbled about in −70°F temperatures, covered with ice and sleet, his body bruised by hailstones. Fortunately, his parachute opened at 10,000 feet and he landed intact in a tree in North Carolina, 65 miles from where he'd bailed out. He made a complete recovery.

# The Tale of the Hobberdehoy

One morning, a valgus hobberdehoy was cornobbled by a very old leptorrhinian calcographer. "You twiddlepoopy liripoop!" faffled the hobberdehoy, "You've given me a wem that smells of bodewash!"

"So sorry," belched the saprostomous calcographer. "I was unaware that my jumentous mundungus was cornobbling you."

"Whatever, you spodogenous whipjack! Now I must go to my xystus and run my balbriggan galligaskin through my chirogymnasts to get this wem out!"

The calcographer felt like a dasypygal pismire. "I have lost my toxophily," he said sadly.

"Wait a second," faffled the hobberdehoy. "Did you say toxophily? You remind me of my toxophillic atmatertera. You have the same anisognathous mouth as she."

"Does she go by Esmerelda?" asked the calcographer.

"Why yes, yes she does. She was brideloped by a calcographer many moons ago."

And then they looked at each other.

"Bob?"

"Jim?"

And then Bob and his great-great-great grandfather Jim went to Bob's xystus to de-wem his ballbriggan galligaskin.

*(What the heck is going on here? Turn the page to find out.)*

# I've Been Cornobbled!

*Did you just try to decipher that odd story on the previous page? If not, go back and read it before you look at the definitions of all these archaic words. You won't find them in most dictionaries, but take our word for it—people used to use them. And that's no bodewash!*

**Hobberdehoy:** A youth entering manhood

**Faffle:** To stutter or mumble

**Dasypygal:** Having hairy buttocks

**Cornobbled:** Hit with a fish

**Collieshangie:** A noisy or confused fight

**Wem:** A stain, flaw, or scar

**Calcographer:** One who draws with chalk

**Bodewash:** Cow dung

**Twiddlepoop:** An effeminate-looking man

**Liripoop:** A silly creature

**Leptorrhinian:** Having a long, narrow nose

**Bridelope:** When the new bride is "both symbolically and physically swept off on horseback" to the husband's home

**Mundungus:** Garbage; stinky tobacco

**Chirogymnast:** A finger exercise machine for pianists

**Toxophily:** Love of archery

**Pismire:** An ant

**Valgus:** Bowlegged or knock-kneed

**Xystus:** An indoor porch for exercising in winter

**Jumentous:** Having a strong animal smell

**Saprostomous:** Having bad breath

**Balbriggan:** A fine cotton used mainly for underwear

**Atmatertera:** A great-grandfather's grandmother's sister

**Anisognathous:** Having the upper and lower teeth unlike

**Whipjack:** A beggar pretending to have been shipwrecked

**Spodogenous:** Pertaining to or due to the presence of waste matter

**Crapandina:** A mineral, such as toadstone or bufonite, said to have healing properties

**Galligaskin:** Baggy trousers

# Didn't Hear That Train a-Comin'

Among the many celebrities attending the September 15, 1830, launch of the Liverpool and Manchester Railway in England were the Duke of Wellington and William Huskisson, a member of Parliament. The two men were planning to ride a succession of trains to Liverpool, with the first stop at Parkside railway station to water the steam engine.

Ignoring the engineer's warning to remain on the train, Huskisson joined the other passengers who'd disembarked to gawk at the parade of engines lined up on parallel tracks. He stepped onto an empty track just as an engine called the Rocket barreled into the station. Huskisson fell beneath the wheels of the locomotive and lost his leg. As his own train transported him to the nearest hospital, the MP declared, "My death is near." He died moments later... unaware that he'd made history as the first person ever killed by a train.

# Two More Fatal Firsts

**BY CAR**: On September 14, 1899, Henry Bliss stepped down from a streetcar at West 74th and Central Park West in New York City. As he turned to help a female passenger down the stairs, he was struck by a passing cab, making the 68-year-old man the first pedestrian killed by an automobile in the United States.

**BY PLANE**: Five years after their historic first flight at Kitty Hawk, the Wright brothers took their new plane, the *Wright Flyer*, on a cross-country tour to prove it could safely carry passengers. Their third stop was at Ft. Myer, Virginia, on September 17, 1908. As a crowd of 2,000 cheered, Orville Wright and his passenger, Lieutenant Thomas E. Selfridge of the U.S. Signal Corps, lifted off into the sky. Then the propeller snapped in two and the *Wright Flyer* nose-dived 150 feet to the ground. Selfridge was killed instantly; Wright suffered multiple hip and leg fractures that plagued him with chronic pain for the rest of his life.

# Happy Eostre!

Easter comes from *Eostre*, a pagan festival. Before
Christianity, early Germans held an annual celebration
in honor of Eostre, goddess of spring and fertility. As
Christianity spread across Europe in the first and second
centuries, the Church often modified or adopted pagan
holidays. Because Eostre was the goddess of spring and her
festival celebrated renewal and rebirth, the Church's belief
in Christ's resurrection made for a good match.

So why the bunny? Eostre's association with fertility led
to her frequent depiction with a rabbit's head. But the concept of an Easter bunny originated with the Germans, who
settled in Pennsylvania in the 1700s. Their "Pennsylvania
Dutch" children believed that if they were well-behaved, the
*Oschter Haws* (literally, "Easter Rabbit") would leave a nest
of brightly colored eggs on Easter morning.

So why the eggs? In an old pagan folk tale, Eostre turns
her pet bird into a rabbit to entertain children. The rabbit
performs a trick: It lays colorful eggs—which are a common symbol of rebirth in many ancient cultures, including
those of Egypt, Persia, China, Gaul, and Rome. The first
concrete historical association of colored eggs with Easter
comes from the 1200s, when English servants were given
painted eggs by their masters as Easter gifts.

# The X-Ray Shoe Fitter

In the late 1940s, the Adrian X-Ray Company out of Milwaukee made and sold 10,000 devices to shoe stores all over the United States that allowed customers to see just how well their shoes fit—by X-raying their feet while they were wearing the shoes. The X-Ray Shoe Fitter allowed them to see inside the shoe (and also their bones), via a small window on the unit. The machines were a popular novelty—especially among children. Although the box where you rested your feet was lead-lined, neither the compartment nor the viewing windows were sealed. Result: persistent radiation leakage.

As the nuclear age dawned and the dangerous effects of radiation came to be known, these machines slowly started disappearing from shoe stores, but they weren't actually banned by the federal government until 1970. Even then, it took many more years before they were officially phased out. The last radiation-leaking X-ray Shoe Fitter was still being used in a Madison, West Virginia, shoe store in 1981.

# ARMY OF THE DEAD

The first known use of a plague as a weapon took place in 1346 when Mongol emperor Janiberg Khan's troops held the town of Kaffa (now Feodosiya, Ukraine) under siege. Bubonic plague had devastated the emperor's troops, so he ordered the surviving soldiers to catapult the plague-ridden corpses over the walls of Kaffa in an effort to spread the disease. It worked, and the locals got sick.

But Khan wasn't able to take advantage of Kaffa's suffering: He was forced to retreat because so many of his own men were dying. Once the Mongols were gone, the residents of Kaffa (many of whom were traders from Italy) tried to escape the contagion by fleeing back to Europe on flea-ridden, rat-infested ships.

Some historians believe that Khan's use of biological warfare launched the Black Death, the plague epidemic that hit Europe in the 14th century and killed about 30 million people.

# Wu Who?

China's first and only woman emperor was Wu Zetian, who ruled during the Tang dynasty in the 600s. Born into a noble and wealthy family, Wu was educated from an early age in music, art, literature, and philosophy.

Beginning her political career as a concubine, she had two sons by the emperor—two possible heirs to the emperor's throne if she got rid of the two women in her way. So that's what she did. When Wu's newborn daughter died during childbirth, Wu accused Empress Wang of infanticide. Some versions of the story say that Wu actually killed her own daughter and then blamed it on the empress. In any case, in 655 the emperor imprisoned his wife and made Wu empress. She quickly used her new power to have the former empress and the first concubine, Xiaoshu, executed. Wu Zhao now became Empress Wu Zetian. But she wanted more.

She began to eliminate anyone who dared oppose her, replacing them with her supporters. By 690 Wu Zetian had eliminated enough of her enemies to do what had never been done by a woman in Chinese history: She deposed her puppet son and declared herself the sole ruler of China—giving herself the male name Emperor Shengshen.

Emperor Shengshen declared the end of the Tang dynasty and a return to the Zhou dynasty (she believed she was descended from the ancient Zhou emperors).

Wu Zetian ruled China for the next 15 years. It was an ironically brutal rule during which she spread the compassionate teachings of Buddhism while ruthlessly butchering her enemies. In 695 she expanded her royal name, taking the Buddhist title Emperor Tiance Jinlun Shengshen—the Divine Emperor Who Rules the Universe. In 705, when Wu was 80 years old, her rule was ended by a palace coup. In all, the former concubine ruled China for nearly 45 years, 15 of them as emperor. No woman has ruled China since.

# "Independence is happiness."
# —Susan B. Anthony

# Two More Sordid Tales from the Mütter Museum

**THE SOAP LADY:** Early in the 19th century, a morbidly obese Philadelphia woman was buried in a downtown cemetery. Many years later, when the cemetery was being relocated as part of an urban renewal project, the excavators made a grim discovery: The environment in which the woman had been buried—damp soil with just the right chemical makeup—turned her remains into *adipocere*, a substance similar to soap. The woman's body was never claimed by relatives; the "Soap Lady" was later acquired by Philadelphia's Mütter Museum for the princely sum of $7.50.

**THE DR. CHEVALIER JACKSON COLLECTION OF FOREIGN BODIES:** Chevalier Jackson was one of the leading throat doctors at the beginning of the 20th century, and part of his job was removing objects that people had swallowed. He apparently kept every object he ever fished out of a gullet, and plenty that others had, too; today more than 2,000 of them are kept in drawers at the Mütter Museum with labels like "Buttons," "Pins," "Nuts, Seeds, Shells or Other Vegetal Substances," "Toys," "Dental materials" (dentures), and "Meat."

# FULL OF SOUND AND FURY...

## SIGNIFYING NOTHING

In 1918, 21-year-old Billy Falkner from Mississippi—at only 5'5" tall—was too short to join the U.S. Army to fight in World War I. So he went to Canada and changed his name to the more fancy-sounding "William Faulkner," but Great Britain's Royal Flying Corps wouldn't take him, either. So Faulkner decided to stay in Canada for the duration of the war. During the Armistice Day celebration in Toronto, he commandeered some bourbon and a biplane and performed a series of trick maneuvers—culminating in an upside-down loop that was executed perfectly...until he crashed into an airplane hangar. The young man emerged with a limp that would plague him for years.

At least, that's how Faulkner himself told it. But historians tell a different story: Faulkner never even got near a military biplane. They even think he faked his limp. But that's what Faulkner did best: tell stories, including his seminal 1929 novel *The Sound and the Fury*, frequently named one of the top ten novels of the 20th century.

**BOTCHED**

**HISTORY**

"For all you kids watching at home, Santa is white. Just because it makes you uncomfortable doesn't mean it has to change. Jesus was a white man, too."

—Fox News host Megyn Kelly. Most historians agree that Jesus, being of Middle Eastern descent, would have had a dark complexion.

# Bug Bombs Awayyyy!

- In the days of high-walled castles, hornet nests were used as weapons—hurled via catapults over town and castle walls. The Romans especially liked to use bees and other stinging insects in their naval battles. They'd catapult the nests and hives onto ships and wait for chaos to break out and the sailors to jump overboard.

- In the second century B.C., the Romans found themselves the victims, though. When they tried to climb the walls of the ancient fortified city of Hatra in Iraq, the defenders threw clay pots at them containing not just bees and wasps but—some historians believe— venomous scorpions.

- The Vietcong used scorpions against American troops during the Vietnam War. Because the North Vietnamese often operated out of a network of underground tunnels, any U.S. soldier unlucky enough to have found one of the tunnels might be surprised by trip wires and booby traps. If a trip wire were hit, a grenade might go off...or a box filled with angry scorpions might just fall on the soldier's head.

# The Line That Almost Killed the Beatles

*"We're more popular than Jesus now. I don't know which will go first—rock 'n' roll or Christianity. Jesus was all right, but his disciples were thick and ordinary. It's them twisting it that ruins it for me."*

That's an excerpt from an interview that John Lennon gave to the *Evening Standard* in March 1966, during the height of Beatlemania. Lennon had spent an entire day at his mansion with reporter Maureen Cleave, during which time he rambled on about books, music, politics, and religion. The interview was printed in full and the statement—taken in context—reveals that Lennon was lamenting the sad state of modern religion, and not trying to deify the Beatles. There was no reaction to it whatsoever in England.

A few months later in July, an American teen magazine called *Datebook* ran a cover story called "The Ten Adults You Dig/Hate the Most." In the section on John Lennon, they reprinted the quote by itself, without the rest of the interview. The result was quick and severe: Christians denounced the Beatles and began a campaign to destroy everything associated with the Fab Four.

Dozens of radio stations, especially in the South and Midwest, stopped playing their records and even organized

Beatles bonfires. Some churches threatened to excommunicate members who listened to the "devil music."

Even the other Beatles received death threats. And the timing couldn't have been worse—this all went down while the band was on an American tour that took them right through the Bible Belt. The Ku Klux Klan even tried to set up a barrier and stop an August 13 concert in Memphis, to no avail.

Lennon, for his part, was shocked that such a seemingly innocuous statement could have created such havoc. He held a press conference in Chicago to try to put things right. "I'm not saying that we're better or greater, or comparing us with Jesus Christ as a person or God as a thing or whatever it is. I wasn't saying whatever they're saying I was saying. I'm sorry I said it really. I never meant it to be a lousy anti-religious thing. I apologize if that will make you happy. I still don't know quite what I've done. I've tried to tell you what I did do, but if you want me to apologize, if that will make you happy, then OK, I'm sorry."

The fervor eventually died down, but many fans never forgave Lennon, and the bubblegum image of the early Beatles was all but gone. As were their U.S. touring days— the Beatles never played another concert in the United States after that tumultuous tour.

# Who Discovered Antarctica?

History tells us that the explorer James Cook discovered Antarctica in 1773. But did someone beat him to it?

A map found in a library in Istanbul in 1929, drawn by Piri Reis, a Turkish admiral, appears to show the topography of Antarctica. But the map dates to 1513... more than 200 years before Cook's expedition. Even stranger, the continent was completely covered by ice in the 1500s. The land that Reis seems to have depicted (underneath the ice) hadn't been visible since perhaps 4000 B.C.

The map, drawn on camel-skin parchment, has been certified as genuine, and Reis was renowned for his accuracy. His map shows specific details of South America's coastline and geography that were thought to be unknown to the Turks. Although skeptics point out that the crudely drawn land to the south isn't necessarily Antarctica, the U.S. Hydrographic Office confirmed that the map accurately depicts part of the continent: "This indicates the coastline had been mapped before it was covered by the ice-cap...We have no idea how the data on this map can be reconciled with the supposed state of geographical knowledge in 1513."

# Who Invented the Safety Pin?

In 1849 a New York inventor named Walter Hunt had a problem: He was too broke to pay an employee the $15 he owed him. But the employee gave him an out—he'd forgive the $15 debt if he could have the rights to whatever Hunt could invent from a single piece of wire. Hunt was a prolific inventor—he'd designed a fire engine warning gong, a stove that burned hard coal, and even an early sewing machine (which he decided not to market because he didn't want to put seamstresses out of work). But for all his skill, he seemed unable to profit from any of his inventions. Hunt had no money, so he had no choice—he accepted the employee's challenge. After three hours of twisting an eight-inch piece of brass wire, Hunt had created the world's first safety pin. It had a clasp at one end, a point on the other, and a coil in the middle to act as a spring and keep the point tucked into the clasp.

So did Hunt hand over his "dress pin," as he called it, to the employee? No—he reneged on the deal and patented the safety pin himself. Then he sold the rights to his new invention for $400 (about $5,000 today), from which he paid his draftsman the $15, keeping the rest. Millions of safety pins have been made and sold since then, but Hunt never made another cent on his invention.

## FIVE FREAKY FACTS ABOUT...
# ROYAL FLUSHERS

- King James I of England (1566–1625) loved hunting so much that he wouldn't leave the saddle, even to go to the bathroom.

- In 1606 Henry IV of France passed a law forbidding anyone to urinate or defecate in the corners of his palace in Paris. That same day, his son, the Dauphin (Louis XIII), was caught peeing against the wall of his bedroom.

- King Louis XIV of France (1638–1715) often greeted guests while seated on the throne.

- De-throned: In 1760 King George II fell to his death from a toilet seat.

- Elvis "the King" Presley proposed to Ginger Alden while he was sitting on the toilet.

# OUTDATED CONCEPTS:
## The King's Touch

A sort of royalist equivalent of faith healing, this was the belief that the touch of a king or queen, who ruled by divine right, could actually cure diseases. The theory dates back to the 1200s in Europe and persisted for more than 600 years. The royal touch was thought to be especially effective in curing scrofula, a form of tuberculosis that causes swelling of the lymph nodes in the neck. Scrofula sores can disappear without treatment, which likely explains why the king's touch was thought to be so effective with this particular ailment.

### 10 Plagues of Egypt

1. Blood (the waters of the Nile ran red)
2. Frogs
3. Lice
4. Flies
5. Diseased livestock
6. Boils
7. Hail (mixed with fire)
8. Locusts
9. Darkness
10. Death of firstborns

# More Words of the Gods

**HELIUM:** This element, found in the gaseous atmosphere of the sun, is named after Helios, the Greek god of the sun.

**IRIDESCENT:** Named after Iris, the Greek goddess of the rainbow.

**BROWNIE:** These cousins of the Girl Scouts are named after the Celtic brownies, small, brown-cloaked fairies that perform household chores while the family sleeps.

**APHRODISIAC:** Named after Aphrodite, the Greek goddess of love. Her specialty: stirring up feelings of desire among the other gods.

**GHOUL:** From the Arabic word *ghul*, which was an evil spirit that robbed tombs and ate corpses. Today the name is given to anyone with an unhealthy interest in the deceased.

**LETHARGY:** Named after Lethe, the mythical Greek river of forgetfulness.

**AEGIS:** Originally the name of the shield of Zeus; today, anything that's protected by something else is said to be under its aegis.

**MONEY:** Named after Juno Moneta, the Roman goddess of money.

**EROTIC:** Named after Eros, the Greek god of...you guessed it: love.

# Skating Through History

In 1975 Rick Wakeman, keyboardist for the British progressive-rock band Yes, recorded *The Myths and Legends of King Arthur and the Knights of the Round Table,* a concept album that told the story of the British folk hero.

Wakeman decided to stage the historical musical... on ice. Not surprisingly, he couldn't find any backers, so at his own expense, the virtuoso keyboardist rented out London's Wembley Stadium and produced the show— with a full orchestra and rock band—in which King Arthur, Lancelot, Guinevere, and Merlin were all portrayed by figure skaters. Although the critics "crucified it," according to Wakeman, the show was a huge hit, and the keyboard- ist calls it a "highlight of my musical career."

# Stonehenges

- **THE FAMOUS STONEHENGE:** The first ancient monument to be identified as an astronomical observatory was England's Stonehenge. Researchers theorize that the circle of massive rocks was built and then rebuilt by three separate cultures between 5,000 and 3,000 years ago. While it's not clear exactly what Stonehenge was used for, the astronomical alignments of the rocks are unquestionable: They mark out the sunrise at midsummer and midwinter, and the rising and setting of the moon (which repeats in a cycle of 8.6 years).

- **STONEHENGE SOUTH:** Predating Stonehenge is the recently discovered stone circle of Nabta, Egypt, which at 7,000 years old is the oldest astronomical observatory discovered to date. Like Stonehenge, it marks sunrise and sunset at midsummer, but other than that, no one knows who built it or what else it might have been used for. The site was abandoned after 2,000 years, just before the rise of the Egyptian Old Kingdom. Did the ancient Egyptians get their astronomical knowledge from an older civilization in the Sahara?

- **STONEHENGE WEST:** In the hills of Wyoming, there's an ancient stone monument called the Big Horn Medicine Wheel. A similar structure is the Moose Mountain Wheel

in Saskatchewan, Canada. Both were sacred sites for Native Americans, but archaeologists date them from before the Plains Indians arrived, to some unknown indigenous people. The Big Horn wheel has been dated to A.D. 1000–1400, and Moose Mountain to about 2,000 years ago. The piles of stones point out the summer solstice and the rising of the bright stars Aldebaran, Rigel, Sirius, and Fomalhaut. There are many other medicine wheels and similar structures in North America, many of which are so damaged that it's impossible to reconstruct their original alignments. But because the positions of dawn and the risings of stars have changed a little over the centuries, it's possible to date the construction of them (and all the others) by accurate scientific methods.

The true relationship between ancient peoples and the heavens may never be known.

# Operation Exploding Chicken

In 1957 the British Army was worried that the Soviet Union would invade West Germany, so the Brits hatched a plan called Operation Blue Peacock to secretly bury nuclear land mines there. Each mine would have half the capacity as the bomb dropped on Nagasaki.

But there was a problem to overcome: The mines required warmth to detonate, and German winters are cold. So the British considered wrapping the mines in fiberglass pillows to keep them toasty. Another proposal involved packing live chickens in the bomb casings with enough seed and water to keep the chickens alive.

Secretly burying nuclear weapons (and chickens) in an allied country is generally frowned upon. Ultimately, the Ministry of Defence concluded that Operation Blue Peacock was "politically flawed" and that the risk of nuclear fallout contaminating the rest of Europe was "unacceptable." The project was canceled in 1958.

**HOW TO CRASH: THE ENGLISH WAY**
*This actual advice was given to British pilots during World War II:* "When a prang (crash) seems inevitable, endeavor to strike the softest, cheapest object in the vicinity as slow and gently as possible."

# Magnum P.U.

*Hey, privy diggers, it's time for the final "Outhouse Detectives" mystery!*

**DISCOVERY:** A wide variety of items recovered from a "two-holer" (an outhouse with two holes to sit on instead of just one)

**MYSTERY:** Underneath one of the holes were perfume bottles, pieces of china, and containers of Ruby Foam tooth powder. Underneath the other hole: a pile of beer bottles. Why the difference?

**THEORY:** Two-holers, like modern public restrooms, were segregated according to sex. One side—with the perfume bottles, china, and tooth powder—was for females; the side with all the beer bottles was for males. Apparently, the outhouse was the only place where the men could enjoy a beer in peace.

> Random Fact: Spoons were such a rare novelty in Elizabethan England that wealthy aristocrats would bring their own folding spoons to fancy banquets.

# The Great Gold Scam of 1896

One day in late 1896, the Reverend Prescott F. Jernegan told a Connecticut jeweler named Arthur P. Ryan that God had come to him in a vision and told him how to build a device that could extract gold from seawater. So the two men went into business with a man named Charles E. Fisher and founded the Electrolytic Marine Salts Company. Within weeks their accumulators were taking $150 worth of gold from the sea every day, and as the news traveled, the price of the company stock made all three men very rich.

But then, in July 1898, Fisher disappeared. And, strangely, the gold accumulators stopped working. Why? Fisher wasn't there to seed them anymore. He was a trained deep-sea diver; he'd been diving down to the accumulators at night and seeding them with gold that he and Jernegan had purchased earlier.

When investors went to Jernegan to find out what was wrong, he told them he'd get to the bottom of it...and fled to France with his family. He was found there, but disappeared again before he could be arrested. (He eventually ended up in the Philippines, where he became a teacher.) Fisher was never seen again, though some reports say he went to Australia. The scam made the men in the neighborhood of $200,000 each...millions in today's money. It remains one of the most successful financial hoaxes in U.S. history.

# THE BYZANTINE BLUNDER

The Byzantine-Ottoman Wars had been going strong since 1265. In the 1450s, the famous gunsmith Urban of Hungary crafted the "Basilic," the largest cannon ever built. The 19-ton behemoth required 100 men to move and could shoot a 1,200-pound cannonball over a mile. Urban tried to sell the Basilic to Byzantine emperor Constantine XI, but Constantine turned it down on grounds that the cannon was too expensive. So Urban sold it to Ottoman Turk leader Sultan Mehmed II, who used the cannon to blow down the walls of Constantinople in 1453 and take over the city.

 World Leaders and Their Pet Bears

- **King Henry III** owned a polar bear. It was a gift from King Haakon of Norway in 1252.

- **Thomas Jefferson** was given two grizzly cubs by Captain Zebulon Pike in 1807.

- Russia's **Ivan the Terrible** (1530–84) executed his foes by feeding them to his pet bears.

# Gilleland's Double-Barreled Cannon

What's better than a cannon with one barrel? Two! In 1862 Athens, Georgia, carpenter John Gilleland based his design on the naval chain shot, which launched two connected cannonballs out of one barrel. Gilleland's version had two muzzles loaded with one cannonball each, and a 10-foot-long chain that connected them. When fired simultaneously, the balls-and-chain would (theoretically) mow down the Union lines "like a scythe cuts wheat."

For the cannonballs to hit their target, however, they had to exit the muzzles at the same time. At the first test firing, they didn't...and chaos ensued: The unwieldy projectile veered wildly off course and mowed down a cornfield and several trees before the chain broke. The balls kept going; one smashed a chimney, the other killed a cow.

Despite the mishap, Gilleland declared his cannon a success. He sent it to Confederacy commanders for more tests, but their results weren't any better. So they sent the double-barreled cannon back to Georgia. Today, it sits quietly in front of Athens City Hall.

# FIVE FREAKY FACTS ABOUT...
# MONEY

- Ancient Spartans had a creative way of preventing capital flight: They made their coins so large and heavy that it was almost impossible to take them out of the country.

- First woman to appear on a U.S. coin: Spain's Queen Isabella (1893).

- In 1124 King Henry I of England ordered 94 mint workers castrated for producing bad coins.

- Largest and smallest bills in history: the 14th-century Chinese one-kwan note (9 x 13 inches) and the 1917 Rumanian ten-bani note (1.5 square inches).

- Motto on the first U.S. coins (copper cents, 1787): "Mind Your Business."

# The World's First Seismograph?

Domemico Salsano, an Italian clockmaker, is usually credited with inventing the seismograph in 1783. His "geo-sismometro" used an inked brush attached to a pendulum. The brush recorded tectonic vibrations on an ivory slab. It was sensitive enough to register quakes from 200 miles away.

But 1,500 years before that, a Chinese philosopher named Chang Hêng had already invented a device for detecting distant earthquakes. It was shaped like a large wine jar, about six feet across. On the outside were eight dragon heads with an open-mouthed toad beneath each one. Each dragon held a ball in its mouth. When a distant earthquake occurred, the dragon pointing in the direction of the quake dropped the ball into the mouth of the toad. Nobody is sure exactly what mechanism was inside the jar, but modern seismologists assume that a pendulum was connected to the dragons. And, according to ancient records, the dragon jar worked.

# NAN MADOL:
# A Floating Atlantis

Around 1,000 years ago, in Micronesia, a tribe known as the Saudeleur conquered the island of Pohnpei and then built the city of Nan Madol...in the ocean on top of coral reefs. Workers quarried nearly a million tons of basalt blocks, some weighing 100,000 pounds, and transported them offshore—forming 92 artificial islands across 200 acres, complete with columns, huge walls, and underwater tunnels. They connected the islets via a complex series of viaducts and canals.

For 500 years, Nan Madol was a major hub that served as a temple, the seat of Pohnpei's government, and home to the society's elite. Still, no one knows how humans were able to engineer this archaeological wonder in an era before construction machines, diving gear, and concrete. (The Pohnpeians' explanation: A sorcerer built the city.)

> Random Fact: The Cowardly Lion's costume in *The Wizard of Oz* was made from two real lion skins.

# First Jobs of World Leaders

- **Leonid Brezhnev**, Communist Party leader in the 1960s, was once a metallurgical engineer.

- **Mao Zedong**—better known as Chairman Mao, founder of the People's Republic of China—was once a school librarian.

- **Yasser Arafat**, chairman of the Palestine Liberation Organization (PLO), worked as a civil engineer and schoolteacher.

- Russian president **Vladimir Putin** worked for the KGB, monitoring the activities of foreigners in Leningrad.

- **Helmut Kohl**, chancellor of Germany from 1982 to 1998, was an assistant to the director of a foundry.

- Cold War–era Communist Party leader **Nikita Khrushchev** was once a shepherd, brick maker, and metalworker.

- **Idi Amin**, president of Uganda in the 1970s, served as a cook in the British Colonial Army. He was also Uganda's light heavyweight boxing champion from 1951 to 1960.

- Before she was elected Israel's prime minister in 1969, **Golda Meir** (who was born in Kiev) emigrated with her family to the United States. She helped run the family store in Milwaukee, Wisconsin.

- Italian prime minister **Benito Mussolini** may not have made the trains run on time, but years before he dissolved his country's democracy and invented fascism, he was a skilled blacksmith and stonemason.

- North Korean leader **Kim Jong-Il** apprenticed as a builder of roads and television towers.

- Russian president **Boris Yeltsin** worked as a construction foreman and a civil engineer specializing in plumbing and sewage.

- **Andrew Johnson** apprenticed to a tailor, and made his own clothes even while he was president.

# Baseball Bizarre

• Cleveland Indians pitcher Bob Feller and Minnesota Twins outfielder Denard Span have something odd in common: Both hit their mothers in the stands with a foul ball. Feller hit his mom in 1939 (he broke her collarbone); Span hit his during a spring training game in 2010. Both moms made full recoveries.

• From 1936 to 1946, Hall of Famer Joe "Flash" Gordon played exactly 1,000 games for the New York Yankees. In that time, he had exactly 1,000 hits.

• Breaking Babe Ruth's home run record will never be 4-gotten: It happened in the 4th inning of the 4th game of 1974, when the Braves' Hank Aaron, #44, hit a homer off the Dodgers' Al Downing, #44.

• In the 1960s, Kansas City A's owner Charlie Finley installed a mechanical rabbit that popped up out of the ground behind home plate to deliver new baseballs to the umpire. Finley wanted the rest of the owners to install rabbits too, but none did.

• In 1957 the Philadelphia Phillies' Richie Ashburn fouled off a ball that hit a fan named Alice Roth in the face, breaking her nose. As she was being carried away on a stretcher, Ashburn fouled off another pitch...and hit her again. The two later became friends.

# The Haunted Winchester House

Sarah Winchester began to lose her mind after her baby died in 1866. Then, when her husband Will died in 1881, she really lost it. But Will was rich and famous thanks to his Winchester repeating rifle, and Sarah inherited his entire fortune. Even still, she was so depressed that she went to a Boston spiritualist for guidance. Blaming Sarah's misfortune on bad karma (due to the Winchester rifle), the medium told Winchester to move out West and build a mansion that would never be finished. She ended up in San Jose, California, settled into a small farmhouse, set up a séance room, and each night she communicated with the spirits...who told her what to build next.

For nearly four decades, builders worked in shifts 24 hours a day fulfilling Sarah's odd demands. Result: a rambling maze of a mansion with staircases that lead nowhere, more than 2,000 cupboards (some only one inch deep), doorways that opened into nothing, and balconies with no way to get to them. Sarah installed five separate central heating systems—despite California's sunny, warm weather—and strung miles of wire connecting strange communication systems that no one knew how to operate.

She built rooms with 13 windows each, 13 fireplaces in one suite, 13 gas lights on her chandelier, 13 holes in her kitchen drain, and so on. By the end of her life, Sarah's mansion boasted 160 rooms, three elevators, six kitchens, 47 fireplaces, 17 chimneys, 10,000 windows, 467 doors... and just a single shower. Sarah Winchester died at age 83 in 1922, having lived the long life that her spirits had promised her if she kept building.

The Winchester House draws thousands of visitors to San Jose each year. Ghost tours and night-time flashlight tours titillate the tourists. True believers swear that the house is still inhabited. Staff and visitors have reported lights going on and off, and cold spots in certain rooms. Maybe it's vengeful spirits, angry that the building has ceased. Or maybe it's Sarah herself, trying to find that lone shower.

# The Way of the Dodo (and the Auk)

• **THE DODO**, a three-foot-tall flightless bird similar to a large pigeon, once thrived on the island of Mauritius in the Indian Ocean off the east coast of Africa. The birds had been living on the island for thousands of years. So safe was their habitat that—over time—they lost the ability to fly. Then the Europeans arrived.

When the Dutch began using Mauritius as a stopover on their trade routes in the 1600s, their ships brought dogs, cats, rats, and humans. The flightless birds were no match for the Dutch and their beastly companions. By 1681, barely 65 years after it first encountered "civilization," the dodo was completely extinct.

• **THE GREAT AUK**, a three-foot-tall flightless bird similar to the penguin, once thrived on the rocky islands of the North Atlantic. Then the Europeans arrived. They hunted the easy prey for food and fish bait, but mostly for its soft down, which became highly prized.

By the late 1700s, it had become obvious that the great auk was near extinction, prompting some of history's first environmental protection laws...but it was too late. All across Europe, museum curators said, "We must procure a stuffed great auk for our collection before they're all gone!" Result: a great auk killing spree. On July 3, 1844, in Eldey, Iceland, a museum collector killed the last known pair of great auks.

# SOMETHING SMELLS FISHY

Every head of *trimethylaminuria*? People with this metabolic disorder are unable to produce an enzyme used to break down *trimethylamine*, a compound found in many foods. That means trimethylamine builds up in the body, until there is so much of it that it's finally emitted through urine, sweat, and breathing. That's bad news. Why? Trimethylamine smells like stinky fish. In fact, it's the same chemical compound that makes stinky fish smell like stinky fish in the first place. People with this disorder can smell so strongly of stinky fish that—as you can imagine—it can make work and social situations difficult. Trimethylaminuria is a genetic disease, and there is no cure, though the strength of the fishy odor can be made less powerful through diet.

The gene mutation that causes trimethylaminuria was discovered in 1997, but the disease has been around for a long time. The earliest known mention of it may come from the ancient Sanskrit epic, *The Mahabharata*, a collection of Indian folk tales more than 2,000 years old. One of those tales describes an unfortunate maiden who "grew to be comely and fair, but a fishy odor ever clung to her."

## BOTCHED HISTORY

"When Newfoundland finally joined with us in Confederation in 1867, it was like a family reunion."

—Stephen Harper, Canadian prime minister, forgetting that Newfoundland didn't join the Canadian Confederation until 1949

# Worst. Pope. Ever.

Pope Benedict IX (1012–56) was a bad pope. How bad?
According to a later pope, Victor III, Benedict IX committed "rapes, murders, and other unspeakable acts." (Those
were, reportedly, bestiality.) How could such a horrible man
ascend to a level of such prominence? Corruption.

Benedict was born Theophylactus of Tusculum into a
wealthy Roman family, and two of his uncles had previously
served as pope. His rich father basically bought Benedict
the papacy—through bribes and political pressure—in
1032 when Benedict was a teenager. Unspeakable acts
commenced.

Four years later, Benedict was forced out of Rome by
outraged clerics, only to return a few months later and forc-
ibly retake his position. In 1044 he was deposed again, until
his armed forces regained control. Less than a year later,
Benedict had become bored, so he sold the papacy to his
uncle. Then he changed his mind and took it back by force.

By this point, Holy Roman Emperor Henry III had
tired of all the papal shenanigans and ordered his army to
remove Benedict once and for all. Henry promoted John,
bishop of Sabinato, to pope (John served as Sylvester III and
was later charged with bribing his way into the position).
Meanwhile, the excommunicated Benedict slunk home to
Tusculum as just Theophylactus again. And then he died.

# THE RIDDLE OF THE SPHINX

The most famous riddle of all (yes, even more famous than "Why did the chicken cross the road?") is the one that the Sphinx asked every human she met. A fierce creature, the Sphinx had a woman's head and breasts, a lion's claws, an animal's body, a dragon's tail, and a bird's wings. And if you couldn't answer her riddle, she ate you:

*What walks on four feet in the morning,*
*two feet at noon, and three feet in the evening?*

The only man to answer this correctly was Oedipus Rex, the king who accidentally married his mother and then poked his own eyes out. As for the Sphinx, once Oedipus bested her, she killed herself.

The answer, if you didn't know it already, is "a man"—he crawls at the beginning of life, walks upright in midlife, and walks with a cane in old age.

# The Futuristic World of...1960

*"Come tour America of 1960 with General Motors! See a view of tomorrow's cities, a panorama of tomorrow's countryside, on moving sound-chairs while the friendly voice of an unseen guide describes the wonders that can happen here!" That's an excerpt from the New York World's Fair catalog in 1939. Here's what GM thought 1960 would look like:*

- The food supply is endless, as scientists have developed methods to artificially pollinate plants and flowers. All fruit and vegetable farming is done under giant glass domes.

- Nobody lives in big cities in the 1960s. Everybody lives in suburbs or the country. Futuristic cities are devoted to industry, business, and cultural pursuits.

- Those who don't work in the city or live in the suburbs reside in small villages. Each such village is home to one factory that produces one industrial item.

- All skyscrapers are outfitted with landing decks for helicopters and flying cars called "autogyros."

- The average highway of 1960 is 14 lanes wide—seven in each direction. But all the lanes don't have the same speed limit: Four lanes are for driving at 50 mph, two are for 75 mph, and one is for 100 mph. And the road isn't flat—the edges of the road curve up to create barriers on each side so each lane remains separate and the fast-moving cars don't veer into each other.

- To prevent accidents, radio waves ensure that cars travel at equal distances from each other, never getting too close.

- These superfast highways will enable coast-to-coast travel in about 24 hours, allowing Americans to spend their two-month compulsory vacation virtually anywhere they please.

- Airports are hubs for car, rail, and air travel. They're also round and built on rivers in the middle of cities. The water makes it easier for a dirigible (blimp) to turn around in the airport's large underwater hangar.

> "So many centuries after the Creation it is unlikely that anyone could find hitherto unknown lands of any value."
>
> —**Committee advising King Ferdinand and Queen Isabella of Spain, regarding a proposal by Christopher Columbus (1486)**

# THE LOUISIANA CATAHOULA LEOPARD DOG

The official canine of Louisiana has an amazing story that began in 1539 when Spanish conquistador Hernando de Soto crossed what is now the southern United States looking for gold. Dogs always traveled with the Spanish troops: mastiffs for use in battle and greyhounds to hunt game. When de Soto died in 1542, his army retreated back to Mexico, leaving their sick and wounded animals behind. The native tribes adopted the dogs, which then interbred with the local red wolf.

Eventually a new cross emerged—tough, wily, quick, and known as the "wolf-dog." When French settlers arrived in the 1600s, they brought the Beauceron, a boar-hunting hound. This was bred with the "wolf-dog" to create the Catahoula cur, which looks like a dog designed by committee: Its motley short fur is multicolored in irregular spots, and its eyes are unusually glassy. But owners swear by the intelligence and uncanny abilities of these dogs as herders, guard dogs, and hunters. They've even been called "cat-dogs" because they like to climb trees.

# Psychos on Acid

In 1968 Dr. Elliott Barker, a Canadian psychiatrist at the Oak Ridge Hospital for the criminally insane in Penetanguishene, Ontario, believed that he found a method to cure psychopaths: nude psychotherapy sessions, fueled by LSD, lasting for 11-day stretches.

The patients, all males with violent criminal histories, volunteered to be placed in a windowless room that Barker called the "Total Encounter Capsule." The soundproof room had a sink and toilet and a one-way mirror in the ceiling. The men were fed through straws in the door. There were no beds, no privacy, and no clothes. And the lights were never turned off. Barker hoped the therapy would allow the men to "reveal their inner selves" and then be "born again" as empathetic human beings.

Did it work? Not really. On average, 60 percent of criminal psychopaths released into the outside world will become repeat offenders. However, when it came to Barker's patients, that rate hit 80 percent.

Ironically, the naked LSD capsule treatments made most of the psychopaths more psychopathic.

# Ancient Power

The National Museum of Iraq has a collection of clay jars made by the Parthians, who once ruled the Middle East. One jar, however, dating from about 200 B.C., is not your ordinary container. It's just over five inches high by three inches across. The opening was once sealed with asphalt, with a narrow iron rod sticking through it. Inside the jar was a copper sheet rolled into a tube and closed at the bottom with a copper disk. The iron rod hung down in the center of the tube.

The odd artifact didn't attract much attention until 1960, when researchers discovered that if the jar was filled with an acidic liquid—such as vinegar or fermented grape juice—it actually generated a small current, between 1.5 and 2 volts. Their conclusion: The jar was an electric battery, used more than 2,000 years ago. In the acidic liquid, electrons flowed from the copper tube to the iron rod—much like the batteries invented by Italian physicist Alessandro Volta around 1800. But what, the researchers wondered, would anyone in ancient Baghdad use a battery for?

The most likely explanation: The Parthians used the batteries to electroplate gold onto silver (covering a silver object to make it appear to be solid gold). Experiments have shown that electroplating can indeed be done with modern batteries similar to that ancient jar.

# Time Zones? What Are Those?

In April 1961, the CIA attempted to overthrow Fidel Castro by leading a surprise attack on Cuban bases. The plan: Paratroopers would land, disrupt transportation, and fight off the Cuban soldiers. Then 1,400 soldiers would invade the Bay of Pigs on Cuba's southern coast at the same time that their cohorts would land on the east side to create confusion.

But the plan went awry from the get-go: Paratroopers landed in the wrong place, and the CIA failed to notice that a Cuban radio station announced the location of their "secret" operation. And when President Kennedy dispatched a fleet of B-26 bombers, the pilots didn't know that there was a time difference between Nicaragua, where the planes departed, and Cuba. The bombers arrived an hour late and were shot down. The mission—known as the Bay of Pigs—was not only a total failure, but it strengthened the USSR's presence in the region, making the Cold War even colder.

# FIVE FREAKY FACTS ABOUT...
# U.S. PRESIDENTS

- Ronald Reagan once lost a movie role because he "didn't have the presidential look."

- The Marquis de Lafayette gave John Quincy Adams two alligators. The president kept his two "pets" in the White House bathtub.

- Richard Nixon was raised as a pacifist Quaker.

- As a young man, President Rutherford B. Hayes had lyssophobia, the fear of going insane.

- Millie the White House dog earned more than four times as much as President Bush in 1991.

STRANGE HISTORY

# Presidential Last Words

"I die hard, but am not afraid to go."

—GEORGE WASHINGTON, 1799

"This is the last of earth. I am content."

—JOHN QUINCY ADAMS, 1848

**Mary Todd Lincoln:** What will Miss Harris think of my hanging on to you so?

**Abraham Lincoln:** She won't think anything about it.

—WHILE WATCHING A PLAY AT FORD'S THEATRE, 1865

"History will vindicate my memory."

—JAMES BUCHANAN, 1868

"I love you, Sarah. For all eternity, I love you."

—JAMES K. POLK, TO HIS WIFE, 1849

"Oh, do not cry. Be good children and we will all meet in heaven."

—ANDREW JACKSON, 1845

"Is it the Fourth?"

—THOMAS JEFFERSON, JULY 4, 1826

"The nourishment is palatable."

—Millard Fillmore, 1874

"Water."

—Ulysses S. Grant, 1885

"I always talk better lying down."

—James Madison, 1836

"Put out the light."

—Theodore Roosevelt, 1919

"I am ready."

—Woodrow Wilson, 1924

"I have a terrific headache."

—Franklin Delano Roosevelt, 1945

"That's obvious."

—John F. Kennedy, when told by Texas First Lady
Nellie Connally, "You can't say that Dallas doesn't
love you," 1963

# Tracking Down History's First Song

In about 1500 B.C., someone carved words and symbols onto a clay tablet in the port city of Ugarit, now known as Ras Shamra in modern-day Syria, a cosmopolitan urban center. About 3,400 years later, in the 1950s, Professor Anne Draffkorn Kilmer of the University of California at Berkeley began studying the tablet, which had been found at an archaeological site. The writing was Hurrian cuneiform script (the Hurrians settled Ugarit), and Professor Kilmer spent the next 15 years working to translate the symbols, finally finishing in 1972. It turned out to be the oldest known notated song in history. And it had not only words (to a hymn to "Nikkal," the wife of the moon god), it had musical notes—and they weren't that dissimilar to the notes used in the diatonic do-re-mi scale that is the bedrock of Western music. Before the discovery, musicologists believed that no such scale existed until the ancient Greeks devised one some 1,100 years later.

# Elvis Lives

Dr. Jukka Ammondt, a professor of literature at Finland's University of Jyväskylä, translated several of Elvis Presley's greatest songs into Latin. "It's Now or Never" became *"Nunc Hic Aut Numquam."* And then, going even further back in time, Ammondt recorded an album of Elvis songs in ancient Sumerian—a language spoken in Mesopotamia around 4000 B.C. "Lay off of my blue suede shoes" translated as "My sandals of sky-blue, do not touch."

# Things Really Do Change

*A follow-up to the quotations on page 5, which revealed how much we 21st-century people have in common with those who came before us. These facts illustrate the opposite.*

- Ancient Egyptians used slabs of stones as pillows.

- Medieval women wore breastbags to flatten and draw attention away from their chests.

- Surgery goes all the way back to the Stone Age. However, it has only been since the mid-1800s that patients were given anesthesia.

- Assyrians who parked their chariots on the king's road were killed and impaled.

- Ancient beer was a thick, sour brew that tasted like vinegar and was served at room temperature.

- If you want to drive across the United States today, you can do it in a few days. A century ago, that road trip would have taken about two months.

- The first speeding ticket came in 1896, when a Brit was fined one shilling for going 8 mph. (In 2010 a Swiss driver going 180 mph got a ticket for $1 million.)

- Next time your kid starts griping, tell him about an ancient Sabaen (Yemeni) religious festival that featured the slaughter and consumption of a male newborn. He was "boiled and deboned; the flesh was rolled in flour, oil, saffron, raisins, and spices and then oven-baked." Then priests ate him.

- In a 1914 U.S. government pamphlet, "health experts" discouraged parents from interacting with or kissing their babies: "The rule that parents should not play with the baby may seem hard, but it is without doubt a safe one."

- Is your closet so full that you have to get rid of a bunch of old shirts you never wear anymore? By history's standards, you're rich. Until quite recently, most people only owned one or two sets of clothes.

- Before the advent of antibiotics, syphilis was treated with mercury and arsenic.

- And finally, way back in the early 1990s, if you were away from home and someone tried to call you on the phone, they would have no way to reach you! Scary times indeed.

*Fin*